"AN EXTREMELY INTERESTING AND HUMOROUS INSIDER'S LOOK AT AN AMERICAN LEGEND, THE SUPREMES."
—Scherrie Payne, formerly of the Supremes

"I LOVED IT! A powerful book that should be read by all!"
—Eddie Kendrick, formerly of the Temptations

"OUTSTANDING! TRUTHFUL! A MUST READ! It's not gonna make everybody happy, but that's how books are."
—Dennis Edwards, formerly of the Temptations

"A startling look at the Ladies, the Legend, and finally the Truth, about the Supremes."
—David Ruffin, formerly of the Temptations

"I've lived through nasty situations with groups in this business, but never one like this! This book is hot! Read it! If you can hold it!"
—Richard Barrett, Three Degrees Enterprises

ALL THAT GLITTERED

My Life with the Supremes

◆ ◆ ◆

Tony Turner
with Barbara Aria

AN ONYX BOOK

ONYX
Published by the Penguin Group
Penguin Books USA Inc., 375 Hudson Street,
New York, New York 10014, U.S.A.
Penguin Books Ltd, 27 Wrights Lane,
London W8 5TZ, England
Penguin Books Australia Ltd, Ringwood,
Victoria, Australia
Penguin Books Canada Ltd, 2801 John Street,
Markham, Ontario, Canada L3R 1B4
Penguin Books (N.Z.) Ltd, 182–190 Wairau Road,
Auckland 10, New Zealand

Penguin Books Ltd, Registered Offices:
Harmondsworth, Middlesex, England

Published by Onyx, an imprint of New American Library, a division of
Penguin Books USA Inc. Previously published in a Dutton edition.

First Onyx Printing, July, 1991
10 9 8 7 6 5 4 3 2 1

My memoirs, my story, my book,
are dedicated to
my grandmother Vera, my mother Eleanor,
and my niece Serene.
From where I got it, to whom I give it.

Acknowledgments

Speak the truth without fear,
Candidly and openly,
Unafraid to look anyone in the eye.
Mean what you say, and say what you mean!

By the grace of God, I have always tried to live by this statement, and even more so in writing my memoirs. By speaking my mind candidly I have often landed myself in difficulty, for sometimes the truth is better left unsaid. Nevertheless, I have tried wholeheartedly to do just that and only that in this instance, and let the chips fall where they may.

By the grace of God, I have been extremely fortunate in the people I have encountered in my efforts to bring my book to life. Therefore, I cannot begin without taking the time to thank you, those of you who have known me a long time, as well as those who I met through this project.

Diana Mancher and Mary Anne Mazzola, of St. Martin's Press, who encouraged me to get started and set me on the right path.

Madeleine Morel of 2M Communications, Ltd., my agent, who believed in me, my story, and my instincts.

Leslie Wells, my first editor, who kindly received me with great enthusiasm and brought me to Dutton.

Joyce Engleson, Vice President and Editor-in-Chief at Dutton, who had the unbelievable insight to sign an unknown author, with an unwritten manuscript. I thank you especially!

Jean Martinet, my second editor at Dutton, who weathered the storm as the book progressed.

Gary Luke, Executive Editor at New American Library, whose expertise and high standards have been greatly beneficial and crucial to my finished manuscript.

Richard Barrett, manager extraordinaire, and his wife Julie, for their belief in me and constant encouragement.

Susan Taylor, Editor-in-Chief of *Essence* magazine, a classy executive who took the time to answer my call for help, thanks!

Zachary T. Wobensmith III, Esq., one of the finest attorneys I have ever met.

Pam Jackson in Florida, and Alfred Fariello in New York, whose skillful services transformed tons of taped interviews into professional transcripts.

Rafaela Cepeda, my advisor, for teaching me ''When one door closes, another one opens, KEEP GOING.''

Pat Newson, my office manager, and her mom Julia Parker, for getting me to the point where I wanted to tell my story.

Linda Burton, my sincere gratitude to the best master stylist in Tampa, Florida.

D.J. of Salon Etc., for being one of the nicest guys, with the best salon in Tampa.

Bill Baker, photographer, and Lisa Goldman, make-up artist, for MLD III, in Dunedin, Florida, thanks for putting me at ease and giving me your best.

To my godparents, Lucy and Lonnie Burdette, and my friend Sherry Page, for keeping the dreamboy going.

Barbara Aria, my co-writer, who I have on a special thank-you list of her own. Barbara, maybe it was because you, Flo, and I are the same sign that in every situation you understood me and what I revealed about the Supremes, immediately. Thanks for rescuing me from one who did not. From the day you rushed into the penthouse at the Beekman Tower I knew I was in good hands.

A loving thank you to my family, close friends, guardian angels, and of course, J.R. With you all, I'd do it again, if I had to live my life all over.

My heartfelt gratitude to the late Florence "Flo" Ballard, the Supreme angel who left me and a generation hopelessly enchanted; Diana Ross, for being the supreme Supreme as well as a perfectionist and an astute businesswoman; and Mary Wilson, for being the quintessential Supreme. None of you ever gave us less than too much!

I've heard, "When the legend conflicts with the truth, print the legend." But remember, you don't have to.

By the grace of God.

Tony Turnor
Gulf of Mexico
1990

Contents

Prologue

Every September when school started again, every teacher I could remember gave us the assignment to report on "What I did for my summer vacation." And every year I wrote a composition about going to stay with my grandparents in Buffalo. I hated my summer exiles to upstate New York because that was the boondocks. I, after all, was from New York City.

The routine continued until 1966, eighth grade, because that September I didn't write about Buffalo, I wrote about my trip to Detroit, all about staying with Florence Ballard and going to Motown. By eighth grade that didn't surprise anyone because I'd been doing Detroit and Motown and the Supremes for show-and-tell ever since I met Flo in 1964 and got caught up in her Supremes dream life.

Before that, I wasn't buying records or following the hit parade or anything like that. I was just learning to play "The Star-Spangled Banner" in piano lessons Monday to Friday after school, and sometimes I was going to the Apollo with my mother for amateur night because it was cheaper than getting a baby-sitter. Anyway, before that Motown's Sound of Young America was just starting to be the biggest thing happening in music next to the British Invasion, and at that time hardly anyone had even heard of the Supremes.

That eighth-grade report was probably the best one I ever did. It was the whole story from day one, from the second Flo said they had a whole week off and I should come stay in her house. She told me, "We'll have a grand time, honey. Flo's gonna do a mess of cookin' mixed up with a heap of partying, it'll be too fabulous!" Things were taking a swing for the worse between Flo and Diana and Mary that summer but I had no inkling. I was just thrilled to be going to Detroit and excited to be going on a plane for the first time. I'd been to the airport a couple of times with the Supremes, but never further than the terminal.

Of course, all the kids in the projects knew about it, my mother was telling the whole world, and I'd been bragging to everybody in the projects and in school, oh, I'm flying to Detroit this summer to spend a week with Florence Ballard in her mansion and hang out with the Supremes and a bunch of Motown stars.

When Flo first invited me my mother said no, she said I had to go to Buffalo. But I told her there was no way I was going back there. I was interested in music, in glitter and glamor, in style and taste, in the Temptations, in limousines, in hotel suites, I did *not* want to be out there playing in the dirt trying to shoot marbles in holes when I could be sitting up in Florence Ballard's mansion minding her business, eating off of Limoges china and Baccarat crystal, and jumping up in a limo, and rolling my eyes at Diana Ross, and playing at being grown-up, and eating in fancy restaurants like Flo said we were going to do. "We're gonna go to the Twenty Grand when you get up here, we're gonna go to the Roostertail when the Tempts are gonna be working there. And honey, we'll be the talk of the town!"

Now why would I want to be going to Buffalo to shoot marbles, or go on the church picnic to the lake when I could be going to Detroit, and my mother thought this was just the most disgusting attitude to have, that despite all of her efforts I was growing up to be nothing but trash and garbage. But in the end my mother relented, "You can just go to Flo's house because you're considered too wild in Buffalo." So off I went.

My parents drove me to the airport in my stepfather's black Bonneville. All my friends in the projects were out there to watch me go, and after I got on the plane my parents had to wait and wave, and try to see which little window I'd be looking out of. Then I just watched the people sitting near me on the plane, and every time someone asked for a blanket, or a soda or anything I'd press my little call button and I'd ask for the same thing. And why not!

As soon as the plane landed somebody came on and announced that one of the Supremes was at the gate waiting, and I was taken off the plane first. Everybody else had to sit back down and they were all turning around this way and that way and saying, who's coming here to meet the Supremes? Then, walking through the airport with Flo all the airport employees and shopkeepers and waitresses kept rushing up and saying Hi Flo! Because all the Motown stars passed through that airport about a million times every month so everyone knew them, and they were whispering, there's one of the Supremes! Flo's head was held very high and she was parading through, she was in her summer chiffon outfit with billowing yards of material, and her high heels always made a lot of noise, like click click click click click.

We got to the luggage area and right away Flo said, "We shouldn't be kept waiting like this." She started tapping her foot and demanding of the porters, like she was the queen of England and I was the Prince of Wales, "Where Is His Luggage? It should be the first off, IMMEDIATELY!" They got it quick as a wink, and we were sped off out of there.

Right outside Flo winked her eye and she said, "Didn't I do that just like Diana would do?" And when I laughed she said, "Well, imitation *is* the sincerest form of flattery." A big limo was waiting by the curb, it took us directly to Flo's house and when I saw that house I couldn't believe it. It really was like a mansion, like nothing I'd ever seen before. The whole neighborhood looked just like a picture postcard. This neighborhood was like twenty square blocks of big, tall, stately trees and brick Tudor homes, perfectly manicured. I remember every day that I was there being just weather perfect, the sun just bright enough, the grass just green enough, perfect mansions with perfect Supremes living inside.

When I saw that house it looked so big. It was a two-story brick house and she had stained-glass windows in the front. The front porch had a fancy green canvas awning that was like the one on the Park Avenue buildings, and when I went inside the carpet seemed like it came up to my ankles, that's how thick it was.

I was scared and nervous to meet Flo's family, who lived upstairs in Flo's house. They'd moved from the projects together and there were so many of them, but after an hour or so I just felt myself fitting right in. We hung around, we went shopping, Flo took me nightclubbing, there was a constant flow of relatives going in and out screaming and carrying on and fawning over Flo.

Everywhere they went people knew them so they had to always appear very ladylike, Supreme-like. Reporters from the Detroit press came to Flo's house to interview her, she'd make these big entrances all sweeping and flowing in some fabulous outfit that she would call "my little cost*ume*," and they'd want to see the seventeen-foot sofa and the marbled end tables that hung down from the ceiling on gold chains, they'd want to hear about Japan, about Germany, about England, all the same things I wanted to hear about. The Supremes were at home but they were still on stage, it was a different type of performance, that's all.

Right across the street from Flo's was Diana Ross's house. It was a similar but slightly different style. She lived on one floor and her parents and brothers and sisters lived on the other. I went over there the first day and Diana was pretty nice to me, they were not working that particular week so she was just home, she was pretty relaxed, she was practicing make-up tricks surrounded by clothes and mirrors. Diana told me, ''I might not see much of you on your little visit here, Tony. I'll be in meetings and I'll be studying and rehearsing on my own. But *do* have a nice time.'' Well, she smiled, and I smiled and left in a hurry.

Mary Wilson lived on the same street too, about one and a half blocks farther down in a semi-attached house. She rented one half to Cholly Atkins, the famous choreographer who invented all the Supremes' shimmies and hand movements and turns. Mary was the only one who didn't have family living with her.

When Flo first got her house in '65 she told me how it happened that they all ended up living on the same street. Someone from Motown had gone out while they were away and found maybe eight or ten houses that looked like the right kind of home setting for an ''ingenue,'' as Flo liked to call herself, and when the girls got back they had each selected one, and after they'd picked they realized they were all on Buena Vista, which didn't surprise me at the time because they seemed to me almost like sisters.

It wasn't until the summer of '66 when I went to Detroit that I really started to see the Supremes as three separate girls living three separate lives. There was Flo in her glorious kind of Liberace-style mansion, it was so pretty, so romantic, all white and powder blue with touches of gold, and she had her own private nightclub in the basement with little cocktail tables set up. Diana's house was much plainer, kind of modern, and just lined with closets all filled to the brim. All her clothes were perfectly arranged by color, by style, everything was perfectly organized. And then there was Mary in her house, which was like a girl's version of Hugh Hefner's Playboy-style, all swirling, sectional couches and deep, deep shag carpet. She had a round bed, and if you pressed a button next to the bed these sheer curtains came around it.

Mary's house seemed to be the party house, the place where Everybody wanted to be and Mary would call Flo, she'd say, "Oh girl, the Tempts are stopping by, and I'm cooking up a big old thing of food, and Duke and the rest of the Four Tops are already here." So Flo and I would go down to Mary's. Even though it was just in the next block we'd drive in Flo's Cadillac, which meant you had to come out the block and go around and go up and come back.

Mary had a little dance studio in her basement where they'd rehearse routines. Cholly would come from next door, they would all stop by, the whole Motown stable, and they'd show everybody their latest steps, they'd compete with steps, and then they'd argue and drink, food would be served, they'd talk about this show and that show, and who stole which steps from whom, and it was fun for them. Even then, Diana was seldom part of the crowd.

There was a Motown company picnic that we went on. Everybody was there with their families, I guess it was just like any big company picnic except that everybody was immaculately dressed. Berry Gordy was there holding court with a throng around him. They were all trying real hard to get close to Mr. Gordy and being really quite obvious, I thought.

Even I could tell that the Supremes were the first ladies of this picnic because here we are at the Supremes' table and we're eating off of china, we've got silverware and crystal glassware and cloth napkins, and a huge arrangement of fresh-cut flowers, Flo had brought all this stuff in several wicker hampers. And then there were the Marvelettes and the Vandellas, they were at a table close by drinking beer right out of the can and eating off of paper plates, Diana commented on it, all she said was "How common!"

I was just sitting there watching them go by, there's Eddie Kendricks, there's Smokey, Levi Stubbs, there's Martha Reeves, and I was thinking, all these people are stars, they're on television, they're riding around in Cadillacs and flashy Lincolns. I asked Mary, "Why are they having a picnic?'' I was wondering, why are they having barbecued ribs and steaks and potato salad, and why are some of the men getting drunk and acting silly, and they've got volleyball teams, some of them are jumping rope and playing cards just like the church picnic? Mary didn't say anything, Flo answered. She said, ''We're stars, honey, but we're people first.''

It looked to me like one big happy family. Of course, later I realized that there had to be some rivalry, some jealousies just like in any family. But then, it was great, it was special, it was the place to be. These people were the envy of all Detroit because they were stars, they all had hits on the charts that summer.

So when I first saw Motown I was really surprised. I had expected a huge, glamorous glass building with stars gliding in and out. It was like an old, Archie Bunker-style house in Queens except that there were Cadillacs and luxury cars lined up outside. And they had a sign over the top that said Hitsville USA. But I was just happy to be there, what did I know, I was coming from the projects in East Harlem, and there really were stars gliding in and out.

Flo took me to Berry Gordy's office, which was tiny, and Mr. Gordy was very nice, he stood up from his desk and shook my hand and said hello my good friend, which is what he used to call me at the time. And he let me sit in his great big chair.

While we were there Flo told me, ''The Four Tops are laying down some tracks in the recording studio, let's go see them,'' and I'd never heard this expression but I wanted to appear very grown so I just said, ''Yeah, let's go see them lay down some tracks,'' like it was the most natural thing in the world. I'd never seen a recording studio, but I've heard people say, how could they get that big Motown sound out of that little recording studio? It didn't matter to me that the studio was so small, it was Motown baby.

That trip was like a dream for me. When the Supremes walked into a place, people's attitudes changed immediately and people were just too thrilled to wait on them and too thrilled to indulge them and too thrilled to run and fetch something, too thrilled to see if they needed anything done. This was what they'd grown accustomed to. They expected it, and nobody thought it wouldn't last.

You become spoiled from living like that with everybody fussing over you, everything arrives for you, you don't ever have to reach. It was like *Star Trek,* if they wanted something it seemed to just materialize. The Supremes didn't just walk into a room, they sort of appeared, it was such an image for me as a young boy to see all of this glamor, money, beauty, makeup, furs, cars, everything being sprayed out like perfume all at once. I never even conceived the possibility that this would end up being too much too soon.

I returned to Detroit several times to see Flo and the worst time was in the early seventies when for Flo it was all but gone; Flo had lost everything. The neighborhood around Buena Vista was still picture-perfect but Flo's mansion was a wreck, all boarded up and falling apart. Diana and Mary had quietly moved. Diana was living in a stark, expensive home in Beverly Hills and Mary's home was high on a Hollywood hillside on Rising Glen Road.

Motown was gone too. Berry Gordy had moved the whole thing to L.A. and now the old Motown building on West Grand Boulevard is a sort of pitiful museum. People come from all over the world to see it, they make pilgrimages there as if it were Mecca, they come to see where the Sound of Young America was born, where the stars recorded the sound that dominated the airwaves for all those golden years. They come to find the gutter-to-glitter story of people like the Supremes, and then they go to contemplate the meaning of that story at Florence Ballard's graveside.

CHAPTER 1

———— ◆ ◆ ◆ ————

1964—Never Go with Strangers

It was past nine o'clock at night, and I was riding the uptown A train all alone. I knew this was way too late for a twelve-year-old boy to be out by himself, and I kept on thinking, what is my mother gonna say? My mother was pretty strict.

My mother told me never to go with strangers and never to take money from a stranger. She was always telling me, don't you ever get into a car with any stranger, never let me catch you taking candy from anyone you don't personally know. She told me to watch out. Soon I was going to graduate from sixth grade, she said, and then I'd have to leave the neighborhood every day, I'd have to take the crosstown bus from where I lived in the Wagner Projects on 123rd Street and Second Avenue to Junior High School Number 43 over on the West Side of Manhattan where they had a special program for gifted kids. I was always a good reader, and I had a real good memory. Junior high was still six, seven months away but my mother was already telling me, "Watch out, some fresh man or woman might try to you know, feel you on one of those crowded Number 29 buses."

When I graduated from sixth grade my mother promised to buy me a "nice" camera, but I hadn't graduated yet. I was only twelve, which is why I was

21

riding home on the A train so late on a cold Saturday night in December 1964, and I was wondering just what my mother was going to do to me when I got back, and I was thinking, I should have had a camera. I kept telling myself, I wish I had that camera and I wish I'd brought one of my friends with me, because nobody in the neighborhood is going to believe this. And of course I was right—the kids in school all thought I'd signed those autographs myself.

I never collected autographs. I wasn't one of those kids who took autographs to school or read fan magazines or any of those things. I guess I hadn't reached the age yet where as a teenager you go out and buy records, I didn't know from Stevie Wonder to the Temptations. I only knew what my mother was playing in the house and I really didn't listen to that, I was into other things. I'd heard of Mary Wells, she was a big hit, and Johnny Mathis I knew because my mother loved him, and I was familiar with the big names like James Brown, Ella Fitzgerald, Sara Vaughan, Sammy Davis, Jr.

I'd been going to the Apollo Theater since I was nine or ten. My mother used to take me Wednesday nights, amateur night, and I always had to scooch down because it was only a quarter to get in if you were under ten. You watched the stars perform and then you had the amateur show so your parents got to see who they wanted and I got to see James Brown throw off his cape singing "Please, Please, Please" for what seemed like a whole hour and people screaming and women crying and passing out, and I didn't quite know what was going on.

Then I saw Eartha Kitt, I saw Sammy Davis, Jr., I saw Duke Ellington, I saw Jackie Wilson, I got to see all these greats. But I was mostly interested in seeing the amateur shows. I thought it was so funny when someone would come on and be so bad that the audience would start hissing and booing and yelling all kinds of names and throwing things and then this guy named Puerto Rico would come out with the hook.

Puerto Rico was great. He would come on the stage dressed maybe in a bra and towel, a woman's wig on backward, every time he came out he had on an outrageous outfit, a bathrobe or a ladies' half slip pulled up or a big farmer's suit. I never understood why these performers didn't just get off the stage—why wait for the audience to throw things and Puerto Rico to come in with the hook. When somebody was good, they were really good and they'd turn the whole place out, but when they were bad that's where the real fun was.

Sometimes I went to the Apollo with my Aunt Estelle. Estelle wasn't like my mother, she'd go backstage, she knew the man and he'd let her in. She even performed in the amateur show a couple of times, but she wasn't too good. "You know, your auntie is a showgirl," she used to tell me. I thought Estelle was really beautiful, and I loved to go out with her.

My Aunt Estelle was the first one in the neighborhood to come out wearing a blonde wig and huge, hoop earrings back in '62. She was fabulous about everything. She'd wear a mink stole and a short little cocktail dress, and she always knew where the best parties were, where the best dances were, she was always sewing up some flaming red ballgown that didn't quite make it, it didn't really look like the one in *Vogue* that she'd copied.

From when I was nine or ten she'd take me on midnight boat rides to Bear Mountain. It'd be a bunch of adults and they'd all say, that kid is so cute, he's on the moonlight boat ride, and everyone thought it was just the funniest thing in the world. Or she'd say, "I'm having my birthday party up at the Baby Grand Lounge and it's gonna be a great big affair," and she'd take me along. My mother would say, "Estelle, I don't know why I let that boy go with you to all those things you do so late at night," she'd say. "I just hope you're not taking this kid into none of those bars uptown."

I wouldn't tell, and Estelle wouldn't tell, she had two kids of her own but they were younger so she'd leave them with my mother and I'd tag along with her, and we'd go to the Baby Grand Lounge, which was the top bar in Harlem. They'd say to her, you can't bring that kid in here, and she'd tell them off and we'd just go sailing in, and I loved it. I watched all the big-time money men in the sharkskin suits and alligator shoes pulling fifty-dollar bills from gold money clips. Everybody who walked in was grander than the last one. These people were *different*.

My aunt wasn't like my parents at all. They were pretty strict, less interested in having a fun time than in trying to get ahead, to get out of the projects, to get a new washing machine or two TVs or a dishwasher. Like most parents, they didn't want their kids getting into any kind of trouble. Usually I had to be home by seven every night, and I had to go to piano lessons every day, Monday to Friday right after school.

Life in the projects was pretty normal, pretty sheltered. The school was right there, so you didn't even have to leave the projects. Everybody's mother was home and sitting out on the bench when you got home. Life in the projects was biking, it was roller skating, it was trick or treat, it was running from one apartment to another. Most of the kids never left the neighborhood except to go to the Bronx Zoo or Coney Island in the summertime, or to pile into somebody's car for a picnic way up at Pelham Bay with a bunch of other kids and sandwiches and Kool-Aid, those were the places to go, it was family life and it was fun. But by the time I was twelve I'd already seen a whole other life from tagging along with my Aunt Estelle and I guess I was born curious, I liked to live on the edge. I got used to being a kid amongst adults and I always had my eyes and ears open.

My stepfather was always telling me, "Think before you act, think before you speak!" He told me I was too nosy for my own good. But I was smart and my parents trusted me. It was my job to take my sister, Ramona, downtown to dance class every Saturday, at a place called Startime, which was in the same building as the Ed Sullivan Theater on Broadway and Fifty-first Street. Instead of waiting for her inside I'd go with some of the other guys who'd brought sisters, and we'd explore. Unlike the predominantly black crowd at school, these guys were white, Chinese, Hispanic, a real mixed group—and some of them were older and slicker and wiser—and we'd go into the penny arcades on Forty-second Street and we'd check out the record stores and clothing stores and get all sorts of stuff to eat. It was fun to hang out with them. I liked to mix with the bigger kids in the projects too, and they let me, maybe because I was so tall. I was almost their height.

When I got out of Harlem, I began to see a whole new world, and I started exploring on my own. That was always my way. I remember the play area in the projects, it was right where my mother could see it from her kitchen window. She could watch out the window and check up on us playing out there but she was way upstairs on the third floor and I was way downstairs, so I'd sneak off. First I went round the block a couple of times, then I went a bit farther, and then I started taking the bus, putting that money in and going straight down, riding all the way to the end of the line which was all the way at the bottom of Manhattan. Then I would pay another fare and ride the First Avenue bus right back up, just sitting there looking out the window. As I got more adventurous I'd get off at Thirty-fourth or Fourteenth Street, look around, and get back on. There was a lot of life beyond the twenty-two buildings of Wagner projects.

I have friends that are still there in the projects who are sitting on the bench, who never finished high school. Maybe if I hadn't been so adventurous, if I hadn't had my Aunt Estelle, if my parents hadn't wanted to get ahead, if my sister hadn't gone to Startime, and maybe if I hadn't been in the right place at the right time I would have stayed in the projects just like some of the other kids and when they started smoking dope or taking heroin I would have been right there along with them. But that would have been a whole other story.

It was the day after Christmas, a Saturday, and as usual I hadn't even told my mother I was going downtown. If she'd have known I was wandering around Thirty-fourth Street by myself without even telling her she would have had a fit.

It was Christmas sales time, crowded, freezing cold, and I had money to burn. I'd been saving up for a few weeks, I had over fifty bucks and now I was going to spend it. This was 1964 and fifty bucks was a lot of money in those days. As a kid I was always looking for ways to make money, like my supermarket shopping service. It started out, I would go to the A & P and I'd hang around outside for somebody to come out and I'd say, need some help with those bags, ma'am. So I'd carry the bags and they'd give me a quarter, a dollar, and I'd put it in my pocket and go back and wait some more. I already knew the stores like the back of my hand because I used to help my grandmother Vera and she went to them all, to the A & P, to the Safeway, to the E & B, picking out the sales items in each store.

Soon I realized I could make a lot more money by just going around to people in my building and saying, give me your list, and doing their shopping for them. So my shopping service started getting popular, and I got other kids to work for me. Pretty soon those dollars and quarters added up so by the time I paid the other kids I'd made about thirty dollars on an average Saturday, which was a lot of money in those days for a twelve-year-old kid. Most of it went on clothes—nice sweaters, tailored pants, shoes, sharp, button-down shirts with tapered sides, and all the rest.

I was into fashion. I loved to dress, I wanted to be the best-dressed, most popular kid in school and I always thought I looked kind of clutzy because I was so tall and I wore these thick, thick Mr. Magoo glasses. Kids thought I looked sort of intelligent, sort of intel-

lectual, sort of smart and to me that wasn't anything
to be proud of, I didn't want to look smart, not like
those bookworms. I wanted to look cool, that's why I
always liked a lot of different clothes. I thought that
nice clothes would cover a multitude of sins, like
breakouts and glasses.

So there I was on Thirty-fourth Street with a little
wad of green bills secured in a fake gold money clip,
I knew my way around and all week I'd been plotting
this, how I was going to sneak down on the A train
and run around checking out the after-Christmas sales
because I wanted to go back to school after the Christmas vacation with some new clothes, but I didn't want
the same clothes everybody else had. Everybody's
mother shopped in the same neighborhood stores or
they'd go to Alexander's in the Bronx and I wanted to
look different from my classmates. Then I thought
maybe I'd find a talking doll for Ramona too, a fake
diamond pin for my mother, a real silk tie for my
stepdad.

So I was plotting how I was going to go home car
rying a bunch of these fancy shopping bags you get
from midtown stores and my mother was going to say,
WHERE HAVE YOU BEEN, ANTHONY, and I was
going to empty those bags out right on the table and
they were all going to say ooh and aah. I was thinking,
maybe I'll even buy one of those transistor radios with
the little batteries, like the kind everybody's suddenly
been getting that are selling on Thirty-fourth Street for
five bucks or so.

I stopped in front of Macy's, right in front of the
revolving doors; the reason I had come directly here
was because I knew this store, this store was familiar
to me because it was my grandmother Minnie's favorite place to shop. But every other time I went to
Macy's and we got to these revolving doors my grandmother would snatch me and jam me in front of her
into that door and pull me into the store just at the
right time.

So I jumped into the door and it spun me around I

don't know how many times, 'til I was spun right out onto the selling floor with all the lights and mirrors and signs and flashing and faces glaring down at me from ten-foot-high people who were all around me in this tide of Christmas sales shopping that was sweeping through the store.

I made it onto the escalator for the boy's department. But even though I had my eyes fixed right in front of me I knew that everyone was looking at me, everyone was giving me the evil eye, and halfway up I thought, oh God I've got to get out of here while I can. So as soon as I got up I got right back on the down escalator and just by standing there I was swept all the way back down through the store and spat out, spinning through those revolving doors onto Thirty-fourth Street.

This was something else. This was like no other time I had been downtown, so first I just stood there outside Macy's watching the steam of my breath. First I watched it close up where it came out of my mouth, then further away where it curled away into the crowds because whoever in the world wasn't in Macy's was out here, loaded with shopping bags, jumping in and out of cabs, honking horns.

I started walking. I went into Woolworth's right across the street, I went into Ohrbach's but this place was even scarier than Macy's and I felt even stranger here because I had never come here before. I walked some more, gawking up through my glasses to see bits of the top of the Empire State building, and gazing into the windows of those little electronics stores, comparison shopping for transistor radios. I told myself, I have to get the absolute best buy!

Then I see this huge, grand department store and a big, big sign that says B. Altman & Company. It looks like a castle to me with the steps going up and the limos lined up outside idling at the curb, and ladies in minks and jewels. I've got to see inside. So I go striding in just like I've been here a hundred times, in through these big glass doors, right past the doorman, into a kind of lobby and immediately I'm caught up with the smell of perfume. I look to my left and there, right there almost by my side in this glittering lobby is standing a goddess of a black woman. Really young, very gorgeous.

She's a total vision. This woman is all done up. She has on what looks to me like tons of hair all teased up and bouffed up and immediately I think of Bunny's Wigwam, the hottest wig shop in Harlem, where ladies disappear into little teepees so the hairdresser can do their wigs without nobody seeing. I know this woman's been to Bunny's Wigwam and her eyelashes come from there too. I know because they're incredibly long just like the lashes on those mannequins in the window on 125th Street.

But this woman looks like nobody I've ever seen before, she's even more fabulous than my Aunt Estelle and I haven't seen many like *her*. She's all wig and lashes and fur, fur up around her ears, she's a fabulous being rising up out of a mountain of shiny Christmas shopping bags. She looks at me and believe me, time stops.

She starts talking to me over that huge fur collar of hers, she's saying, can I help her get a cab?

I know how to get cabs. I've even made money getting cabs for people in front of my building. But I'm in another world now so I say, well, all you have to do is go outside, put your hand up and say "TAXI"— you know, flag it down. How she got this far with all those bags I don't understand.

"You look like a trustworthy kid," she says. "Do me a favor and watch my bags." And she steps out from her mountain of shopping bags and glides through the door like she's somebody special.

This woman doesn't know how to get a cab. From where I'm standing trying to peek into her bunch of bags I can see she doesn't know, because you cannot get a cab in midtown in Manhattan on a busy Saturday unless you venture out into the middle of oncoming traffic so they can see you and most of the cabs won't stop for you anyway because you're black and they don't want to be going up to Harlem. So in minutes she comes gliding back in out of the cold, and she says, ''Oh I don't know how to do it can you help me?'' Without a second's hesitation, as if the whole thing were some prearranged plan I say yes and pick up some of her bags.

So we struggle through the doors together with all her shopping bags and every single person looking at her. She's like a painted doll. She's beautiful, she's beautifully dressed, and even I can tell that these are expensive clothes she's wearing. How come this woman who walks like she's gliding has the money to shop in this kind of a store with all these gleaming limos idling outside and the chauffeurs waiting? And then I figure, maybe she's one of these women my mother talks about when she sends me out of the room. One of those, you know, Ladies of the Evening!

I'm all set to jump into the street and hail a cab for her when suddenly she tells me she's hungry, she's heard of a place in New York where they have good hot dogs. She must be talking about Nathan's because Nathan's is famous but then she says they have orange drink too. Now I know she wants Nedick's.

''That's right down the street,'' I tell her.

''Well,'' she says, ''why don't you help me there with my bags? We can get a cab better over there and we'll get some hot dogs.''

My mother's words came rushing into my head, but this woman fascinated me. Maybe she's a woman spy like in *The Man from U.N.C.L.E.* and they've sent her here to kill me with one of those poisoned Nedick's franks. I just had to find out. I'd seen that show on TV a million times so I knew all the tricks. Everybody was always telling me, aw you're too big for those *Man from U.N.C.L.E.* spy toys, but I loved that show and I knew all about their spy briefcases and their hidden radios and I'd even seen those spy radios and things in the mail order section of the newspapers.

So we're walking along and talking about not-much

and I'm thinking, how did she know I was going to B. Altman & Company when anyway I was going to Macy's? She must have followed me from Macy's but she was already inside the store when I got there plus she had time to do all that shopping. How did she beat me to B. Altman's? Why would she want to kill me? She doesn't even know me, and on and on until my mind's looping but I know what I'm going to do. I'm going to see if she takes the first bite. There's always a lot of franks rolling around on the grill at Nedick's and they can't all be poisoned because then all the other people sitting there would get killed too.

We get to Nedick's and she orders two franks and two orange drinks. She doesn't appear to favor any particular frank when the man serves them up and she doesn't appear to know the man. Then, when she goes to pay the man she takes this huge, bulging wad of money out of her pocketbook—even the man's eyes jump right out of his head. I tell her,

"You shouldn't ought to take your money out like that! Somebody might rob you!"

She pays the man, she doesn't seem to care, and we go stand over at the lunch counter. She must be the only woman wearing a fur in Nedick's. She starts talking about how it's so cold, she bought things for her family, she has a lot of sisters and brothers, and I'm watching her as she very delicately takes a bite of her frank, a sip of her orange drink.

"How many people you got in your family?" she asks me.

"Just me and one sister."

"Oh!" she says, "Mine's a *big* family, we've got twelve kids."

I can't believe it. What does this woman mean twelve kids? Nobody's got twelve kids. Even Mrs. Chris upstairs in my building, Jimmy's family, even she's just got five and that's the biggest family I know. But she's still not falling over from her frank so I take my first bite, she's telling me she bought Christmas gifts and she's so excited to be in New York.

"Where do you live?" she asks me.

"Oh, in the projects." I don't tell her Wagner projects, I just say the projects, I figure that's a smart move, don't give anything away.

"Oh," she says, "I live in the projects too!" And I'm thinking, sure, sure this woman lives in the projects. But I say, What's the name of your projects?

"I live in the Brewster projects. But hopefully soon I'm going to be moving into a big, fancy house."

I never heard of no Brewster projects. And nobody moves out of the projects into no big fancy house. This woman is lying. I'm starting to pick up she has an accent and a strange style of talking. She sure talks a lot, and she's kinda nosy.

Then she tells me she has to go to rehearsal because she's going to be on the *Ed Sullivan Show* and I nearly choke to death. Now I've got her. I know she's not going to be on no *Ed Sullivan Show*. I happened to know the Ed Sullivan Theater from taking Ramona to dance school, and some weeks I'd see crowds of girls lined up outside that theater hooting and hollering and screaming, jumping up and down, flashing cameras, then I'd see a limo pull up, some star like maybe Tony Bennett or Sammy Davis, Jr., get out, and girls start grabbing and pushing, trying to get near the star. Even some policemen got knocked over the barricade sometimes.

Who does this woman think she is, saying she's going to be on *Ed Sullivan*. She's not one of those stars. And another thing, nobody who's going to be on the *Ed Sullivan Show* is going to be standing up in Nedick's right now eating hot dogs with some twelve-year-old kid who they don't even know. This woman is lying, she's a spy, she's up to no good.

So I say, "Oh really?" And she tells me a whole story about how she has a singing group that she formed and she named them the Supremes and now it's their first time on the show. I'm so excited, she's telling me, I'm so excited to be going on the *Ed Sullivan Show*.

"Didn't you ever hear of us honey? We've got a record out called "Baby Love." Didn't you hear it? And now we just had a new one out, maybe you heard it, it's called 'Come See About Me.' "

"No ma'am, I never heard that," and I'm telling myself, this woman sure can lie!

"We've been here before, we were at the Apollo, the Motown Revue—that's where I'm from, it's called the Motor City."

"The Motor City! I never heard of that."

"Well that's what we call it, the people who are from there. Don't they teach you geography in school?"

"Yeah."

"Well it's called Detroit—Detroit, Michigan, and that's where I'm from."

I know she's lying. I never even heard of Detroit. But she seems kind of nice, she's not the axe murderer, in fact she's beginning to remind me of my Aunt Estelle so I figure I'll do my little spy routine on her, I'll get some more information out of her so I say, "I know where the Ed Sullivan Theater is! I know exactly where it is because my sister takes dance class there!"

"Oh!" she says, "Maybe you want to ride up there with me."

Well, I have nothing better to do and immediately my mother's face flashes inside my head. We finish, we go outside, we both raise our hands and a taxicab screeches to a halt.

"Oh, you gave me good luck!" she says. I'm thinking, if my mother knew I was getting in a strange car with a strange woman she'd kill me before the stranger killed me. But the cabdriver's putting all her millions of shopping bags in the trunk and the woman's telling me to make sure she gets those bags out when we stop.

"Honey," she says all sweet and nice, "otherwise Flo might forget her things in there!" This is the first time I heard her name.

I sit right on the edge, right next to the door with a few packages and her huge, huge pocketbook in between us so that if she tries to feel me like my mother said, I can jump out screaming. And I'm thinking, funny how we got a cab so fast. Maybe this driver's her partner and they're going to kidnap me or they're going to murder me like you hear about them doing to little kids.

So then she tells me her name's Florence Ballard, but she says, "Everybody calls me Flo, or sometimes Blondie because I was always kind of light-haired. What's your name?"

"Anthony." That's what everybody called me.

"Anthony," she's laughing. "That sounds like Mark Anthony of Anthony and Cleopatra fame, chil' that's too cute that suits you. You look so smart, like a Mark Anthony." Then she says, "But I'm going to call you Tony, it's more casual, more sporty."

That's when she starts telling me more about her group the Supremes, how she started it and they've been singing together since they were fourteen, since they were in school and they were called the Primettes, and how she picked the name Supremes, how the group used to have four girls but, she said, twice they lost the fourth girl and no new one joined so now there's two other girls that sing named Mary Wilson, that's who was in it from the beginning, and Diana Ross, who came later and they take turns singing lead, and my head's spinning—

"You'll like Mary," she says. "Diana's kind of stuck up but she's okay too."

Then she told me they just came back from playing in England with a whole bunch of other groups called the Motown Revue, and they were big hits, and everyone just went wild over them, and they met Paul McCartney and Ringo Starr, and on and on she was going like a motormouth and of course I'm not believing a word of it, not one freakin' word.

She's telling me about when they first came to New York and played the Apollo, and I'm remembering this one night not that long ago when they had a whole bunch of out-of-town acts. I remember because a couple of my mother's favorite stars were on. She's reeling off this list of names, Martha Reeves and the Vandellas, and Mary Wells—

"I remember, I remember seeing that show!"

"Well we were on that show, honey. We were the first ones out, we had on the best dresses and we sang the best, we got a great reception. You know, we weren't really known then, honey, but now we're getting big and soon we're going to be famous!" And she tells me how they used to play sockhops and they were always never getting anywhere and for the longest time everybody called them the no-hit Supremes until they got their first big hit single just last summer.

"We did a big show Christmas Day," she says, which I find very odd—who works on Christmas Day? "It was at the Brooklyn Fox Theatre," she says, "with Marvin Gaye and the Temptations and the Marvelettes, and Little Stevie Wonder. You ever been there, to the Brooklyn Fox?" I'd been to the Brooklyn Fox Theatre but I had never seen or heard any of these guys All I knew about the Brooklyn Fox was that my mother went there to hear gospel. But Flo's still going, she never stops talking—

"And soon we're going to England again."

England *again?* Nobody just goes to England *again.* She can't fool me. This woman sure can cook up a story!

We pull up outside the Ed Sullivan Theater and it's getting real dark. I'm going to be late home, I'm going to be late late, I'll get it from my mother but I'm going to watch this woman try to get in the door of the Ed Sullivan Theater after we pull all her bags out of the trunk. She tells me to wait outside and somebody's going to come out and get me in a few minutes. I don't believe the old man at the door is really letting her in, maybe she's a cleaning woman or something, or maybe I'm going to watch her come flying back out on her ear, or some other body part.

The cab's gone, she's gone, the sky's getting darker every minute and I'm standing out on the street, I've got to get on that A train and get uptown to 125th Street and get on that 29 bus and get across town to Second Avenue. So I head toward the corner, I get halfway toward the corner, I turn back, I'm looking and looking and stamping my feet to keep warm and blowing in my hands and it seems like hours, I'm thinking, this woman ain't never coming back, but finally this old guy comes out and says, "You Tony?"

And in I march, fully prepared for the slaughterhouse.

"Okay, DON'T TOUCH ANYTHING, DON'T GO ANYWHERE, DON'T DO ANYTHING, STAND RIGHT HERE IN THIS SPOT!" the man says and disappears.

Inside there's people running around barking orders at each other, there's a metal staircase like the one in school, and after what seems like another eternity a man comes dashing down and says, "You, Tony, come on upstairs, Flo wants you to meet everybody."

So I go upstairs into this room and there's Flo and a whole bunch of other people sitting around, and Flo's busy unwrapping all those packages that were so beautifully wrapped with bold, shiny paper and bows like I never saw before, and she's telling them, I got this for this one, and that for that one. Everybody's oohing and aahing and comparing purchases and I'm standing here watching this whole scene when all of a sudden Flo turns around and sees me.

"Oh, there you are!" she says, just as if this is the most natural thing, and she introduces me to two other girls. As soon as she says their names I've forgotten them. Then she introduces me around to some other people, there are a few guys and an older lady, she tells them how she met me at B. Altman's and I helped her carry her bags I was so nice, and there's so much happening I can't remember any of these names. Then one of the women, the one with the real light powder makeup starts unwrapping her packages and she says she went to Saks Fifth Avenue.

I was just struck dumb. I never knew anybody who

could shop at Saks Fifth Avenue. What was I doing here with all these big, flashy people. Then Flo told this woman who went to Saks, "I don't think that's going to look right on you, honey, not with your legs." And the woman told Flo, "Oh it'll be fine, it'll be fine. I'll wear boots." It sounded kind of bitchy to me, like sisters kind of bitchy, but I wasn't paying much attention. I was focused on Flo.

Then they all went clickety-clacketing down that little metal staircase to rehearsal and I just tagged along, nobody told me not to. We went into this place that was all wires, wires everywhere, millions of wires snaking around and I was surprised because this place was so small. One side of the studio was floor-to-ceiling mirrored so I figured, that's why it looks a lot bigger on TV. If I didn't know I was in the Ed Sullivan Theater I probably wouldn't believe it because it's so small.

They started rehearsing, but this was nothing like the rehearsals I knew from piano lessons or Ramona's dance class. Everything was happening at once and all these men sitting near me with big notepads were shouting move left move right move up move down stand this way stand that way put the mike higher check the sound sing this song sing that song and everybody was in constant motion except me. I was just sitting there thinking, my God, my God! This lady is really going to be on the *Ed Sullivan Show,* and she does have a singing group and a bunch of people fussing all around her! And suddenly it occurred to me, she's my friend.

They started singing a song that went ". . . so come on hurry, come on come see about me . . ." and it registered. I'd heard this before, I'd heard this on the radio! I must have heard it lots of times. How come I never before heard of the Supremes?

By now it was nine o'clock at night and the whole thing was over, they were packing up. Nobody was saying anything to me. I was just sitting there and they were all starting to leave so I just got up and went back upstairs with them. That's when Flo realized that I was still there. She came up to me with that look like, shouldn't you be home? But she was very nice, she asked me, did I want to come down tomorrow early and watch the regular show? But I knew she was thinking—they were all thinking—who is this kid and what's he doing still here at nine o'clock in the night he should be gone home long ago.

I could tell they were worried. Flo started saying, "You want me to call your mother?" And quick as a flash I told her, "No no! Please, there's no need. I'll just jump on the A train and be home in no time, you don't have to call my mother." So then Flo gave me ten dollars for a cab and she asked me if that was enough to get home, "Promise me you'll take a cab." She told the others, "If there's one thing this kid knows how to do it's hail a cab!" I watched them take off in this big limo, then I ran right down the subway steps with my head whirling and my heart slapping against my inside. I bought a token, and I put the rest of the money with the little wad in my pocket.

I figured, whatever beating I get when I get home, this day was surely worth it. I'd met a stranger who was a star, I'd been inside the Ed Sullivan Theater, and I'd even turned a small profit.

CHAPTER 2

◆ ◆ ◆

Close as Sisters

So that's how I happened to be riding home on the A train past nine o'clock that Saturday night, all the way up to 125th Street, wondering how I was going to tell my mother and wishing I'd had a camera because I knew she'd be the first one that wasn't going to believe this story. I could hardly believe it myself.

But I didn't have a camera because I was still in grade school and suddenly here I was back in the subway, it was late, and I didn't know if I felt very big and grown like when I'd stepped out of the subway that morning, out onto Thirty-fourth Street with my wad of money, or if I just felt kind of scared and excited. I was sitting there on the A train all by myself past dark, I still had to get that 29 bus crosstown, I still had to face my mother and not a single package did I have from my big midtown shopping expedition.

When I finally got back home it was about an hour later. My mother was furious, she was standing right in the lobby of the building with her belt, ranting and raving, she was waving that belt around, shouting and crying and some of her friends were there trying to console her—they must have called the housing police because if anything happened you didn't call the regular police, you called the housing police and they'd look in the basement, on the roof, in the laundry room.

When my mother first saw me she was relieved, it was all hugs and kisses and tears but after about ten seconds of that she started screaming, "GET UPSTAIRS ANTHONY! Don't Even Wait for the Elevator! WALK up to the third floor!" And on and on she goes, I'm trying to tell her my story, I can hardly get a word in, she's screaming it's all a big lie, she doesn't believe a word of it.

Then my stepfather butted in, he said nobody could have just made this story up. Nobody's going to make up that they just met this person and this person's going to be on *Ed Sullivan* because everybody in every one of the twenty-two buildings of these projects watches *Ed Sullivan*.

"Get Me The TV Guide!" ordered my mother. "Somebody named the Supremes better be in there." Well, needless to say the *TV Guide* didn't have any Supremes on *Ed Sullivan*. The Supremes just weren't that famous, they weren't headlined, they were like the Russian circus or the ballet acts or Topo Gigio or whoever you had to sit through for a whole hour before the big acts came on. My mother said, "Let's wait and see if they're on TV tomorrow night and they'd better be on." But that was no good because like I told her, they wanted me to come down tomorrow afternoon and see the rehearsal.

"NO you're not going. FINAL. No Way are you going down there, there's something very fishy going on!" Then she called my grandmother Vera and she told *her* the whole story, and my grandmother came right over and *she* said there was something odd going on, something seriously suspicious about grown women wanting a mere child around and anyway she'd heard of this group the Supremes (God knows where my grandmother had heard of the Supremes) and she thought they wore *sleeveless* dresses, "sleeveless dresses that show All of their Business." At which her eyebrows sort of arched up.

Then I remembered. I'd seen so many new names and faces coming at me at one time, I'd forgotten but now I was remembering and I told my mother, "Florence Ballard! That was her name but she calls herself Flo. And they're staying at the Warwick Hotel!"

My mother went directly to the phone. I was holding my breath for ever while she dialed information, she got the number of the Warwick Hotel, she dialed that number, waited for them to pick up, and announced real matter-of-fact, "Let me speak with Florence Ballard please. Is she registered there?" . . . (Now my heart was pounding) . . . "She IS?"

My mother put down the phone, she didn't even wait to speak with Florence Ballard, she just sat down like she was in shock and I let out my breath. After that, for some strange reason, I didn't even have to plead with her any more, she just said I could go back down there tomorrow, she even relented and said that tomorrow, just for tomorrow, I could skip church and go straight from Sunday school to the rehearsal. She was very strict but she knew I could be trusted to do things on my own, and she knew that if she didn't let me go I'd be a miserable person to live with for the next couple of months. I would have been so evil I would not have spoken a single word to anybody.

I wanted to be downtown early, I didn't even know if they would let me in, I didn't know why they were being so nice to me, letting me in there, letting me in when all those other kids were stuck outside just trying to get a glimpse of all that glamor. Maybe they didn't mean it, maybe Flo had forgotten, maybe anything, but nothing was going to stop me from trying.

I didn't sleep all that night and all through Sunday school I couldn't stop wondering, I don't know if I heard ten words of the lesson that morning. I was so busy whispering to all the other kids about what had happened to me, it made me jump up in the air when Reverend Lance Martin informed me loud and clear, "Anthony, this is *not* your personal chitchat hour. This, young man, is Sunday school."

Right after Sunday school let out, still dressed in my Sunday suit and tie, I leaped on that 29 bus, jumped on the A train to Fifty-ninth and Columbus Circle, ran for the D train, one stop and I'm at Fifty-first running up the steps out onto the street and I'm there. But the Supremes aren't there yet, maybe they're not coming.

Well, it didn't take me long to figure out that it wouldn't be smart to get bunched up with all the other kids that were waiting there, because I knew from past experience that these kids were no way getting in the Ed Sullivan Theater, not ever. So I said to myself, I'm going to go to that hotel. I raced over to the Warwick Hotel, just in time to see the elevator doors open on the other side of the lobby, and these three women stepped out of the elevator looking something like glamorous triplet sisters wearing the clothes of life.

"Tony! You made it!" Flo says in that bubbly kind of voice. "I'm so glad you made it, honey!" The other two just smile, then the one with all the light powder makeup says, "How nice," but kind of curtly, like she doesn't really mean it.

Flo really did seem glad. She told me she'd called her mother in Detroit, that she told her mother all about me, she told me I reminded her of her brother back home. She was so friendly, sort of sisterly, and I guess I was too young to see it then but later I knew that even a grown person, even a star like Flo might feel kind of homesick sometimes, might even feel overwhelmed by all the whirl and excitement and strange places and everything else that was new. But right now I was not thinking anything like that, I was just thinking, these women are fabulous! This is AmAzing!

There was this big, shiny limousine waiting outside and the three girls got in the back, then Flo pulled down a jump seat for me to sit on. Now, I had been in limos before, this was not my first time in a limo because every time there was a big wedding or a big funeral in my family, which was often, there'd be a limo. But this was the first time for me in a limo when there wasn't any wedding and there wasn't any funeral, so I was learning something, that this was just another method of transportation (even if the trip was only three blocks). This was part of life in the big time.

I had forgotten the other two girls' names, but sitting up there in the limo I thought they all looked like Flo, they all looked like dolls. They were all made up with the hair, the lashes, everybody's face had on all this powder and lipstick and lashes, they were all perfumed and coiffed, all decked out in furs, they all had on sunglasses and jewels and their bracelets were jing-jangling as we went driving off in that limousine to the Ed Sullivan Theater. They told me they didn't do a full makeup because they were going to have a dress rehearsal and they did special makeup for TV. To me they looked as if they were in full makeup, but underneath all that powder and pancake makeup their faces still had a kind of a happy glow.

We got to the theater and the first thing that struck me when we walked into the dressing room was this big, long make-up table. Everything was already set up on the table, big towels all over the place, everything was neat and beautiful like in a department store. All the eyebrow pencils were laid out together, all the eyelashes, the lipsticks in every shade of red and pink, the pancake makeup, they were all arranged in rows with ten or twelve of each item. In years to come this would be something I would do, ordering by the dozen and laying everything out immaculately on make-up tables in dressing rooms in cities all over the world, from L.A. to Malaysia.

I stayed around there all day. Everybody was fussing and carrying on, and everybody was a little nervous. Flo told me this was such an important event for them. I met Gregory the hairdresser—he was a tall, very good-looking guy—everyone else was like a sea of faces to me, but I did notice that everyone, all the men and all the women were beautifully dressed, very elegant.

I watched them all, but mainly I watched Flo. I was

real quiet trying to keep out of the way and trying to take it all in because I'd never ever been around this kind of thing before, I didn't know what to do with myself, I didn't want anyone looking at me or wondering what I was doing there. So, when I heard somebody say they wanted a cup of coffee I just jumped right in. The coffee was upstairs because you couldn't bring food into the stage area. I leaped up, "I'll go get it!"

Nobody drank coffee in my house, I didn't know anything about cream and sugar and how it's taken. I didn't know when a person says, I want black coffee, that meant don't put anything in it. So I figured, pour the coffee in, put in some milk, some sugar, I didn't know how much sugar, I must have put in about ten spoonfuls. That was my first little job for the Supremes.

Then somebody wanted some cigarettes from the store, a little after that Flo wanted a cheeseburger, someone else wanted a hot dog, and on and on it went and I was thinking, why don't they just make a list, but it almost seemed like they were creating things for me to do, little errands to keep me busy which was fine because I couldn't wait to get outside, I was so nervous I needed a break to get away from all of these grown people, to get out in the street so I could say to myself, WOW! I don't believe this! I actually made it inside the Ed Sullivan Theater! Wow! Wait till I tell those guys next Saturday at dancing school they'll have a fit, they'll never believe it!

Running in and out getting things for people I was starting to notice this crowd of kids my own age gathering outside the door of the theater, just like I'd seen on Saturdays but this time there were boys as well as girls. I never saw a boy fan there before, and they were yelling and screaming for the Supremes! Every time I went to the store I had to march quick as I could through these fans with my mouth shut tight because they were all pleading with me to get them autographs, or to get them inside, and that's when I really began to know what a fan was because before, on Saturdays, I used to think they were just crazy girls, crazy about the guys. Then it dawned on me that these girls, these Supremes were really famous, they were stars and *I was with them*—stop and imagine that!

In the middle of it all I had to call my mother. She'd made me promise to call her from the theater right after the dress rehearsal, I guess she only half believed my story. She wanted to know exactly and in every detail what they'd be wearing, what style of dresses, how they'd be standing, who was in the middle and she said, "When Ed Sullivan comes on, these girls better have on the same dresses and they better do exactly what you said they'd do." Well, I sure hoped I told her right because I was so busy running errands for everyone, and I was so excited—mainly I was excited to be inside the actual Ed Sullivan Theater—that I could have made a big mistake and said three steps instead of four.

Flo was too busy most of the time to pay me much attention and it seemed like the three of them were always surrounded, always being fussed over for one thing or another. But not too long before the show Flo said they were going back to the hotel to get something to eat. I couldn't figure out why because it seemed like they'd been eating all day, I know *I'd* gone to the store enough times, but there was the limo waiting outside, and the crowd of fans right outside the door, so I just tried to hold onto Florence so as not to get separated and lost in the mob, I just stuck real close and I got whisked along right into the back seat of the limo.

I went up to Flo's room with her and she had room service bring soup while she made up some wild concoction of tea and honey and lemon she said was for her throat. I just took to her, we hit it off like we were kindred spirits. It seemed like I'd known this lady all my life. Every minute she was reminding me more of my Aunt Estelle, she was always laughing and she had this way of talking that was kind of sweet and tough and funny at the same time. She must have been nervous about the show, about being on Ed Sullivan for the first time but she'd say, "Chil', we're gonna show them we're the best, we're the Supremes! And Flo's gonna sing like she's singing for the sun to come up!" She was always saying, Flo this and Flo that and at first I thought she was talking to me like some people talk to little kids, but then I noticed she talked that way to everybody.

The show was beautiful. They were wearing these short chiffon dresses made in three layers, with thin little straps and a little pinched-in waist, very simple, sleeveless (how'd my grandma know?), and they did these very demure movements, very graceful, very cute, just these little shimmies and turns and a lot of stuff with the hands. I thought it was the living end, I thought they were just gorgeous with the makeup and the hair and everything.

Someone from Ed Sullivan had done their makeup before the dress rehearsal, but when they saw it in the mirror they looked horrified, they ran right back in the dressing room and took it all off and started all over again. Flo told me they'd always done their own makeup. She told me Diana had studied this kind of thing in school and Diana used to make all their outfits and used to cut their hair for them all, of course she charged them for it.

So there they stood, all together in a neat little line on the stage, the one with the light powder, who I now knew was Diana, she stood in the middle and they all shared one microphone. They were doing "Come See About Me" and the audience went wild for them. It seemed like a lot of them knew it already.

When their part of the show was over I went back in the dressing room to meet them and they all seemed so thrilled, except Diana was saying how Ed Sullivan had kind of rushed them off the stage, he hadn't stood and talked to them like he did with the headlined acts. But even that couldn't really crush their excitement. I heard Diana Ross say, "We'll be back!" The way she said it sounded to me almost like a vow.

Flo asked for my phone number, she said she'd call me when they came back to town, she said that might not be until they came back from Europe. The girls gave me photos and records and autographs to take to school, and they gave me about six 45s, each with a little dark blue label in the middle that had a map on it of the Motor City, Detroit. It was as if they'd given me a million dollars.

So this time when I left there it was with one of those fancy shopping bags full of goodies that would keep me going until the next time, except until it happened I really didn't think there was going to be a next time. I thought it was like a single weekend's adventure, I hoped they'd call me but I was most concerned that I didn't have any witnesses, I should have brought one of my best friends with me.

Of course they gave me money for a cab again and I took the subway again and pocketed the change. It was ten o'clock when I got home. But this time my mother and all her friends were up in the apartment waiting for me. My mother had called everyone right after I called her to report on what the girls were going to be wearing and how they were going to be standing and what they were going to sing. She'd called everyone to predescribe it and they were all so amazed and so thrilled because I had described it exactly. She'd spread the whole story, she'd called everybody and she'd said, "Oh yeah, I just spoke to my son and he's down there with the Supremes, he's down there with them right now, the one he knows is on the left. Oh, you haven't heard of them? Oh girl, they're big stars!"

So they were all up there, and they'd all brought their children and the children were still running around the apartment, climbing over the furniture and everyone was waiting for me, waiting for me to tell them every little detail of my day with the Supremes.

"Which is the one you know?"

"I know the taller one, the one on the left, her name's Florence."

"Who was that one in the middle?"

"Oh, her name is Diana."

"Oh yeah, those girls are cute, I never heard of them you know. But the one in the middle, she looked like she was doing a little extra, she was wiggling a little more or something."

I said, "She's the lead singer."

"You couldn't really see them too good because the TV set wasn't that clear but that one in the middle, she opened her mouth real big. She's good though, she's good."

They kept hammering questions at me.

"Oh, the one on the right, she looks really quiet but she's cute. Who's she?"

"That's Mary Wilson."

"The one in the middle, she's got a tooth missing in the back, she oughta get that tooth fixed. She's got those big bubbly eyes. Why's she so *skinny?*"

I hadn't really paid much mind to Diana and Mary, Flo was my link, she was my friend and I concentrated pretty much on her. But right now in my mother's living room they were all picking out this girl or that girl, and most of them were picking Diana.

For the next few weeks, as the Supremes' record shot to the top of the charts and they became more and more famous, I became a star in the projects, just for knowing them. It felt real good, and I intended for it to stay that way.

From now on my whole life started to turn around the Supremes—when were they coming back, where were they now, where were they going next, what were they doing, what had they done? I started doing things I'd never done, I started going to record shops looking for posters and things like that, I looked for records. They'd given me those six copies of "Come See About Me" but that was all I had to hang on to, and now that I was going back in their history and I was checking out whatever was new, I was discovering that they had other songs.

I started hanging out in record stores and looking. Not all the stores had their records, I had to go all the way downtown to Colony Records and I found out they already had LPs out, there was *Meet the Supremes* that I knew nothing about. I bought it and I pinned the sleeve on my wall at home, it had a moody picture of the three girls in identical, plain blue sleeveless dresses. I discovered that record had already been out a whole year!

They also had *A Bit of Liverpool,* which had a lot of Beatles songs on it and a funny picture of the three of them in these smart suits and ties and umbrellas, with bowler hats on their heads. In the picture I thought Flo looked like she was trying not to break up laughing, but I didn't like this record as much as the others. They already had a huge seller with "Where Did Our Love Go," they already had a hit with "Baby Love," and when I heard that song I realized it had been on the radio. Then, just a few weeks later I found a brand new LP, *Where Did Our Love Go.* I studied the pictures on the sleeves, I noticed that on each one Diana was a little bit in front of the other two, I also noticed that Diana and Flo both seemed to be looking right at you out of the picture, whereas Mary was not looking exactly at you. I started spending my money on these records and by the time they came back I knew every word.

I knew everything. I read everything I could possibly find on the Supremes and at that time there was a lot being written. I found out about different magazines, *Jet* magazine and *Ebony* magazine, and I started reading these and discovering there was such a thing as Motown, Motown was big, Motown had the latest sound that was called the Detroit sound

In February I was still waiting when I heard "Stop! In the Name Of Love" on the radio. By the time I got down to Colony Records it was number one, it was heading toward being a million-seller—their third, I found out. I thought it was fabulous, it was great for dancing. Then there were interviews with the Supremes, and little Supremes stories, and Supremes fact sheets with pullout double-page photos and stuff. So I learned everything all at once.

I learned their ages, I found out they were all twenty-one years old. I learned that they *all* lived in the projects, I learned how many brothers and sisters they all had, how tall they were, what their hobbies were, that Flo and Mary were friends since elementary school, that they'd been singing together since they were fourteen, which seemed like forever to me.

I cut out their pictures. They were always in these little dresses, all dressed the same, or sometimes off-stage they'd be in stylish matching suits with hats and gloves, the whole bit, they always had the wigs and the makeup and the eyelashes and the jewelry, they were always standing in a little line like triplets.

Of course, after about three weeks of talking non-stop about the Supremes and carrying my clippings and photos around everywhere I went so I could show my friends, and playing the same records over and over, singing along trying to learn the words—every time the record finished I'd just put the needle back at the beginning again—after about three weeks of this my stepfather started screaming that he couldn't stand it any more, he'd yell at me, "YOU SOUND LIKE A FROG!" And my mother said, enough. She said she was not going to have any more of it, there was more to life than Supremes and if I didn't start concentrating on my school work there was gonna be Trouble.

So I just had to bite my tongue and go to school and stop showing the pictures round school so much and whispering in class so much. Christmas was over, I went back to Scouts and piano lessons, I went back to helping after school at the Head Start program they ran at the church. I used to help the younger kids with their reading. The state funded it and the church paid me about twenty-five dollars a week which, added to my delivery service, was just what I needed so I could keep buying records and buying clothes, so I'd be ready when Flo came back. I had to bide my time, waiting to pounce, waiting for the very next time these Supremes came to town.

CHAPTER 3

◆ ◆ ◆

Gutter To Glitter

I learned everything there was to know just waiting for the Supremes to come back to town. I started seeing headlines, like "THE SUPREMES MAKE IT BIG," and then "SUPREMES WOW EUROPE TOO." I was still thinking, how do you just go to Europe? Europe was very foreign, I didn't know how someone just went to Europe. I read about their European tour, which was with the same Motown Revue Flo had told me was at the Apollo. I read how they were just as big as the Beatles and I knew what kind of reception the Beatles had received when they came to New York, with all the cops there to protect them from the fans, the ever screaming fans.

By the spring of '65—this was four months since I'd first met Flo and her Supremes and spent that day with them at Ed Sullivan, and it seemed like an eternity—by now I was beginning to wonder if Flo would ever call. I'd given her my number but maybe she'd lost it, maybe she didn't want to take the time to get it from directory, maybe by now they were just too busy, or too famous.

I could tell the Supremes were getting more famous even than when I first met them, I could tell because I was getting to be more and more of a star around the projects, everybody thought I was the last word on

the Supremes and I thought so too. They had just had
yet another hit single, "Back in My Arms Again," I
thought this one was just great because it had Flo's
and Mary's names in the song, they were part of the
story, and this song was on the radio *all* the time, I
would get so excited every time it came on. The Supremes were now being played on all the black stations
and everybody was talking about them, about their
sound, their moves, their style, they were the sweet-
hearts of soul, picture-perfect dolls. Everything I heard
or read made them out to be these black, glittering,
vocal Barbie dolls living a new kind of gutter-to-glitter
American dream come true.

So I was always thinking, oh God, how am I going
to get in touch with these people again, I'm just going
to have to keep watching every Saturday. So every Saturday when I would go downtown to take Ramona to
dance class, I'd be checking the marquee at Ed Sullivan to see if the Supremes were up there, every week
I'd be religiously going through the *TV Guide*, I'd be
thinking, maybe now they're big stars they'll be put in
there, and finally one week I saw it and my brain
screamed, IT'S SHOW TIME AGAIN!

I started by calling the studio to see when rehearsals
were, I'd just pick up the phone, "Do you know what
time it's scheduled for?" I would try to talk very deep,
"I'm calling about the Supremes rehearsal." "Oh, that
reheasal's at one o'clock and they are having the night
rehearsal Friday night at seven o'clock." That was it.

So I just went down there that next time. I thought
I knew what to expect as far as looks went, how they
would dress, how they would look and everything, I
expected them to be just like before, just as beautiful,
just as nice, but the next time I went down there they
looked different, they looked a hundred times better.
More hair, more makeup, more perfume, longer eyelashes. And instead of maybe thirty fans outside the
door there were now about a hundred.

They had all these incredibly stylish outfits they said
they'd bought in Europe, they'd bought miniskirts and

high boots that were not like anything I'd seen in New York. And it wasn't only appearances. Just the way they acted was a hundred times more fabulous and they were even more surrounded, they seemed to have about a hundred different people with them who were even more perfectly dressed then the last time, and this would be the case every single time that I saw them in those early days, there was always more of everything. They also had something new, they had an itinerary, I'd never heard that word *itinerary* before but Flo said, "Honey, now Flo can tell you exactly when we're gonna be in town and you can just come right on down and meet us because Flo wants you around."

In the course of the next couple of months the Supremes kept coming back to New York, and every time they came I would almost die waiting for the end of my piano lesson, the end of the church service, the end of whatever I had to do that day so I could race down and see them. They came and did *Ed Sullivan,* they came back to do *Hullabaloo,* they recorded two songs for Coca-Cola commercials. Then they came right back and did a big, big show on Memorial Day at the Steel Pier in Atlantic City.

So it seemed as if the Supremes were in New York every other week, and when they weren't I couldn't wait because my friends started to hang on every word I said. I started making a scrapbook, using tons of Scotch tape, I worked on it for hours. I used to bring Supremes clippings into school. Every Friday in English class they had show-and-tell, everybody had to get up and talk about something they'd brought in, you had to think of something original.

I was always the most popular in show-and-tell because I always had the latest Supremes story or the latest photo. Maybe I'd bring in the latest album and talk about the liner notes on the back, and my teacher started to warn me, "You know, if you want to get a good grade you have to really do something else. You can't just talk Supremes all the time, Anthony. The idea of show-and-tell is to talk about a lot of different things.'' I gave her a look I saw Flo do and believe me, she got the message. I wasn't about to stop doing the Supremes just because everybody else was doing stuff about the tail end of a hurricane or a planned space mission, or some kind of dead, supposedly rare leaf they'd found while they went on their merry way. I wasn't really interested, I just kept bringing in those Supremes things for show-and-tell anyway, then I'd take them home and tape them in my scrapbook.

During this time I started really, really getting close to the Supremes, mainly with Flo because she was my link. I never really paid that much attention at that time to Mary Wilson, she seemed very quiet and very nice and very sweet and she never really seemed to say much. However, I did start noticing things: Diana Ross and Florence Ballard were always competing with each other in what looked to me like a friendly way, they were both always looking to get in the thick of things, especially with the fans outside. As soon as they came out they would be surrounded. I would still be hanging on to Flo, trying to get through the crush and the fans would be rushing up to get Flo's auto-graph, to get Diana's autograph, then after this big hullabaloo was created around Diana and Flo, if they had time the fans would say, ooh, there's the other Supreme, and they'd run over to Mary. She'd be stand-ing there calmly, she'd give them a nice smile, nobody ever rushed her. Her manner was more laid back, more of a just-happy-to-be-here type of thing.

I started to notice that even though these three girls did everything together and dressed and looked pretty much the same way, they didn't all act the same. I could ask Flo for a favor because I knew her, I was getting to know her very fast, and Mary always smiled warmly at me, I just thought she was shy, but Diana Ross was another story. I was frankly kind of scared of her. She did not seem friendly to me. Of course, I didn't say anything about it to anyone, I remembered what Flo had told me in the cab that first day about

Diana seeming stuck up. But I wanted to be friendly with everybody, everybody around them seemed very nice, everybody was nice to me and they all said when I first met them that Flo had told them all about me.

I'd met Gregory, the hairdresser and make-up man, but now I started hanging around with him and watching him work. He was always easy to talk to, he was always washing or styling one of the wigs that I would see lined up on the mannequin heads all around the dressing room, or he'd be setting out the makeup. And there was Don Foster, he was introduced to me as the Supremes' road manager. He was always very civil, always in a suit and tie. He was very friendly to me, and I was very quickly getting to feel more comfortable around these people, still making myself useful by running to the store and getting coffee and passing messages, so I started asking Don all kinds of questions about his job. What do you do? How do you like traveling? What's your job like? I was beginning to understand all these different jobs that were being done and all this staff that was required so the Supremes could perform and sing and just be plain fabulous.

I met Mrs. Powell, the notoriously grand Mrs. Powell, a charming, very sophisticated lady who was the girls' chaperone. She took charge of their huge stage wardrobe, she made sure everything was always correct. This lady is the last of the great etiquette teachers. Flo told me Mrs. Powell taught everybody at Motown how to do everything right so they could feel perfectly comfortable around kings and queens and high society, and she said when they were on the road Mrs. Powell would make sure there were no undesirable people trying to hang around the Supremes.

Flo told me that Mrs. Powell used to run one of the best modeling and charm schools in Detroit, but she was now working for what Flo called Motown Artist Development. The first time I met Mrs. Powell, she said, "Oh, I have heard of you, my dear, I have heard you're quite a nice young man, I have heard you have wonderful manners and my dear, manners can take

you places money cannot." This is how she introduced herself to me and personally, I was happy to
stay out of her way, she made me nervous. To me she
was total royalty, a real whirlwind of elegance but—
wait a minute, you could see underneath all those
manners this lady was *not* to be taken lightly!

I also met Berry Gordy. It was that second time the
Supremes were in town, they were doing *Ed Sullivan*,
it was late in the evening and all day long I'd heard,
"Mr. Gordy's here," "Mr. Gordy's here," "Mr. Gordy's
going to come down," "Mr. Gordy said to do this,"
"Somebody better call Mr. Gordy," "Somebody better see what Gordy wants to do," "Does Gordy know
that we're leaving," "Does Mr. Gordy know . . ."
Everybody was very worried and concerned about Mr.
Gordy this, Mr. Gordy that, and I'd also heard that he
didn't approve of strangers or outsiders, so of course
I was afraid of this man and what was going to happen
when he came down, I thought he might take one look
at me and say, what the hell are you doing here, kid?

Flo said, "Oh, you'll meet him when he comes,
you'll get to see him." That's all she really said. Then
finally he came and I thought he was just like the rest
of them, beautifully dressed, pleasant smile, and
strangely enough he appeared to be glad to see me.
He said that Florence and some of the other people
had told him about me. It seems they had told him the
story of this kid they had met in New York, he had
heard of me and he came right up to me and said, "So
you're the kid." We started talking, he said, "My God
you're tall, how old are you? You're almost my
height!" He was not a tall man, but he was very gracious and cordial. Then he went about his business,
but I saw that everybody was much more careful of
what they said and did when Mr. Gordy was around.

Right after that I always knew it would be different
if Mr. Gordy was there. Later, when I was really
known around the Supremes and I would just go down
to where the musicians were setting up for rehearsal,
sometimes they would tell me right away, "Mr. Gor-

dy's in town. Mr. Gordy's with us.'' Because sometimes I could get real silly, I liked to clown around,
but when he was around there was no letting me go
up on the stage at rehearsal before the girls came down
so I could play the piano and bang on the drums, and
all those kinds of things a kid is interested in doing.

I knew that when Mr. Gordy was there I went to
rehearsal, that was cool, but I sat down at the table. I
wasn't up on the stage messing with things and looking
at the charts and leaning over the music conductor,
Gil Askey's shoulder or doing things like that. I just
sat at the table trying to look very sophisticated and
quiet. My brain clicked, no going up on stage, no
playing the latest thing I learned at piano lesson today,
my ''Star-Spangled Banner'' jazz version or something like that, because you never knew when he was
going to come in. This was serious business, and just
as long as I went along with that Mr. Gordy never
showed me anything but respect.

Another regular around the Supremes' entourage
that I got to know early on was Phil, the chauffeur.
Motown used to use the Carey Limousine Company
every time the Supremes were in New York and they
always sent Phil, a real nice, real down-to-earth Italian
guy. He used to drive the girls around to and from the
hotel, and then to the stores to go shopping, to the
House of Kenneth beauty salon or wherever. At this
time they were going everywhere together, they did
everything together like three sisters. They were always laughing and giggling together, they seemed to
live and travel as a trio.

Sometimes, when I would be running out to the store
for yet another order of fries or another soda, Phil
would be waiting in the car, he'd be reading the newspaper or listening to the radio because he couldn't leave
the car, so he'd ask me to get him a coffee or a pastry,
and sometimes he'd invite me to sit in the limo and
talk for a few minutes before I faced all those fans in
front of the door.

A lot of the fans didn't like me because I wouldn't

get chummy with them but they'd still hound me and hang around me because now it was me who got to choose which fans received the autographed pictures that Flo would sometimes send down with me. She'd say, "Now mind you're fair with those pictures, Tony." She was the one that really enjoyed the fans, she would love it when they swarmed around her with the autograph books and the photos, she'd stop and talk to them for a couple of minutes and Phil would be holding the limo door, Diana, Mary, Mr. Gordy, everyone would be waiting. Diana would shake her head. I once heard Diana comment something about not getting too close to the fans. "One must create an illusion of mystery with the fans to be sought after," she said. "It keeps them guessing, darling." Even then I knew she was right. She'd say, "Don't be too open like Flo, keep them guessing."

One time, it was a weekend rehearsal day and I was sitting in the limo talking to Phil when Diana came dashing out to the limo in a big hurry. She was in some fabulous fur and the fans were swamping her, she signed about three autographs trying to get the ten feet from the door to the limo. Some security guys were helping her, they helped her into the limo and I heard her tell Phil she wanted to go shopping. Phil asked her, "Miss Ross, what about the other two ladies?" "Oh," she said, "they're not coming. You can drive off. Let's go."

Diana shot me a look and I got out, and Diana was driven off by Phil. When I got back inside Florence said, "Oh, we were just coming down, we're going to go shopping, Diana's waiting for us and we're all going to Bergdorf Goodman."

"She left!" I just blurted it out.

"What do you mean she left?"

"I was sitting outside and she came and she said you and Mary weren't coming."

"Well that's a fine how-do-you-do!" Flo said. "What are we supposed to do, walk? Well ain't that nothing!" And Flo went on and on. "That limo is not for Miss Ross's exclusive use, you know. Tony, you'll just have to get us a cab quick. Mary and I'll wait inside till you have one at the stage door. We'll catch up with her over there, that heifer." I was shocked at Flo's comment but I ran for a cab, I thought, isn't this where I came in?

So we got in a cab and we went to Bergdorf Goodman, there was a whole line of limos idling outside, any one of them could have been Phil's so naturally the girls glided into Bergdorf's and told me to peek in limo windows looking for Phil. I went all along this line of limos, and the drivers inside were looking at me from behind their newspapers like, what's he peeking at me for? But I didn't see no Phil.

Then I went into the store, of course I didn't see Flo and Mary, they hadn't waited. I planned on using a trick from my spy days, I was going to follow the scent of their perfume—being Supremes they were easy to track down. But right away a saleslady came up to me, "Oh you must be with those ladies," they must have been the only black women in Bergdorf's, "they just went up to the second floor!" When I found them I told them Phil was nowhere to be seen.

Flo just looked at Mary, "Mm hmm! I told you, girl." And that's all she said.

They did their shopping, they bought up what appeared to be half the store and nobody was looking at a price tag either. My mother would always look at the tag before she looked at the garment, and she wouldn't even look at the tag unless the garment was on a sale or clearance rack. But Flo and Mary were taking six of these and three of those. Flo would say, "Oh that looks great! Ooh I think that looks good on you Mary! Get two, they've got two colors, get both colors." This is how they shopped, and they never waited for anything to be wrapped, they moved on to the next floor or the next department, picking and choosing seemingly at random, leaving all this great stuff behind and then when they were ready to leave, everything had by some miracle been all wrapped up and got down to the first floor all at the same time.

When we got back to Ed Sullivan there was Phil in the limo, looking very nervous, and the moment he saw Flo and Mary he shrieked, "What are you girls doing in a cab!"

Florence said, "Honey—please, you left us!"

He looked panic-stricken, "Miss Ballard, I didn't leave you. When Miss Ross got in she said that you ladies weren't going." Then he turned to me, "Tony, I asked her didn't I?" I said, "Mm hmm," very matter-of-factly and Flo knew I was just about to jump up and tell him the whole story, she shot me one of her, I'll handle this if you don't mind, looks.

"Oh she *did?*" said Flo. "Well we were going, she knew that. So *she* left us behind on purpose but honey, we got left and this is the last time Flo's gonna get left. Why didn't you send Tony in there to tell us to hurry up, Phil?"

He said, "No, Miss Ballard, I'm very sorry but when Miss Ross got in she told me very definitely, take me to Saks right away. She said you ladies had some more rehearsing to do."

Diana seemed a little edgy and very apologetic when we got inside. Florence came right in and said, "Well thank *God* there are taxis here!" And Diana said, "Ohh! I thought you girls were going to re-hearse! I'm so *sorry*. I didn't *know!* It was all a misunderstanding. Besides," she added looking a little sideways at me, "you girls have paid staff here to assist you, I *knew* you were in good hands." Flo just shook her head and rolled her eyes, "THAT, Diana Ross, is NOT the point. Fair is Fair."

Nobody said anything more about it. I was amazed that Diana would do that, and I thought Flo was really something when she got mad. Clearly, you wouldn't want to mess with her. But after that I started picking up on little conversations between Flo and Mary—I started hearing, Diana did this, Diana did that. I didn't pay it any mind, to me it was just like sisters or best friends, this kind of thing was happening every day in school, there was always some of that, I heard she said you told her he said, kind of crap.

Flo was just a talkative person. She always had plenty to tell me about whatever exciting thing was happening. Every time I saw her it was, I'm so thrilled, I'm so excited, I'm so happy to be in New York, my group's gonna do good, we're gonna do great, we're going through the roof, we've been on the move and everybody likes us. Or sometimes it would be, "Honey, you know it's kind of exhausting going nonstop all the time."

When they were in New York one time that spring she told me she'd just bought a new house, a red brick English Tudor, a fantastic, big house in a beautiful neighborhood of Detroit. She'd moved out of the projects, and so had Mary and Diana. "And you know honey," she said, "we're still neighbors! We're all on the same street!"

It seemed incredible to me still that you could move straight out of the projects into a fancy house. Flo told me her house cost near fifty thousand dollars, plus she was spending a fortune on renovations and interior decorating so the new house would suit her to a T. That much money could have bought *three* houses! People dreamed of just moving out of the projects. It was a big thing for us when the weather was good to go for a ride on a Sunday afternoon, ride out to Long Island, go into Queens looking at houses for when your parents had saved enough. When your stepdad's saved enough we're gonna move to Queens, we're gonna put a down payment on one of those little homes they're building out there and move, my mother would promise.

But these girls had bought houses and moved their *parents* out of the projects. Flo had seven glorious rooms all to herself downstairs, and an eight-room apartment upstairs for her mother and her younger brothers and sisters, and then they were going out buying all this fancy furniture to fill up their big houses.

Of course when I told my mother about Flo's house she decided she just had to have one too, and soon. My Aunt Debbie told my mother, "Girl, that's the way to go." And Estelle advised my mother, "Eleanor, you'd better buy something new because you know you won't have enough money to renovate like Flo Ballard. Everybody knows there's no end to the Supremes' money."

Flo talked a lot about the projects and it was the exact same kind of place I was living in, just in somewhere called Detroit. They were going in and out of each others' apartments, nobody locked their door, nobody rapped on the door, it was just turn the handle and walk in and borrow whatever you need, it's okay. They would braid each other's hair on the front steps, somebody's mother was mixing lemonade for everyone on a hot night, to cool things down. You could stay out late on a Saturday night, you could listen to the doowop groups competing with each other and people would be dancing.

She was telling me about how she and Mary and Diana got to be heroines in their projects when they had their first hit, how they heard their song blasting from transistor radios in all those different apartments and kids whispered as they walked by.

She told me about Eddie Kendrick and his group the Temptations and how they were all friends, how they used to sing around the projects. We had that too, there were people singing under my mother's window every night in the summer, they'd heard about Detroit and people like the Supremes, the Four Tops, the Tempts, and they thought maybe this was the way out. The guys were hanging out doing doowop, singing practically nothing but Motown songs, the Latin guys were beating the bongos, adding their beat to the already hot Motown rhythms, the girls were singing. Some of them were terrific.

We had all that but we didn't have Berry Gordy, somebody who knew how to do things, who knew where to go. We had people doing full shows, we had a great male group called the Elegants—they ended up in Vietnam—their first look at the world outside Harlem was the rice paddies because there was nobody with a company on 125th street in Harlem where they could go and get signed and they didn't know there was a world beyond Harlem, that there were record companies just a subway ride away.

That was the difference, and I was only just beginning to see it. I thought all these new people I was meeting were just great because they knew how to do it, they knew how to get over, and I was going to learn too. I planned to watch and learn, and ask Flo all the questions I could think of. I knew she'd help.

Flo would just sit and talk to me and tell me these things anyway, I don't know why. Maybe she was used to having all those brothers and sisters running around the house. She was like a big sister to me. She'd tell me about show business, places they'd been. "And when you get big you'll go, I'm gonna take you one way or another, you'll see these places." She encouraged me to learn.

One time during one of these visits Flo took me aside and said to me, "Well, what do you want to be? Can you sing? You should be in a band or something like that."

I said, "Listen, I cannot sing, I go to piano lessons every day, I like it, I play some piano." I was trained in classical piano and how to play Chopin and Beethoven, but I couldn't play doowop or bebop. Besides, I wouldn't dare. My mother had gotten the piano from Macy's when you could rent a piano with the option to buy; it was about $8.50 a month plus $125 delivery, which was big money to add to the household bills for several years to come. It was a big sacrifice and my mother was not having anybody playing that crap on a perfectly tuned Baldwin in her living room.

So I told Flo, "No, I'm not really interested in that. What I really want to be is a road manager, I want to be like Don, I want to be in the office and be in charge and things like that." She said, "Really? Well, honey with those glasses you've got the look."

Recently I had been telling a few people that I wanted to be a road manager, it was always a big thing in school, what are you going to be, and when I would tell them they'd say, "A road manager? What's that?" Everybody wanted to be a police officer, a fireman. You had your crew of would-be doctors and lawyers and these were always the most stupid kids in the class, and of course nearly all the girls wanted to be models or Diana Ross. So I would answer, "That's somebody who, if you are a famous star or a singer and you travel all around the world singing songs and stuff, the road manager goes out and makes sure that everything is taken care of."

"Well, Mr. Turner," my teacher told me, "I don't think that there is a big call for road managers, so you should just come right out of your dream world and think of something a little more normal and respectable, like a schoolteacher. How many road managers are there?"

I'd been picking up some quick wit from Flo to add to what I already had so I answered him, "I have *no* idea, but I'll tell you what. I'll send you a postcard from the road."

I had seen road managers in action and I really had quite an idea of what it was. I knew I wanted to be a road manager like Don Foster, but I didn't want to wear a suit and tie like Don Foster, and Don had already told me, "You know, if you're going to be a road manager and be a professional, you should wear a suit and tie, you have to watch everything the girls do, you have to watch who is around the girls and things like that."

So I told Flo what I wanted to be and she said, "Honey, you've got to know a lot about everything to be a road manager, now."

I loved her, the way she talked. She went on, "You should go ahead honey, and you should talk to Gregory."

"Gregory, he's a hairdresser!"

"That doesn't hurt. You should hang around Gregory and let him teach you how to style hair, how to do makeup. Find out everything you can about that, about rollers, about what kind of eyebrow pencils, what colors of makeup we wear." She added, "Baby, if someone is willing to give you information about their profession, then it would be to your advantage to get it."

Then she reminded me about that first *Ed Sullivan Show*. "Remember the dress rehearsal, they had to put all that horrible makeup on us, we had to let them do it because they said they were professionals but they didn't know how to work with black skin and they put all the wrong colors on and we looked like clowns, we had to take it all off and do it ourselves? What if we didn't know how to do makeup, we would have went on like that, looking like total fools!"

She looked at me very seriously, "Don't get upset when I tell you to learn how to do makeup, how to do hair. And also, talk with Mrs. Powell."

I answered, "Oh yeah, Mrs. Powell, she seems kind of strict, she's always giving directions to everybody, even you."

"But honey she can teach you all about charm and acting properly in different situations. Anyway, you have good manners and she'd like to teach you. She's really a nice lady. Flo will ask her to give you some lessons, I don't feel you need extensive training like some of the department store divas around here, but every little bit helps."

I guess she saw the look on my face, because I didn't know the first thing about what a department store diva was, but Flo didn't tell me that Diana had worked in a top Detroit department store, she just kept on, "Tony, there ain't nothing wrong with a future road manager knowing about such things, it will help you with your singing group one day, it will help you keep them looking good." She added, "Mrs. Powell can give you lots of pointers in manners and how to greet people, because I think you're kind of shy like me. You seem very outward, but I think you're kinda shy. She can tell you, you know, how you're supposed to sit, how you're supposed to eat, she teaches everybody at Motown.'' I was a little surprised to hear Flo saying she was shy. She was always talking, she always came right out, how could she be shy?

So Flo sent me to Mrs. Powell, and Mrs. Powell said she'd teach me in her spare time. The first thing I learned was how to shake hands, how to extend your hand and say, ''Hi. How are you. My name is Tony Turner, please come in.'' She got me all practiced up in how to do that and she said you had to do it with a certain diction, a certain tone of voice that was enthusiastic and bubbly, the way I heard the girls talking a lot, and you had to smile, ''always showing your upper teeth only.'' She would instruct me, ''You have very good posture. Sit correctly and learn how to talk to people.'' She just started right in.

I still didn't know how all this was going to help me be a road manager, but it didn't much matter anyway because now Mrs. Powell said she was preparing me for something special, a big surprise. She said, ''I'm going to prepare you, because I know you are going to be around and soon the girls are going to be at the Copacabana, that's a very important engagement and I am going to find a job for you. I'm going to get it okayed with Mr. Gordy first, maybe you can man the dressing room door.'' I didn't know why she had to clear something as trivial as that with Mr. Gordy, but I later realized that he wanted to know everybody and everything that came within twenty thousand feet of the Supremes.

This is what she trained me to do. She said, ''It's a two-week engagement and there are going to be parties. A lot of people will be coming up. Don't say anything, they'll knock at the dressing room door— you can feel safe that they're okay to come in because otherwise security wouldn't have let them get as far as the door—they'll knock, you'll open the door, and all you'll say is, Hi, how are you, my name is Tony Turner, please come in. Always extend your hand first and shake their hand, and if they have a coat or something like that, you'll take it. Always smile, always be up. Be a real people person!''

I must have practiced that a million times. I would practice at home in front of the mirror, trying to make my upper teeth show, I would practice with Mrs. Powell, I was very nervous and finally I said, "Mrs. Powell, you have to teach me something else because I'm so nervous that when I say this to people and the people respond to me they'll say, Oh what a charming young fellow and who are you, and how old are you? And I'll be stumped because I'm programmed and I won't know what to say next.''

But she said, "It'll be fine, don't worry, I'll develop you like a flower. Stand perfectly erect, smile, and if somebody asks you something you don't know, come and get me." She spoke to me about the type of shirt and tie I should have, the color, she said I needed a starched white shirt, button-down collar preferred, baby-blue tie, and a black suit with a pocket handkerchief to match the tie. She said, "Try to buy a set so it's matched, and black socks, lace-up shoes, no loafers they're too casual." She just sort of came on, boom, boom, boom, she took charge of everything.

Of course this meant I would have to buy these things, I would have to work extra hard and save up, I thought maybe my mother's cousin James Knight would help me out. He was the manager of a custom designer menswear store in Harlem called Mr. Tony's for Men, and sometimes he would let me have some real nice, expensive suit for fifteen dollars, or maybe Estelle would treat me, she was getting nearly as excited about this Supremes thing as I was, she was showing up in copies of all the latest outfits the girls were wearing. The Supremes style had become her style. She never missed a chance to comment on how she and Flo looked so much alike.

So that was it. I was going to be helping at the Copacabana. I was going to hang out with Gregory so he could teach me, and since this was to be in July, there would be no school. My job was to open the door and help in the dressing room—a big deal indeed. The Supremes at the Copa was going to be a lavish production.

I had a pretty good idea what the Copacabana was even before Flo told me. I knew it was a swanky midtown nightclub, it was tuxedos and Sinatra and Cuban cigars. Flo was so excited, she said it was a thousand times better than the Apollo, a thousand times more important, it was their dream come true and she would be singing a lead part, she said it was a Streisand song and it was one of her favorites. But she wouldn't tell me what it was, she said she wanted it to be a surprise.

But she did play me their new album, *We Remember Sam Cooke*. She said there was one song on it called "Ain't That Good News" where she sang lead. Flo sounded fabulous, her voice was big, it was like the singing in church, but it was also like her talking voice, the way she would enunciate every word and the ends of words, like sta*tion*. So she was very happy about this lead vocal and she was bubbling over about singing lead at the Copacabana.

The Copacabana was *the* New York supper club, it was big time for sure, it was sophistication and nonchalance at its height, it was their first major New York nightclub engagement and they were all too excited. Suddenly everything was happening so fast I could hardly keep up with the news. *Time* magazine had just come out with a big story about the Supremes, they'd bought big, expensive houses, they had left the projects for good. All those hits and gold records, all that money, they'd finally left Martha and the Vandellas and the Marvelettes far and fast behind, they were on the move, and I was going with them. Of course, it didn't occur to me that they might not all three be going the same way.

CHAPTER 4

◆ ◆ ◆

"People": A Matter of Taste, A Question of Style

S chool was out for the summer!

Up around the projects it was, hey, let's go biking, let's go roller skating, let's go down by the East River! It was, "Hey Tony! The hydrant's open and if your Aunt Estelle comes by with her boyfriend CG maybe we can drive through in his Eldorado with the top down!"

But I was hardly thinking about that. I wasn't thinking about graduating from junior high school or about getting that camera my mother had been promising me, or about going to Buffalo or the church-run summer camp that I went to every year, or even about my thirteenth birthday in July that was getting to be so close it should've been countdown time. Something in my mind kept saying, you can move beyond that. It sounded real right to me.

I was thinking about the Copa. I was still practicing in front of the mirror, rehearsing my smile and trying "Hi! My name is Tony! Pleased to meet you, won't you come in!" in all sorts of different voices, and I was doing extra time on my grocery delivery service so that I'd have money for the black suit and the baby-blue tie and that whole uniform Miss Powell wanted me to have, plus some fabulous clothes for the month they'd be in town.

I knew the Supremes would be coming to town early for this engagement, Flo had told me they'd be coming about two weeks ahead of time so that everybody could get all rehearsed up and ready for the Copa, since this was to be such a prestigious and important engagement. They were also planning to record an album, *At the Copa,* which meant that everything had to be even more perfect than perfect.

So when the day finally rolled around I got all dressed up in my best clothes and went racing downtown to the Copacabana on Sixtieth Street. This was in the afternoon because I knew they would be doing afternoon rehearsals at the Copa right up until the day of the show.

I didn't know how I was going to get into this place, but I was all dressed up and by now I was also feeling pretty confident about things, I was one of the regular faces around the Supremes and when I got down to Sixtieth Street there was one of the band members about to go into the club, so I just sailed right in with him and as soon as I was inside someone came right up to me and announced, "Flo ain't here! She ain't coming." I panicked. No Flo, no fun.

They told me Flo was still in Detroit, she was sick and she'd be arriving in about a week, that's all they said. Later I overheard Diana quietly telling somebody, "She is *not* that sick. All Flo has is a slight cold, if that. I have worked when I was at Death's Door. *I* have collapsed on stage!" Then she turned to somebody else. "Were you there that time I collapsed on stage?"

So I hung out for a while watching rehearsals and checking out the club. I was pretty disappointed. The place was small and kind of dingy. It was in the basement of a small building, you had to go down these steps to get in there, I couldn't even see a dressing room. I had imagined a big, big stage but the stage looked tiny and I kept on thinking, this ain't hardly fabulous.

I had never been to a nightclub in the daytime before

and I was really shocked by this place. The tables looked all beat up, I could see that the seats were worn, that the carpet had been tracked on, there were chairs stacked on top of the tables and people were vacuuming. I thought, this is a dump. Compared to what I had seen at some of the hot nightspots in Harlem the Copa didn't look like anything. The band was just sitting around, people were running around in sloppy workclothes—what kind of a place is this? Where's all the glamor?

Of course all the Motown people were dressed impeccably as usual. All the big shots were there fussing around the girls, I was introduced to them all and they seemed friendly enough but busy, busy. Gil Askey, the musical director was there; Cholly Atkins was there going through all these intricate movements with Diana and Mary; Johnnie Allen the musical arranger was there; Mrs. Powell was of course there—I gave her my best handshake. Berry Gordy's youngest sister Gwen Gordy Fuqua was there to help the Supremes with their wardrobe, and Harvey Fuqua was there, he was introduced to me as the head of Artist Development, and he seemed to be involved in everything. It seemed like Florence was the only person that wasn't there.

Mr. Gordy was there of course, but he didn't seem to be dealing with anything directly. He would watch what was going on and then he'd call Harvey Fuqua or Cholly over and say something real low, and then they'd go back and take care of it, and as usual when Mr. Gordy was around there was not so much fooling around, everybody went about their business like wooden soldiers.

For the next few days I kept going back for afternoon rehearsals at the Copa, I kept myself busy by doing the usual trying to be helpful. I was running out for errands, helping them unwind cable, just moving things around. It wasn't so strict that you had to have a union card. Everybody from the Copa or from the orchestra they'd hired thought I was just somebody's kid so nobody said anything to me and I just kept pretty quiet and watched it all happen, I'd never seen such a big production, so many people taking care of anything that had anything to do with the Supremes. It looked like all *they* had to do was get up there and be cute and sing.

When Flo finally arrived about a week before the Copa debut I jumped on that subway and went dashing straight down to the Plaza Hotel to meet her. When I got to the Plaza I looked up and immediately I thought, Jesus, how am I gonna get in this place!

It looked to me like a huge palace or a castle. It looked so big, with the horses and carriages all lined up outside, the coachmen in their uniforms, the fountain, and I'm just standing there gazing at all of this, I'm kind of frightened to go in because the doormen look very tough and they have on these coats with the little capes, even in the heat of summer they're in these incredible uniforms.

As soon as I got inside I was lost. It was so huge, the ceiling looked five stories tall, there were huge potted palms and people just gliding around, and I was thinking, how am I going to find out where Flo is, who do I ask, where's the front desk? I was used to the Warwick. The Warwick had a really small lobby and you just went right to the front desk, but here, I couldn't even see where they had an elevator in this place. There were people sitting right in the middle of the lobby having tea or coffee at these little tables with waiters running around like in a restaurant, I saw signs for the Persian Room and I was telling myself, this place is SO big I don't know what I'm going to do.

As I was looking around I saw Gil Askey and he came up to me, "You look like you're lost." I told him I was supposed to meet Flo. "Oh, she's in suite 811." I told him, "I don't even know where the elevators are." So he showed me the elevators and left me, and when I got out I was in yet another huge hall with tapestry carpet on the floor, and ornate chairs and mirrors and I thought, this place is just fabulous! What a place to be living in!

I knocked on Flo's door, "It's Tony, Miss Flo!" and she flew open these huge double doors, "COME IN!" She spun around like Loretta Young and walked away all in a breeze, like this place was the most natural place in the world for her to be. It was so grand, she had a beautiful suite with a view of Central Park and I thought this was really quite a large suite for one person. "I was just getting ready to come downstairs, honey! You coming to rehearsal?"

Flo was so happy to be at the Plaza. The way she walked through that hotel, she had a way of walking that wasn't like a normal walk, her head would be high up in the air and her shoulders would be thrust back and she would be parading, strutting, giving all this attitude and her outfits were all sensational. She walked through that hotel like she owned it, and all the way down she was telling me how fabulous this show was going to be, how they were going to be such a big hit at the Copa. And all the time I'm thinking, how did I get here? I'm in the Plaza Hotel, I'm walking through the Plaza Hotel with Florence Ballard and this place is a palace.

How did I get here?

Flo's telling me about how she's kind of sad to have missed all that rehearsal time but she's excited too, because she's going to be singing lead on this song and now she tells me the song is "People," this is her song, she's been singing it while they've been touring the last couple of months, she sang it in Detroit and she said she stopped the show. I had heard Barbra Streisand's "People" on the radio, it was a big hit just then from the Broadway show *Funny Girl,* and I knew it was a big deal for Flo. This was her song, and it was also going to be on the *At the Copa* album.

Over at the Copa everybody seemed to be a bit jumpy. Diana was being very businesslike about everything, I thought she was being a bit bossy the way she'd tell some of the Motown people, Get Me this and Get Me that, monopolizing as much time as she could for herself. And I realized Flo was kind of nervous because she had a lot of stuff to catch up on, there had been changes in the act to suit the Copa stage, it was all rush, rush, rush.

Flo was having trouble getting some of the new moves. Diana and Mary had been practicing while Flo was sick and now Flo was struggling to catch up. I could tell she was upset about it, she was frustrated but I heard Cholly Atkins say, "When Flo gets it, she gets it perfect, it just takes her time." It seemed like Cholly was especially close to Flo, almost as if he and his wife Maye looked at her as a daughter.

After rehearsal it was back to the Plaza so the girls could change, then it was dinner, we went out and I had lobster for the first time which I thought was a whole lot of trouble for what it was worth but Flo told me, "Honey, next time just order the tail." Then it was more rehearsing up in a suite at the Plaza, and I didn't leave until it was all over at about two in the morning.

The next day was the same. We went to the Copa at one o'clock, I made myself useful and watched rehearsal, Flo was still having trouble, she was getting more upset, Diana would say, "Oh, it goes like this," and she'd do a quick spin with her hat twirling away, "Girl, you can't get that?" Or "That's such an easy step, Flo. Look!" and she'd demonstrate, but sometimes Cholly would have to correct her because Diana seemed to be always doing it a little different, she was always adding a little extra here or lingering longer on a pose there, so she wasn't staying in sync with the other two. Cholly kept telling Diana that some of the changes she had improvised wouldn't work or didn't look right, and he insisted that she do the routine as taught.

It went on like this for three or four days, with afternoon rehearsals at the club from one 'til four o'clock, evening rehearsals at the Plaza from seven o'clock, everyone rushing around. Then maybe out to a nightclub, I'd just tag along, nobody said don't come. I was still having my little charm lessons with Mrs.

Powell. Some of the guys in the Supremes' entourage had heard about her coaching me for the door job and they kept coming up to me, they'd put their hand on my shoulder or slap me on the back and they'd make me practice in front of them and tell them about my latest lesson.

I watched rehearsals every day. Flo was catching on good, but to me it seemed almost like Diana was trying to work out her own arrangements. She'd tell Cholly, "I don't think this step is working right, I think I should be a bit further up," and Cholly would say no, do it my way. But then the next day at rehearsal they were doing it the way Diana wanted. Diana would be up a few steps in front of the other two and since they weren't in a line any more Diana's movements didn't have to be exactly the same as Flo's and Mary's. After a couple of days Diana stopped going to the evening rehearsal. Everybody knew why, everybody knew she was thinking, well I have done quite enough rehearsing while Flo's been laying in bed in Detroit claiming illness. It's *Flo* who needs all this extra rehearsal time.

There were a lot of songs being rehearsed that I had never heard before, I'd only see them do current hits, never a full, live stage show of the Supremes. But now they were doing things like "Rock-a-Bye Your Baby With a Dixie Melody." There were also several medleys (I'd never even heard the term *medley*). I was learning.

I was beginning to be less nervous around these people, I was getting used to walking past those doormen in and out of the Plaza hotel and I was getting used to being surrounded by all the adult conversation. After the Copa rehearsal I'd go with Flo and we'd sit at one of the tables in the Plaza lobby restaurant, the Palm Court, which was the place to be seen at four o'clock having high tea. This was one of the things Flo loved, because all the fans would be clamoring outside and a few of them would manage to get into the lobby, they'd come over to the table and Flo would sign autographs, she'd hand out some photos, she'd let these kids sit down at the table and she'd talk to them, answer their questions. Flo really liked to pamper the fans.

After a few days I started telling my friends in the projects, especially the ones who didn't believe me, that Flo and I would leave the hotel at such and such a time, and that we could be seen in the Palm Court around four. I'd see them hanging around outside our building trying to think of something new to do and I'd tell them, "Why don't you just come down and see for yourself?" So they'd come down, then they'd tell their friends and their friends would come down, they'd hang out all day and every day because this was something to do for the summer. This was something altogether different and they all knew none of them had a chance in hell of getting any further than the lobby of the Plaza or into the Copa itself. This was for grown people, this was for sophisticates, not for a bunch of teenage fans—with the exception of myself, I thought.

Back up in Flo's suite I was quickly learning what Flo called a matter of taste and a question of style. Everything had to be first class. The first day I was there Flo showed me how to dial room service, how to speak to the maitre d' and not just order, but very haughtily request that something be sent up at once. "I am calling from Miss Florence Ballard's suite, one of the Supremes, and she would like . . ." and if they didn't have a certain caviar it was, "Well, get it," and they got it. This is the way things were done for the Supremes.

Flo showed me how to set up the bar. She showed me how to get the liquor menu and order a bottle of everything, one scotch, one vodka, one gin, one rum, one rye, and a selection of four or five dozen canapés because people would be coming up to the suite and she wanted to be hospitable. Then she set up a bar on the table, she looked it over, and she said, "This doesn't look right, honey. Call downstairs and tell them to send me half a dozen crystal decanters, and tell them I want a dozen champagne glasses, a dozen water glasses, a dozen highball glasses, some shot glasses.'' She said, ''I want cocktail napkins, I want three ice buckets, and I want all the glassware to match.''

She gave me this whole, big order and when they knocked at the door there were three or four guys pushing room service tables loaded with all of this glassware, and everything matched, everything was perfect. Then she showed me how to pour all of the liquor out of the bottles into the decanters, how to get everything set up just so because this was the way it should be done. She was very, very regal.

I never really saw Florence drink until a couple of days later, which is when I started to see a whole other side to everything. To me, everything changed that day although I guess it was already changing, I just wasn't aware of it, it wasn't out in the open yet.

By now it was about four days into the last week of rehearsal. We were down at the Copa, as usual Cholly was saying, change this, change that, why don't you pull it up and down, and everyone was fussing around. Flo started doing her ''People'' lead and I was listening—this was the first time I'd heard her do it and it sounded fabulous. She was just tearing this song inside out, she was belting it out, it sounded nothing like the Streisand version I'd been hearing on the radio. Everybody was listening and Harvey Fuqua came in, he stood down by the stage and very calmly announced, ''Stop the band. Stop everything.''

Everything stopped, he said, ''There's going to be a scheduling change in the show. 'People' will not be in the performance.'' Nobody said a word but you could see the look of surprise on their faces. Mr. Fuqua said, ''In reviewing the lineup we've decided that there are too many show tunes so we are taking out 'People.' ''

The next mouth I hear is Florence's, which is just screaming, ''SHE'LL NEVER GET AWAY WITH IT'' as she storms out, leaves her pocketbook, leaves everything. I'm running out after her, Phil's waiting outside and when he sees her he jumps out to get the limo door for her but Flo says, "No, Phil. I'm walking."

I go scurrying behind her. I can hear her ranting and raving all the way to the Plaza, "FLO'S NOT TAKING THIS SHIT," people are looking at her as we're going through the street, "Flo's not taking this shit because that girl's going to be doing this song before this engagement is over." We're crossing Fifth Avenue, dodging and ducking traffic, she's screaming, "My voice is hoarse but it ain't so hoarse they should take that song away from me!"

People are slamming on their brakes, she's not waiting on no lights, she's just yelling, "That bitch doesn't even know how to sing that song! I have been doing 'People' all along!" She's not waiting for a car to stop at Fifty-ninth and Fifth, she's just walking right out into the street oblivious to everything and my eyes are just starting to open, I'm just beginning to say to myself, these are not the sweet little darlings you read about in *Ebony,* just like sisters, close as kissin' cousins and all of that.

It wasn't till we got back to the Plaza and all the way up to her suite that she realized she had left her pocketbook behind, she had no key to get in. She told me, "Tony. Go downstairs and get another key so I can get in." I offered to get her a chair, and left her seated outside the door as if she was on a throne. I went downstairs, I was so nervous, I told them what had happened and they took their good slow time waiting on everybody else first until Flo came storming down, banged on the desk and started screaming, "I want the key to my suite NOW! I'm a SUPREME!" and right away they gave her a key real quick and sent a security man upstairs with us

Upstairs she was still talking about this song, People, People, People, and then she said, "Go back and get my pocketbook before one of those BITCHES rifles through my stuff." So I had to go back to the

Copa. When I walked in everybody hushed up and I muttered something about Miss Flo's bag, then I had to walk back through the streets carrying this woman's great big pocketbook, very odd indeed, and all the people were looking at me, thinking, what's this kid doing walking down the street with a big, lady's pocketbook?

I got back to the suite to find the door held wide open with a garbage pail. Inside, Flo was laid out on the long white sofa with her arm draped over her forehead. She had changed her outfit and she was all done up. She told me, "FIX ME MY MEDICINE!" I looked at her like, what's this lady talking about, and she said, "Honey, fix me a drink."

"Miss Flo, I don't know how to fix drinks."

"Baby, just pour. Your wrist will naturally flick back when it's enough. And honey, why don't you just call me Flo, Miss Flo's too formal." Then she added, "Flo's my name and singing's my game."

So I went over to the bar and I poured her a drink out of one of those crystal decanters and gave it to her, and she started telling me, "Tony, it's like the game of concentration. When you get a take card you get to take your opponent's prize. Berry Gordy is Diana's take card." I hadn't the first idea what she meant but she went on, "You know, Tony, Diana never cared about Berry until she knew I was interested in him. He and I used to get along just great until that bitch came along."

She was crying, she got up off the sofa and started marching around the room, she was getting all worked up again, she was screaming, "Flo's not taking this shit. Flo knows nobody's doing this but Diana Ross and Berry Gordy." Then she started calling Mary all kinds of names and she was telling me, "GET MARY ON THE PHONE!" She looked right at me yelling, get Mary, so I quickly picked up and dialed Mary but Mary wasn't there, most likely she was still at the Copa.

Flo cried and she shouted, she kept saying, how

could they drop "People," this was her song, this was the one shining moment that she had. She was telling me, Flo feels like quitting, Flo's not doing this, Flo's not taking this, Flo knows what's going on, Flo knows this is all about Diana Ross and Berry Gordy.

She stayed there with the door open and as everybody came back from rehearsal she just swooped them in, "CHOLLY GET IN HERE! DO YOU REALIZE WHAT THIS BITCH HAS DONE!" Then when Diana and Berry went past she yelled out, "GET WALKING! YOU'D BETTER GET WALKING!"

Cholly Atkins came in, he seemed to be very in sync with Flo's needs, and he tried to calm her down. He said, "Don't worry about it, it's not permanent, it's just for the Copa engagement, it's very important and they just want to make sure the show has the right running order." He said, "The show has too many show tunes, Flo, there's "I Am A Woman" from *Funny Girl* and "Put on a Happy Face," and there's "You're Nobody Until Somebody Loves You"—

"SO TAKE OUT ONE OF MISS THING'S SONGS," she yelled. "Why do they have to cut my one thing, take some of the other stuff! What's all that talking they have Diana doing now, she does all the talking in between the songs and we don't get to do any talking."

Mary had come in. Flo turned to Mary, "Mary, she has all the talking lines, we don't have anything to say, we're just standing there."

Mary just sat there, she didn't say a thing. Flo hardly gave her a chance, she just kept on, she was banging around the room slamming her fists on the oak end tables, knocking down those matched crystal goblets, she was yelling that this was the last straw, she was not going to take it, she was just screaming, screaming, screaming and I couldn't understand half of what was going on.

Diana had the sense not to go near Flo's suite and so did Berry Gordy, but everyone else was going in and out. Flo was screaming, she was crying, everyone was trying to calm her down and she just got worse, and worse, and worse. They were trying to put out her fire, they were trying hard to put it out but Flo was throwing gasoline on it and to me, in a way she was in her glory, she was really having a good old time.

She held up all night ranting and raving, that was the night I was there until three in the morning and I kept thinking, I gotta get home, I gotta get home, but things were too good to be leaving. My mother could've come over with Grandma Vera and twenty housing authority cops with dobermans and handcuffs and they couldn't have moved me out of that suite, I wouldn't be missing this for a hundred thousand dollars, this was better than television or the movies or the time the baby grand piano got thrown into the Hudson River on that drunken moonlight boat ride with Aunt Estelle.

It was one negotiation after another with Cholly going in and out, I guess he went to speak to the higher-ups or to give them reports and Harvey Fuqua was coming in, everyone was trying to calm Florence, but Florence kept yelling because she knew there was nothing to be calm about.

They were all saying, "It's not that bad, it's not going to be in the show but it's just for this time." And Flo kept telling them, "In a few days Diana's gonna be singing that song!" Everyone said, "No Flo, it's just for this engagement," and she'd scream, "NO! It AIN'T for this engagement, honey, don't tell me that SHIT, it's NOT for this engagement!"

She was cursing like a sailor, everyone thought this was getting to be ridiculous because Flo would have her song back soon, her song was a showstopper and why would anybody want to drop it but Flo kept telling them, "It's permanent and I'll bet you that Diana Ross is gonna be up on that Copa stage singing MY GOD-DAM SONG!" Then suddenly she stopped, struck a pose, and said, "Everybody Out!"

* * *

Sure enough, after a few days "People" was put back into the show only now it was Diana up on the stage singing the song and that was it, that was when I said to myself, OK, there seems to be a bit of trouble here.

Nobody said a word about it. Flo said nothing because she had predicted it, she just strode into that dressing room and got right down to business preparing for the second show and you could tell she was thinking, Honey, Flo knows.

But after that first show, when everyone was busy putting on makeup, fixing gowns, combing wigs, the guests were buzzing outside in the reception area, Flo was sitting there in her terry cloth robe retouching her eye makeup and her lipstick, doing her nails, and very nonchalantly she started to belt out "People." She just sat there and at the top of her lungs she sang, "PEOPLE, PEOPLE WHO NEED PEEEOPLE," very dramatically and nobody in that dressing room said a word. Mary Wilson didn't say a word, Diana Ross didn't say a word, Greg just kept right on with his work, the place was frozen.

It was so quiet in there you could hear the glasses clinking out in the reception area and even they sounded kind of quiet. Flo did the whole song. She must have held the last note about five minutes and then from outside the dressing room came this, clap clap clap, all the guests out there were clapping and Flo just started powdering her face with that pressed powder and she said, "Mmm Hmm," she was very satisfied with herself and after that, every now and then when she got good and ready she would just break into a chorus of "People" and nobody would ever say a word, nobody ever said anything much about anything after that except behind backs. Flo was the only one who spoke out to your face.

Flo couldn't help it. Like she always said, "Fair is fair, honey."

CHAPTER 5

◆ ◆ ◆

Battle Stations

When I saw it, I saw it all at once and that was at the Copa.

I started to see what was happening the day they took "People" away from Flo, then every day after that I saw a bit more, because not only was I being educated in style and taste and how to do things right, in what to order and how to order it, I was also having my eyes opened, I was beginning to realize that "the Supremes" was a whole lot more than these three glamorous girls getting up there and singing like sisters and fans screaming and chasing limos three blocks, it was really a lot of pressure and conflict and bitchiness and by the time opening night rolled around the tension in the air was so thick you could've cut it with a knife.

The girls were very nervous. They were nervous about getting up on that stage and performing in front of a ton of New York press and celebrities, they were nervous about doing everything right, and besides that there was no love lost between the girls. Mary and Flo had set up their make-up stations on the left side of the dressing room and Diana had commandeered the entire right side for herself, it was like battle stations and since Florence was not speaking to Diana anyway it really didn't matter.

The atmosphere was tense, but it was exciting too because this was the famous Copacabana and the Supremes were making news. It was big news to have a pop group performing at the one and only Copa, plus they were young, they were black, *and* they were girls so there were TV appearances and magazine articles, and after the opening night it was even more exciting because by the second night they knew they'd been a huge success. All the reviews came in saying how fabulous the trio was, how polished, how graceful, how elegant, and in these reviews nobody was singled out, it was all thought of as a group effort.

So you had that happy mood in there too, like, gee everything's going great, the critics loved us, the press was out in full force, we're stars and everyone loves us. It was all too fabulous baby, it was spectacular but Florence saw this as her biggest nightmare ever, the worst thing that ever happened to her, and backstage in that Copa dressing room she let no one forget it. Flo hardly said a word to anybody, but when she did it was usually nasty and sarcastic, little remarks like, ''Well we all know Miss Diana Ross thinks this is all about *her*.''

So there was all this tension, everybody was walking on ice and the dressing room was hectic, it was total chaos in there. Mr. Gordy came in wanting a change in his show, everybody had to drop everything in a hurry and leave so he could speak to the girls in private but of course just as they were on their way out Flo had to throw in one of her comments. Or he'd come in, ''Good evening ladies,'' and Flo would swipe, ''What the fuck is good about it?''

Mrs. Powell was descending on everybody, giving orders on what to do and what not to do and who should be doing what and who should be speaking to who. She was in everybody's conversation, telling Diana or Flo, ''Young lady, I do NOT like that tone of voice. That is NOT the proper behavior for a Supreme.'' She didn't care who you were, she was like your grandmother. Even Diana and Mr. Gordy called her "Mrs. Powell."

It was the same every night. It was cans of hair spray, it was makeup, it was eyelashes lined up in a row, it was Mr. Gordy coming in, "Those gowns look terrific on you girls," it was Flo snapping, "Who asked you Berry Gordy? What would you know about gowns?"

It was always somebody looking for a needle and thread—with all the bags of stuff they traveled with there was still something they needed. Stockings have been left behind at the hotel, or Mary's putting on her stockings and then as she's getting on her gown, the gown catches on the stocking and makes a run so then the gown has to come off, the stockings have to come off, and it's start all over again.

Then there's maybe five minutes left before they have to go on, the band's already playing, and to get on stage they still have to go down to the basement in this elevator, through a little lobby and into the club. The club's packed, packed. They have to go through the audience and up a couple of steps to get on that little stage, they have to dash down through the crowd, ducking waiters carrying Chinese food, and the crowd's already clapping like crazy. It was always like this, but the first night was the most chaotic and the most tense.

They were having some special gowns made up for this engagement, Gordy's sister Gwen had commissioned these gowns from a theatrical costume designer and fifteen minutes before show time they had still not arrived. Everybody was going crazy, Flo was saying, "Honey, we should've stuck with Saks Fifth Avenue" and Diana shot her a look, like, how ridiculous. Diana didn't want to even think about putting on any of the "emergency" gowns that were hanging on the rack from their previous shows. Then Mrs. Powell came rushing in with the new gowns and the girls took one look at them, at these very plain gowns with huge, artificial tropical flowers around the neck that I guess were supposed to match the Copa's Polynesian-type decor.

The gowns didn't even fit right, but there was no time to fix anything, so the gowns were put on and the girls rushed down for their first show at the Copa. Of course by this time the dressing room was in complete turmoil and I had to stay and help Gregory and Mrs. Powell clean up because in an hour the girls would be back and everything had to be ready and waiting so that the Supremes could prepare for their second show of the night.

The girls would walk in and expect to see the dressing room in complete order. They didn't want to know how it got that way, they just wanted to see each gown hanging regally straight on the rack, everything back in its place, tons and tons of fresh clean towels—hand towels, bath towels, wash cloths, the make-up tables were completely carpeted in white terry cloth towels. Everything was laid out with whatever they needed just within reach. Not that they ever reached for anything either, everything had to be brought to them and they were oblivious to the turmoil, they never commented on it except if they returned and something was out of place, especially Diana. If a towel was out of place or her make-up table didn't look like a display on the first floor of Bloomingdale's, she'd let you know!

Diana had almost a map of where she wanted things to go on her make-up table. She wanted the eyelashes in one particular spot, the lipsticks in another, and it had to be this way every single day. On the first day Gregory set out the makeup and then he taught me how to do it. He said to me, "I'd better do Diana's makeup, because you know how she is."

He said, "You see how I have everything in order, you just look at how I have hers and then you carbon copy it on the other side for Mary and Flo but it doesn't matter if you don't have it exactly right, just make sure you have all like items together, put them neat and leave finger space between them so they can pick things up." Flo and Mary were more easygoing about things like that, but as I learned more I learned that to me Diana's was really the right way. People saw it as, she thinks she's so grand, but I could see that having things organized made it easier to function under all of that pressure.

The girls usually did their own makeup and then Greg would assist them with the finishing touches. Greg was mostly concerned with the wigs. Each girl had maybe twenty wigs apiece so this one guy was working on sixty wigs because who knew what they were going to wear. Everything had to be in a constant state of readiness, like they were getting ready to take off to the moon, so he was forever washing, setting, rolling, teasing, combing, spraying a wig, and all these wigs had to be lined up on wig heads around the dressing room because you never knew which wig they would pick to wear on a particular night.

Greg told me that Diana would always pick the wig that wasn't ready, she would always want to wear that *one* wig, the one that still had the rollers in it or the one that was only halfway rolled, and the other eighteen that were done, those were not suitable, that was not the look she was going for that evening.

Greg loved to bitch about Diana. He'd tell me how stupid her wig looked, how terrible her makeup was, and of course Diana didn't like Greg either. He was really a very popular guy—he would wear these outrageous outfits and sometimes he seemed to be attracting just as much attention as Diana which, Greg said, is why Diana didn't like him. He'd tell me how she powdered herself too light, she was always in this kind of Kabuki mask of very light makeup that stopped right where her neck started, but he said Diana would never listen to anything he said.

The Copa was a real training ground for me and an eye-opening experience. This was the first time I saw the Supremes without their makeup and it was a big shock. They'd sit there in their suites at the end of the night rubbing it all off with cold cream and suddenly they looked just like normal women their age, it made me see them more as people rather than as big stars and I felt more comfortable, I saw that a lot of it was just make-believe, like someone had taken off a suit of armor.

Flo actually looked just as good without her makeup on and I thought Mary looked prettier without it, she was just naturally very pretty, but Diana, I realized that Diana transformed herself like a model with makeup, when she took it off she looked plainer than you'd imagine, she didn't have that cute little innocent look that Mary had. As Flo would later say, "Looks is deceiving. Makeup and phoniness is the art of deception they all practice."

I always thought there was something odd about Diana, she was aggressive but then I'd catch her at moments when I thought she looked very lonely. I'd watch her in the dressing room time and again doing something I used to call sitting up in the mirror. The other girls would be sitting around, ordering something to eat, chatting about clothes and girl talk and Diana would be sitting by herself, all made up in front of the mirror, absolutely still, just staring at herself, just looking at her own utter glory.

She seemed to be concentrating very hard as if she were in a trance, oblivious to what was going on around her. Almost as if she were trying to go into the mirror, she was looking at herself head-on, right in her own eyes and she would sit there fifteen, twenty minutes, expressionless. It seemed to me like she was getting some inner strength from it. Flo and Mary never seemed to notice but I used to wonder about it, I thought she looked very tragic.

A lot of things were packed into that period for me, a lot of hostility, a lot of bitching, a lot of learning, running around and running errands and manning the door and right from the start Gregory told me, "Always appear to be busy, always look like you're doing something. That's the best way to stay around."

I wanted to learn how to do makeup, but before

Gregory would teach me he wanted to see if I send this kid out to buy six number 2 eyeliners in black sable, six in dark burgundy, two dozen pancakes shade number 16, a dozen Monica Simone eyelashes, and if I give him a big, long list and a hundred-dollar bill, will this kid be able to come back with all this stuff and the change without getting it all messed up? Will he be able to do all this without making the ridiculous kinds of mistakes you'd expect a thirteen-year-old to make?

A lot of times I would succeed because I had experience, I had my supermarket shopping service, which made me a pretty capable shopper. I knew that if the lady tells me Del Monte peas, twelve-ounce size, then I get to the supermarket and there's no Del Monte twelve-ounce, don't substitute with Green Giant because she won't want it and then I'm going to have to waste my time taking that can all the way back again.

So when they sent me out to the Make-Up Hut and the lady in the Make-Up Hut said, we don't have this and we don't have that but we could give you this, I knew from experience that maybe shade 17 is a bit darker than 16 and I knew not to bring it, I knew how to say, just let me take one of these so they can see the shade and if they don't want it I'll bring it back. And then of course I'd show it to Greg and he'd say, "That was smart Tony. But this one's fine, why don't you run back and get eleven more." And so I'd have to run back to the Make-Up Hut anyway.

I discovered that each Supreme had her own preferences for certain make-up shades. I used to wonder who dreamed up the names, because they were perfect, the names fitted the girls perfectly. Flo used to wear Light Egyptian, she'd say, "please get my Light Egyp*tion*" and she'd mix it with a touch of Light Creole. Diana would be the Bronze Goddess and Mary, I think Mary had Brown Baby number 3.

The lashes were ordered by number but they had names too, they had the spiky, the extra spiky, the fluttery, the demi-short and I'd look at the lashes and tell Gregory, "These don't look that thick. I guess they look different when you put them on." He told me, "No, they don't wear one pair, they wear three pairs. That's how you get the thickness," and he showed me how. He said, "You just take three pairs and hold them together like this, you put the glue on all three of them"—it was called Eye Lure, it must have been like the Crazy Glue of the eyelash business "you mash them together and they're ready." When they took off their eyelashes they all came off glued together and then the next night it was easier.

But those things were heavy, one night I told Greg, "Put some on me. Let me see." So he put some on me and I could hardly keep my eyes open, I felt like I had a great canvas awning over my eyelid, I said, "How do they see!" He said, "Darling, they're used to it, they can hardly see without them." Then there was the kind of eyelash that stuck up, that would hit you in the eyebrow and the girls would just flutter them as if they didn't weigh a thing, that was after they'd added a ton of mascara. I always thought it was funny how they'd put on the eyelashes and *then* they'd sit there applying the mascara and separating out the lashes with a pin. I wondered, why don't they do that before they put them on, it was almost like they imagined those lashes were real, it was total make-believe. Then they'd drench themselves in perfume, they didn't dab it on. That dressing room would be smelling for days.

Of course, as soon as the dressing room was tidy I would run down and catch part of the Supremes' show. The first time I saw the club at night I was amazed because somehow they'd turned that dump into this fabulous, showy place with the white, white tablecloths and the red napkins, the little candles with shades on them at the tables, the maitre d' and the waiters all in tuxedos, everything set so pretty, everything so dimly lit with pin spots on the band, it was like Cinderella, it didn't even look like the same place any more. It was still small but now it was what you might call intimate. You could hear the tinkling of glasses, the forks hitting the plates, the buzz of conversation while the girls were singing, you can hear it on the album they recorded, *At the Copa.*

Then they had the Copa girls with these kind of Carmen Miranda-type outfits on, they had the cigarette girls walking around with cigarettes and cigars, the hat-check girl with her little hat cocked to one side, so now I was seeing it at night it looked like a *real* nightclub. Then the next day it would look a mess again, it went from beautiful to terrible just like the dressing room, except unlike the dressing room which was like a battleground, on stage the girls were all smiles and everything was wonderful again. They did their routines perfectly, they twirled their canes and their little straw hats, they sang their show tunes and their hits and everyone went wild. Only now, instead of three triplets in a row it was Diana out in front and Mary and Flo standing a few steps back.

Offstage, Flo kept telling me, "Flo is getting tired of standing behind Diana Ross and being forced to hide her own talent." She'd say, "I can sing, I shouldn't have to do that." Flo even bitched about Mary, she'd say, "Mary Wilson has lowered herself to being cute for a living, but I got talent, I'm the one with a voice around here honey, and I want to *sing,* I don't just want to hum. If I can't sing, at least let me talk, I can say good evening ladies and gentlemen."

So she was mad and she let everybody know it but as soon as she got up on that stage she was beautiful and funny, you never knew when she was going to say something. She'd just park herself up next to Diana and Diana would say one of the lines that had been written for her, like, "Gold won't bring you happiness," there would be a little lull, Diana would say, "when you're growing old" and the band would go up tempo for the song to start but just in that fraction of a second Flo would jump right in with, "I don't know about all of that, honey." Or Diana would say,

"Thin is in," this was the time when everybody was starting to catch on to Twiggy and that fashionable, bone-thin look that Diana had. And Flo would just say, "Thin might be in, honey, but fat is where it's at," and she'd wiggle her body suggestively.

The audience just loved it, they loved it, the men were always attracted to Florence because she had that very shapely, Marilyn Monroe-type figure, very curvy and voluptuous. So when Flo threw in these lines everybody roared. Flo was a real sensation during the Copa engagement and people were saying how funny she was, what a wit she had, how she was such a natural comic and she had perfect timing, perfect delivery. But all Flo could think about when they were offstage was how Diana had stolen her song, Diana had stolen the limelight and it was Just Not Fair.

It was rough riding for Flo, she was very moody this whole time, she didn't want to be around a lot of people but of course it was summer, the fans were out in full force every day outside the Plaza Hotel and it was, hey, let's run behind the girls. These fans were not beneath running behind a limo, and baby they could run clear down to Saks Fifth Avenue and usually arrive there within thirty seconds of any limo but Flo didn't want to deal with this. She didn't want to deal with any of this stuff so she stayed to herself a lot, she slept a lot, she left her key at the front desk for me and I would just let myself in in the morning, Flo would be asleep in the bedroom and I'd lay down on the couch and watch *I Love Lucy* at ten o'clock on channel five and pick up matching glasses to wash from the night before until Flo woke up at about twelve.

After a few nights of getting home at two o'clock in the morning and racing back to hotel around nine Flo told me to dial my mother and she asked her if I could stay down there. She told me, "Honey, you're starting to look kind of tired, you're not getting enough sleep. You should just come and stay down here. Let's ask your mother to send your clothes up." Of course I had to beg my mother and of course my grandmother thought this whole thing was highly suspicious, but she had to let me so I was now living up at the Plaza, I was running around this fancy hotel having high tea and learning how to mix drinks. That's when I first noticed Flo drinking.

I'd sit up late into the night with Flo, because after the show Mr. Gordy would usually have something for the girls to do, some people to meet or some nightclub to be seen in but Flo would be back at the hotel bitching. Mr. Gordy would have to make something up like, "Oh, Miss Ballard isn't feeling very well." She'd be up in her plush suite, bitching and sipping her liquor.

Flo would be laying out on the couch in some kind of Liz Taylor Cleopatra pose, she'd be sipping her medicine out of a crystal goblet and she'd say, "Honey, Flo's fixing to go into the mystic." Then she'd start telling me about Diana, or about Berry Gordy, or about Diana *and* Mr. Gordy and sometimes I didn't really pay her much mind because I knew Flo was in her medicine. Maybe I'd only poured her a couple of drinks but she'd be well on her way before that second glass was empty, her voice would be getting louder and she'd be very vibrant, she got drunk quick.

Flo didn't drink in the daytime, it was always after the performance. She started drinking at one and two in the morning and we'd sit up half the night, Flo would be sipping her medicine, she'd tell me about the interviews they did, how Diana would always jump in and answer every question making Flo and Mary just sit there like idiots, she'd tell Diana, "You don't *have* to be the spokeswoman you know." Because Diana was always complaining about how *she* had to work so much harder, she had to do this and she had to do that and she wasn't getting any more pay than Flo and Mary.

I was kind of surprised to hear the Supremes talk about money because I saw the way they lived and to me it seemed like they never had the first idea what money was. They just spent it, their pockets were always full, everything was the best. You want a mink coat? You want a Cadillac? Buy it, ship it. One of Flo's mottos was, "Better no mink than cheap mink."

Flo kept pointing out to me how everybody was always fussing over Diana. She'd tell me, Diana's being pushed forward and Mary just refuses to see what's happening, the whole thing's being engineered by Berry Gordy and Diana Ross, what right does that little Hitler have to take control of the group, and Miss Ross wouldn't be nowhere without Flo and Mary doing back-up because that Miss Ross, Flo would say, ain't got no voice worth speaking of.

Any conversation we had always ended up like this, with Flo making quite a speech about Diana or Berry Gordy or even Mary, or just the way things were going. It didn't matter where we were or what we were talking about, it could be anything.

Flo still made a point of having high tea every day in the Plaza lobby, but now it wasn't just so that she could hang out with the fans, it was also because she knew Diana and Mr. Gordy would probably be passing by. One time, we were sitting there looking at these huge menus, you could hide four or five people behind them and they had all sorts of exotic-sounding dishes on them and as usual we were trying to figure out what's what. I saw something called "Spaghetti Bolognaise" and I asked Flo, "What's that?" She said, "Honey, I'm not sure," then when the waiter came over she asked him, "Sweetheart, darling, what is this? What does this consist of?" She always found some classy way of finding out. "Honey," she told me, "that ain't nothing but spaghetti and meat sauce, that's all it is." Then she looked again, *"Twelve dollars fifty?* ORDER IT, I don't care. I'm making the money and it'll be less for Berry Gordy to STEAL."

As soon as Diana and Berry walked by Flo would holler out, "Hey! Napoleon! How are the troops doing?" She'd say things like that because she said Mr. Gordy fancied himself like a dictator and Motown was his country, and he was running it like a king.

Flo told me, "Little Napoleon's holding court." I didn't know what that meant.

"What does that mean, 'holding court'?"

"Well, it's like a place where nothing's real. It's like the general, like Napoleon, like the emperor and his court. When you're in the emperor's court, the emperor's like the big boss. The emperor could be like the schoolteacher and you're the pupils, so you're the court. You want to be nice to the teacher so he'll give you a nice grade. So the court that's around Gordy, the people that work for him, Diana, all of them cater to him as he holds court."

Flo went on, "Mary's getting caught up in it too. But she knows what's going down, I'm gonna have to talk to her. I know she'll be on my side, she won't let Flo down. We go *way* back, honey."

It was getting so the air would freeze any time Diana, Mr. Gordy, and Flo were anywhere near each other. If there were fans at Flo's table they'd get real quiet, I don't think they had any real idea of what was going on, and I was getting pretty confused myself because during this time I never saw Mr. Gordy even raise his voice, he always seemed perfectly gentlemanly, it was Flo who was doing all the shouting. I was starting to wonder why Diana always referred to Flo as "the quiet one."

Everybody knew Flo was bitter. Some of the Motown staffers started asking me on the side, "Tony, how's Flo today? Has she relaxed any yet? What's she saying about Diana and Berry?" Flo told me, "I better not hear you telling them any of my business. If they ask how I'm feeling, you just say, ask Flo!"

When she wasn't sleeping or working or bitching Flo wanted to keep busy, she wanted to see places, she complained about never getting to see places they performed in, even in Europe. "Tony, honey," she said, "on this trip Flo's gonna do some sightseeing, and you're gonna help. I'm not staying shut up in this Plaza Hotel with Miss Diana Ross and her staff of spies, which probably includes Mary. Now, let's start with some shopping.''

Flo was going to lift her spirits by shopping. So for two weeks we went all over the place and wherever we went, we went by limo. We went to Bergdorf's and Bonwit Teller, and although these places were just fifty feet around the corner, we could have walked but we went in the air-conditioned limo because this was how it should be done.

After Bergdorf's we might go to Saks, but first it was back to the Plaza for a complete, head-to-toe costume change. Then maybe she wanted to go to the House of Kenneth for a beauty treatment but it was back to the Plaza again, everything off, another outfit and on to the House of Kenneth only to take all this off again and put on a white terry robe. After a couple of days of this I thought, I gotta get some more clothes! Because I figured, you don't dare wear the same thing to Bergdorf that you were wearing in Saks. I said to Flo, ''I gotta call my mother and tell her to send some more clothes! I didn't bring enough stuff!''

Flo just waved her hand in a generous sweep and said, ''Don't bother.'' So we marched off to the boys' departments in Lord and Taylor, Abercrombie and Fitch, Arnold Constable, Saks Fifth Avenue, and she completely outfitted me from head to toe with a whole bunch of new outfits. She'd tell the salesman, ''Darling, show us something . . . debonair,'' and the salesman would go scurrying. It was so simple.

We started sightseeing. Flo said, ''We have to have some Cul*ture*, we *must* do the museums,'' but it was always back to the hotel in between even though I knew that nobody on the Circle Line had been at the United Nations Building, and nobody at the United Nations was going to be at the Museum of Natural History. Hardly anybody recognized Flo as a Supreme anyway but she did make people stop in their tracks, people saw her as something to look at, they'd stare at us like, *who* is this black woman with this kid in this huge limo with all of these furs in the heat of summer? Of course

I'd take it upon myself to announce, "She's in the Supremes!" and the response would be, "I knew it."

I had seen New York on my little bus adventures and my trips downtown but now I was seeing a whole other New York, it was the New York of money. We would march out of the stores with three or four porters behind us loaded with packages, you could hardly see us for packages. We rode through Central Park in a horse-drawn carriage, we lunched in the best restaurants, and Flo always looked very elegant, very much the lady with the hats, the mink cuffs, the little Chanel suits, and that grand, haughty walk.

The day we went to the Statue of Liberty she was wearing a mink pillbox hat and a little Jackie Kennedy suit—she was a great admirer of Jackie Kennedy. Of course it was so hot outside I thought I was going to melt but Flo insisted on climbing all the way up to Liberty's crown. "Tony, honey," she said, "I've come all this way and we're not leaving till I see the world the way this lady sees it."

Well, I thought they must have a hot dog stand or souvenir shop or something really spectacular at the top but after climbing about a million stairs, which was pretty dangerous with Flo in her high heels, clutching her little pearl-studded handbag, all it was at the top was hot, dark, and tiny. So we stood there staring out over the water and Flo said the oddest thing, she said, "Tony, the Statue of Liberty is a very lonely lady, standing here all alone with her back facing Jersey. They should have positioned her better. We all must position ourselves."

When Flo felt sad about things she usually called her mother in Detroit and talked for hours, I could see she was real close to her family and whenever we went shopping she was always buying things for her mother or her brothers and sisters because she said they had to look a certain way, she told me being a Supreme's sister or mother made you pretty famous in Detroit and you have to live up to it.

Of course, I had to call my mother too, my mother

had to know every single thing that was going down. From the moment I had told her about the Copa engagement she had been wanting to come down and see the show, but of course I knew she couldn't afford this place. Then one day Mr. Gordy told me he would like to meet my parents because I had been so nice, I was such a nice kid and he said he would arrange everything, a table, dinner and drinks, the whole thing.

My parents were thrilled and as soon as my grandmother heard about it she wanted to go too, she was still insisting that something was very, very strange about these girls, she just wanted to get to the bottom of this whole thing. I thought I was going to die of embarrassment. I had to ask the Supremes if my grandmother could come and I was hoping they'd say no, but they said, "Oh sure."

So my mother had to have her new "outfit," my grandmother had to have her new "outfit" and a new mixed-gray, Mahalia Jackson-type wig, it was days of shopping, my mother bought three dresses from Lady Nadine and a beaded jacket that she thought was just like something Diana Ross would wear, and the whole project had to be informed as to the exact time they were leaving to go to the Copa. It was a big production, almost as big as getting the Supremes up on that stage.

Naturally, I was wearing one of my new Flo Ballard suits, and when we got to the Copa everyone treated us like royalty. We had a ringside table for four, I introduced them to the managers and staff, Mr. Gordy came to the table, shook my stepdad's hand, and gave my mother and grandmother a kiss and a hug, which they both agreed was *so* gracious and kind of him. Then he told me to bring them up to the dressing room after the show, at which I sat there thinking, Oh no!

As soon as we got inside the dressing room my grandmother opened up her mouth to speak—this is the woman who was going to investigate the whole thing and now she had seen them on stage wearing dresses with their *backs* out (how disgusting)—she said, "I think you girls are FABULOUS!" I was in total shock. "I told my grandson, I always loved the Supremes! You young ladies are a credit to us all."

Suddenly she was a big fan. She was all over the place chatting up a storm and I felt so embarrassed. Then she saw Flo, "Oh! The lovely Miss Ballard, I know all about you!" They started talking like they were relatives or something and when we finally left all my grandmother wanted to talk about was the Supremes and how lovely they were, "I don't know why people talk about Diana Ross, she's sooo sweet, a very lovely hostess, a staaar. And that Mary is just sooo cute."

My grandmother was taken in, just like everyone else who read the papers or saw them perform or watched them on TV or waited to catch a glimpse of them dashing out of a door into a limo and out of a limo into a store. Everyone loved them. They were just such lovely girls, it all seemed so right, so perfect really.

I was always reading things like, "Their Copa Runneth Over."

"They are an inspiration to us all."

"Laughter is always in the air."

But amongst the inner circle everybody was convinced that Flo hated Diana, and mostly they were on Flo's side. Flo said she didn't really hate her. She said she just disliked her, the way she was gaining power, "the way she uses her feminine wiles like a magic wand around Motown, compensating for her questionable vocal abilities."

Everybody around there whispered, all the staff members, everybody said, "You know that Berry and Diana, they took that song from Florence, that's a damn shame."

Mary tried to make it go away. She told me, "Tony, I know Flo's upset but you really shouldn't pay much attention to what Florence says when she's mad, especially after she's had a couple of cocktails." But Flo was telling me, "You know, Mary's been blinded from sitting up in Berry Gordy's court too long."

Mary said, "The whole thing will blow over in a couple of days and Flo will be back to her old cheerful self."

Mary was wrong. It never happened.

CHAPTER 6

— ◆ ◆ ◆ —

J.F.K. or Bust

When I first met the Supremes they seemed like happy-go-lucky sisters. But once the hits really started to come out one after the other and the money started rolling in, the houses got bought, the entourage got bigger and bigger, the itinerary more and more hectic, then things started to change. From that day in July 1965 when Harvey Fuqua announced that Flo's song was being dropped, nothing was ever the same again. Everything hit the fan at the same time and like Flo said, "All of my temper came up outta control and I went off on those fools."

Before the Supremes left town after the Copa run Florence said she wanted to go uptown and see the project where I lived, so the next day we jumped in the limo, we came up Third Avenue from downtown, we came to 124th Street and when we turned the corner I couldn't believe what I saw. Florence said to me, "Tony, you told every damn body!"

I said, "I told a few people." I was so upset. I'd say there were three or four hundred screaming teenagers, children, and parents out there. Luckily, Florence had a stack of pictures with her that she'd already autographed, so she got out of the limo but she never actually moved away from the door, she just kind of hung her arm on the door and she spoke to everybody and everybody was so excited and she gave out the pictures. It was quite a scene.

She stood there holding onto the car for about fifteen minutes and people asked her questions like, why don't you sing lead sometimes, they said, we like Diana but how come the other girl, Mary doesn't sing lead and Florence answered, "Well, Diana is the lead singer and I'm glad you enjoy her." She answered like a Supreme should answer, very diplomatically. She said, "I'm glad you enjoy the Supremes and I'm happy to be able to come here for a brief visit."

Oddly enough, I only heard a few questions about Mary. They kept asking about Diana and I was thinking, these peoples' mouths are too big. As soon as I could, I butted in, "Flo, tell them the story of how I really met you in B. Altman's, because they don't believe it," and she started laughing. She started telling them that story and it got them off the subject of Diana.

I was upset, because I wanted Flo to come upstairs to my mother's apartment but it was an impossible situation. I was upset that all those people were there, but she wasn't upset, she was very happy because she was by herself. She was a Supreme alone, Diana wasn't there, so I didn't want them asking all those questions like, why does Diana do this or that, I don't like that hair Diana wears, I don't like how Diana does this or that, what's the new record? I wanted her to be happy, things had been rough and I knew that but people in the projects didn't know that there was trouble. All they knew was what they saw and they could see that things were being focused on Diana, which to them seemed only natural.

So I was happy for Flo in that moment, I was happy I could do that for her and she seemed thrilled that there were three or four hundred people out to see her, just her. Then we went back downtown and Flo reported the whole thing to Diana and Mary. All Diana said was, "Oooh, you went to the projects with Tony, oh that was dangerous!" Flo just said, "Well, you used to live in the projects too, didn't you? It's no more dangerous now then it was then, in fact it wasn't that many months ago you moved your whole tribe out, just like we all did, Di-a-na.''

Everyone could see that things were being focused on Diana, and during the Copa run they had released another album, *More Hits by the Supremes*, which was the first one to really separate out the girls. The cover showed a picture of each Supreme, each girl in her own little separate space with her own signature, and this time Diana was in the middle glaring straight out at you, while Mary's and Flo's pictures were on either side and they were both looking toward Diana Ross.

After the Copa debut it seemed to me as if life for the Supremes only got more hectic. They were always flying off to perform or to record somewhere because by now they were not recording only in Detroit, they were recording wherever they were or wherever the schedule would permit. And wherever they were they'd be running off before the show, after the show, whenever they had a spare second that could be filled in with an interview or a promotional appearance, or just to show their faces in some place where the Supremes were expected to be seen so they could get written about in the newspapers. But it was beginning to seem like Diana was the one being interviewed, she was always jumping to answer the questions as if she were the only Supreme, the last star, that's just the way she acted.

I'd see Diana be very bossy and very arrogant, "GET ME A CUP OF TEA, NOW!" "PICK UP MY DIAMOND BRACELET!" Whereas I never saw Mr. Gordy order people around the way Diana did whenever he wasn't in earshot. I heard him dealing with situations where anyone else would be panicking and cursing, but Mr. Gordy would just say, "The lights were not as they should be, I'd like to see the manager, I'd like to see the lighting technician, I think we have some problems that need to be worked out."

When Mr. Gordy was in town he watched everything—the lighting, the choreography, the costumes, the band and especially the audience. He went to rehearsals and he watched everything and then he'd have a private meeting in his suite, he never usually criticized anyone in public. I respected Mr. Gordy, I wanted to be like him, I wanted to be like all those shrewd, well-spoken men who were around the Supremes. So after the Supremes left town I told my friends, "Well, we give shows too, for money! All we have to do is lip-synch to the records."

Then I put together a few of the girls in my building, a few of the guys, and we used some of the shopping service money to fund these big shows. I figured I could have some fun and make some money while the Supremes were away and I figured I had plenty of show biz experience.

First we had to have the outfits. We'd go across the street to the Chinese laundry where they sold mystery packages of unclaimed sheets for seventy-five cents. All it took was a stapler that you stole from school, a pair of scissors you stole from school, nobody knew how to sew but we made gowns and suits out of old sheets that we stapled together. Sometimes in your seventy-five-cent package you'd get shirts or old tablecloths, so you had to work with what you got. That Chinese laundry man wasn't giving no refunds.

I became pretty famous as a "little project Berry Gordy." I never performed or sung, I was always the manager, I'd wear my suit and tie and I'd say, you look good so you can be Eddie Kendrick from the Temptations, you can be David Ruffin. My mother said Ramona *had* to be in it and I kept saying, no, no, she's too little. Because to me, my sister had no talent, she'd be difficult to work with but my mother insisted, she said, "Fair is fair, and you better make her a Supreme." So I let Ramona be Mary Wilson in exchange for letting us use her ballet tutus as wigs.

We printed tickets on little white flash cards, "A TRIBUTE TO MOTOWN 25 CENTS COME ONE COME ALL," just like the quarter parties the bigger teenagers used to organize. My mother would never let us have the shows in her apartment, never ever, so we had to find somebody's mother that was open enough to let all the kids pack into her apartment. I decided to ask Miss Chris—she lived on the fifth floor and her son Jimmy was in the show, her daughters were in the show, so she almost *had* to let us use her apartment. But before I asked her I figured it would be best to put her youngest daughter, Renee, in it too, so overnight Renee became Dionne Warwick.

We did the show one Saturday a month, but sometimes we had to wait until new records came out, a new Marvin Gaye, a new Four Tops, a new Supremes. Just before one of our first shows, Motown released "I Hear a Symphony" by the Supremes and of course we got right to work learning the lines and practicing all the little shimmies and turns I'd watched the girls do. We got so good at it that we were doing two shows a day. We'd take all the furniture out of Miss Chris's living room, struggling with it by ourselves, and put it in the back bedroom. Miss Chris was always sitting in her kitchen so I put her to work selling hot dogs and Kool-Aid and taking the money at the door, I wouldn't trust anyone but Miss Chris with the profits.

Everyone in the show had to bring kitchen chairs from home. First the audience sat on the floor but no, we needed something a little more sophisticated than that so everybody's mother said, okay, you can take my four kitchen chairs. The people who couldn't sing or dance, I made them ushers or backstage staff. We'd put two girls up on chairs and we'd hang colorful party streamers around them to make it look like a cage, those would be your go-go girls wearing boat-neck-style pillowcases. Of course, when the Supremes came on there were never go-go girls, the Supremes were the headliners, the go-go girls went behind Wilson Pickett or James Brown. The show would go on about two hours because everybody did two or three numbers with the flip side, and I of course ran everything.

We used to rehearse after school. I'd yell, I'd rant,

I'd rave, I had my little pad, I'd supervise the stapling of the gowns, I'd get someone to cut up an old towel and make ties for the ushers and I'd fire people in a minute, I wanted perfection. Then the parents started wanting to see the shows because everybody wants to see what their kids are doing, so we introduced Saturday night shows for parents at the price of a dollar a head.

Of course, it was a little hard because I was still running the grocery service and everybody's husband usually got paid Friday, they wanted their groceries Saturday, and they'd say, "What do you mean you can't get my groceries, what are you talking about, what do you mean you're having a Supremes show? oh forget that junk, forget that junk, I want my groceries!" And we'd have to get all the shopping done before twelve so we could do the show at two. It got to be too hectic for some of the kids that worked the shopping service *and* the shows, so just like I'd seen people on the Supremes' staff disappear, anyone on my staff who couldn't cut the mustard disappeared too. All I did was mimic the adults.

So all the time the Supremes were flying around the world being stars I was busy too. Then there was school. I had a private tutor named Oaks Plimpton who was George Plimpton's brother, and with his help I had passed admissions tests to Dalton, Collegiate, Trinity, and Choate, which were all prestigious private schools. But I wanted to stay with most of my old schoolmates, so in the fall I started in the Intellectually Gifted class at Junior High School 43. I was taking that crosstown bus every day, it was so crowded you didn't know if somebody was trying to feel you or not, and I didn't care. Then there was homework and all my little jobs, there were piano lessons and drama lessons at the Curt Surf Theater Workshop where I'd won a full scholarship, and in between I'd be watching for the next record, the next New York appearance or TV show, the next piece of news. And there was plenty of it.

I was still bringing Supremes stories into school except now it was junior high and it wasn't show-and-tell, it was current events and all the other kids in the class were starting to get into political science instead of leaves. NASA's mission control had just beamed "Where Did Our Love Go" up into space for the Gemini V astronauts. It seemed like they were trying to see how long these two guys could stay shut up in a tiny orbiting spaceship without going crazy and I guess they thought the Supremes might keep them going just that little bit longer. So the Supremes were up there in the stars and of course I thought it was fabulous. I brought a clipping into class about it. A couple of other kids brought in clippings about the scientific importance of the mission and the effects of weightlessness and stuff, and I thought, my God, this class is full of boring bookworms. Let's talk Motown!

There must have been something on the Supremes every single month in *Soul* or *Jet* magazine, with readers' comments and reviews and photos. In September I read that the Supremes were booked to perform at the Flamingo in Las Vegas, which was an even bigger deal than the Copa, this was great news, this was show biz. To me Las Vegas sounded like the ultimate in glittering luxury. Also, the girls were about to start on yet another European tour—I was getting used to this kind of thing by now—and I read a rumor that Diana Ross would be leaving the group. I was shocked but strangely thrilled. After all, Diana was by now the most talked-about Supreme.

So when Flo next called I said, "Flo, what's this story about Diana leaving?" and she told me, "Ain't nothing chil'. Maybe that bitch is fixing to be the only diva in this group but she ain't ever leaving, and Flo ain't either." Flo would call from all over the world. I'd be hanging around outside my building with some of the other kids and my mother would call out of the third floor window, "Anthony! It's Flo!" and I'd race up to the phone. "Tony, you'll never guess where I'm at! Amsterdam! Can you hear me?" She called from

London, Paris, Rome, from places I had never even heard of and she'd ask me about the new record, how did I like it, they were going to be in town, she had bought me something. Flo would always buy me T-shirts and souvenirs from different places. Or it would be, "Tony, you know what that Diana did!" Sometimes she was up, sometimes she was down. "Tony, I'm exhausted."

Flo would call at two or three in the morning and she never said, this is long distance I gotta go now, she just talked, she never seemed to think about the money, those Supremes never looked at their phone bills anyway. The bills just got paid. Flo didn't seem to know where the money was coming from or where it was going, she got her weekly allowance from Motown, she said the company was investing the rest of her money, and nobody thought that this wasn't going to go on forever.

One time in the fall Flo called to tell me they were coming to New York. They were going to do *Ed Sullivan* and they were booked to perform at Lincoln Center—at Philharmonic Hall. She sounded very excited, she said they'd be the first pop group *ever* to perform there. At that point I didn't know what the excitement was about, I was more interested in going back down to *Ed Sullivan* and helping out, I was getting to be as much a regular around there as they were.

I'd been given a token job the Supremes laughingly called Fan Control and Patrol, which meant I had to throw the fans off track. By now, there was always a huge mob of fans outside that Ed Sullivan door waiting to throw themselves at the Supremes, and the girls didn't always have time any more to get caught up in a crowd and waste five or ten minutes. So I simply had to tell those kids, "The girls are leaving at two o'clock, everybody should go get something to eat, but be back here by a quarter to two and they'll be leaving by the stage entrance." Whereas, in fact they'd be leaving at one fifteen and Phil would be waiting for them at the main entrance.

So the Supremes came to do *Ed Sullivan* in October, and I could see that now the competition for fans between Flo and Diana was getting very stiff, but they each went about it their their own way. Mary, I thought, was still not getting her fair share of attention from the fans. I'd hear Flo argue with Diana in the dressing room, she'd basically tell Diana that she wasn't having none of it, none of her sneaky tricks and Diana would look at her like, oh please, dear, please, what on earth are you talking about? I heard Flo tell her, "I don't know why you're working so hard, Diana, you're getting the same amount of money we are, I don't know why you're trying to hog up everything. You think it's all about you and I'm tired of you trying to hog the spotlight with the fans and everything else."

I still thought it was kind of like friend fights, like schoolfriends, sometimes you have a rough couple of weeks, I'm not your friend this week, you got a higher mark on the spelling test plus you cheated, you brought the teacher a gift and then two minutes later we're speaking again. To me this argument between Diana Ross and Florence Ballard seemed just like that but better, because it was really much more interesting.

Florence would devise things. After an *Ed Sullivan Show* Diana and Mary would come out and the fans would make a big fuss, Diana would dash into the limo, she'd be looking and acting very grand, usually she didn't have time for fans, it was just a quick, "Oooh, I'm so happy to see you kids here," and into that limo. Then Diana would tell me, "Could you please go back inside and tell Blondie we're waiting on her," that was Flo's nickname.

So I'd go back inside and Flo would say, "Let her wait, let her wait." She'd take her slow time fiddling around in the dressing room, then fifteen minutes later she'd come out, she'd make it her business to talk to each and every fan on the sidewalk, Diana and Mary would be sitting in that car waiting and then Flo would announce, "Oh, you girls can go. I'm gonna walk to the hotel,'' and Diana would see red but she never reacted, she never created a scene in public, she just told Phil, ''Drive on! Drive on, Phil!'' And God only knows what Diana was saying to Mary in the back of that limo at times like this.

Flo now had all the fans to herself and she loved it, she was going to walk to the hotel with this crowd of loyal fans traipsing right behind her all along Fifty-fourth Street. Maybe she would stop at the pizza place with thirty, forty kids and just take it over, buying everybody sodas and pizza with anything you wanted on it. She enchanted them all. Then Flo and I would give them the slip out the back door and the fans loved it, they loved Flo for it. Mr. Gordy on the other hand didn't like it one bit. Flo told me he'd been insisting that the girls no longer went anywhere alone, only with Phil or with someone from Motown, and he also didn't like her being so familiar with the fans. But I could tell that Flo didn't care *what* Mr. Gordy said.

I was by now getting to know some of these fans, the ones that were there almost every time I was there, the loud and pushy ones, the ones that would later call themselves the A fans. These fans exchanged photos, spread the gossip, they called each other with news in between visits and they could be very aggressive, they thought they were stars in their own right and you better not disagree with them!

Some of their parents were fans too. The parents bought the albums and the kids bought the 45s, they had the little record players and transistor radios and they played those songs over and over, blaring out the project windows and the suburban windows too. The Supremes belonged to everybody, these fans were black and white, boys and girls. They came from all over and when October came around they were all waiting for the Supremes at Lincoln Center, which was another big scoop for the Supremes.

All the fans started to scramble for money to buy tickets, the cheap ones, the balcony seats, and although Flo told me, ''You don't have to,'' I decided to buy a top-price ticket for myself. So I bought my ticket, and I made a list of what I would need to make the night perfect because this was going to be a big event for the Supremes and for Motown and for New York, but I thought it was an even bigger deal for me.

The first thing on my list was clothes. I had to have a new suit and some new outfits for rehearsals, something slick and sharp for each day they were going to be around, and I had to have something extra special for Lincoln Center so I had to make more money, I started renting out my bike to kids in the projects who didn't have bikes.

I said, ''I'll rent you my bike for fifty cents a half hour, and you can only ride in a straight line, only where I can see you.'' I had bought a very fancy imported German bike with the money I made on my little enterprises. It was unusual because the handlebars were only about twelve inches across, and everybody on the street kept stopping me to ask where I got this bike. So I let them rent it, but they could only go from my building to the next building, fifty cents a half hour, no tricks no turns and if you fell off once your ride was over, no refunds.

I raised a lot of money doing that, of course I went directly to Mr. Tony's where James Knight recommended the right clothes for a current look and I bought my sharkskin suit, my silk socks, and some great shoes. Then I decided, I'm going to take a Checker cab because I want to look flashy. I wanted to pull up at the door where all the fans could see me. My stepfather had just bought a jet black, shiny, brand-new Bonneville that was just as big as a Cadillac and he offered to drive me down but I didn't think that was such a great idea because I knew the fans would say, oh, there's Tony, his father brought him, ha ha. I figured it would be much more fabulous to arrive all alone in a taxi, it would be a little mysterious and hadn't I heard Diana tell Mary and Flo, ''It's best to keep the fans guessing, darling.''

Naturally, I wanted to get a limo but a Checker cab

was as close as I could get on my budget, and since you couldn't get a Checker cab in Harlem that easy I thought, I'll take the train downtown, go in the side of the Hilton, march out the front door, I'll be all dressed up and the doorman will probably recognize me anyway because he's seen me here with the Supremes and I've seen him get cabs for people. I'll slip him a tip and get a cab there and it'll be cheaper than coming all the way from uptown.

So that's what I did. I had been to the rehearsal, then rushed home to get all dressed and all fixed up so I could make my proper arrival in grand style. But of course I hadn't anticipated such heavy traffic downtown. This wasn't the kind of thing I knew about. I sat in that cab watching the meter tick away eating up my money, and about two blocks from Lincoln Center I finally paid the driver, jumped out, and walked the last two blocks in an evil mood because I'd blown my grand entrance. To make it worse, my shiny new Italian leather shoes were killing my feet and then, just as I was getting near the place I heard footsteps running up behind me and one of the fans tapped me on the shoulder, "Hi Tony! Did you just get off the train?"

I was hurt, I turned around and said, "NOOO, I did NOT get off the train." I knew this kid had balcony seats so I told him, "And I am NOT sitting in the balcony!" Then I marched off in what I thought was appropriately grand Diana Ross style.

When I got inside I was really impressed by all the deep, crimson carpets and the glittering chandeliers and everything else. It was even grander than what I had seen when I went to rehearsal, because that was the back door, and this was the front lobby. Of course, it all made me pretty nervous but I acted like I wasn't. The stage was just huge, and they had a full orchestra with violins and trumpets and trombones. They did their show songs, their ballads, a new song called "I Hear a Symphony," and that audience, they were all dressed so formal but they went wild. Then there were standing ovations left and right and bouquets of roses were presented, it was a huge event and it was perfectly Supreme from beginning to end.

I didn't wait for the applause to die down before I raced off to go backstage. I wanted to be quick but it was a good, long journey to go all the way around the back, then I had to bang on the door forever and after the guards finally came and checked their guest lists and let me in it was another good journey to get upstairs in an elevator, all the way down this hall, then take a left turn, all the way down that hall, then take a right turn and it seemed like it must have taken me about forty-five minutes to get backstage. It also seemed like everyone else in the world was backstage and the girls were surrounded, they were all aglow, they were just glowing with all the showers of applause and the congratulations.

The girls were buoyant and bubbly and bouncing and there was something else too, a kind of amazement. This was a big show for them, bigger than their or Motown's wildest dreams. Of course I didn't realize that because it was such a big show for me to be going down to Lincoln Center. But I did notice that happy mood, Flo was saying, "Honey, we is terrific," and to me it seemed as if some of that old sisterly feeling was there again that night.

Or could it be that I just imagined it? You never knew what was going to happen next.

A couple of days later the Supremes left town to go to Boston and I rode with them to the airport. This was the first time I'd ever been in an airport and it was just me, Phil, and the girls. The road managers had gone on ahead with all the mountains and mountains of luggage that they traveled with.

I was sitting in my usual spot up front with Phil, the girls were sitting in the back kind of tense because they were running late, they had to catch that plane so Phil was driving pretty fast, and halfway to the airport Flo started complaining to Phil that he was going too fast, she said her wig was bumping up against the roof of the car and then she told Phil, "Pull over, Phil. Let me drive this car," and of course she looked at Diana when she said it.

Diana's eyes just rolled to heaven, Mary gave Flo a knowing glance, Phil said, "No, Miss Ballard, you can't drive," and he tried to laugh it off but Flo kept going, she said, "I *know* how to drive. I'm from Detroit where these cars are *made.*" Phil told her, "I can't let you drive. This is a company car, Miss Ballard!" But she kept insisting, "Let me at that wheel!"

So finally Phil tells Flo, okay, when we get near the airport, when we get on the Van Wyck Expressway you can drive and sure enough he pulls over, she gets out, he moves over into the middle, I move over, she gets in the front, grabs hold of the wheel and instead of this woman trying to merge into traffic she just shoots straight across three lanes of the highway and horns are blaring. Flo's laughing, "I like the fast lane!" She's clutching the wheel with her handbag still dangling from her arm, she's peering through the windshield as if she's going to go through that glass, "Ooh, this car's much bigger than I thought," and she just shoots straight to the airport driving like a wild woman. Diana's shrieking, "YOU'RE GOING TO KILL US ALL!" and Flo's lane hopping and zigzagging and cutting. She comes within inches of the car in front and Diana screams, "Oh Jesus!" at which Flo turns full around with the car still going straight ahead at about five hundred miles an hour, Flo glares at Diana and shouts, "NEVER take the Name of the Lord in Vain."

Phil's still trying to laugh it off. He knows this woman never drove no limo before and he keeps telling her, "Okay, Miss Ballard, oh my! You're a good driver, Miss Ballard, now why don't you *please* pull over and let me get back behind the wheel?" Flo's having the time of her life, she's saying "No, no, I'm going straight there. J.F.K. or bust!"

She drove so fast that when we got to the airport she nearly missed our turn-off, she backed up right on the expressway and just ran right up on the soft shoulder, across the grass, and somehow we just sort of ended up at the door, *right* at the door. The limo was halfway up on the sidewalk. A skycap who nearly got knocked down screamed, ''The Supremes!'' and Flo jumped out of the car and stood there beaming, just so, real pleased with herself.

Mary kissed me goodbye, Diana voiced no comment. She very quietly busied herself with fixing her makeup and wig in her little mirror and then she got out of the car and that was all, they were flying off and I was driving back into the city with Phil.

Flo winked at me. She knew Mr. Gordy was going to hear about this because a star does not jump right onto the Van Wyck Expressway and take over the limo from the chauffeur, maybe an Ikette but *not* a Supreme. This was just not done but Flo told me, ''I don't give a damn what that Gordy thinks or what he's going to say. If I'm driving, then I'm driving, honey!''

She just enjoyed it, she was like my Aunt Estelle or better yet Auntie Mame, she wanted adventure. To me, the whole thing was fun, going to the airport for the first time was fun but for her it was the same songs, same shows, same gowns, same routines every day and I guess she needed something to liven it up a bit.

So we said goodbye, and as soon as I got back in the car Phil said, ''I've gotta get this car checked!'' He looked kind of pale, he said he'd been scared half to death, he said, ''I don't care if she is a Supreme, the lady can't drive.'' Phil told me he only let Flo drive because he knew Diana didn't like it, it was Flo's game and he played along because Flo was a paying customer. So was Diana, but Phil said, ''Miss Ballard, she's down to earth, she's always asking me about my wife and how's the kids doing. Miss Wilson's sweet too, I feel sorry for her, always caught in the middle but that Miss Ross, she's a witch, she'll get in the limo and she'll just bark, ''TAKE ME HERE, do this do that, stay here and don't leave from in front of this door.''

Mary and Florence would go to Saks or the House of Kenneth and they'd say, "Phil, we're going to be in here about an hour, hour and a half, go get a coffee or a hot dog if you want but come back." Diana would insist, "Do *not* leave," and she knew when she went in that she wasn't going to be right out. But she wanted that car and I guess she was a star and it was her money, it was her right—the other girls were just more generous. Driving home from the airport Phil told me, "I never know when that Miss Ross woman is going to come out and want to go somewhere, and if I'm not right here in this limo with the engine running I'll lose my job. She won't even let you stop to take a piss!"

I was just a kid. I was the kid who was always around and I was usually very quiet because I didn't want any trouble, I was no fool. I was just there and it was getting to seem like I was invisible or a piece of furniture or something, so people would say anything in front of me and they would tell me all kinds of things. I heard everybody's gossip, I was their sounding board, after all what could I say or do about it, I was just a kid.

So I was quiet, but of course I was real interested in listening to what everybody said and I was always straining my ears to hear because I was so nosy. During the next few months I would hear a lot of stuff coming out of peoples' mouths, and some of it wasn't too pretty.

CHAPTER 7

— ◆ ◆ ◆ —

Stealing Innocence

In November the album, *At the Copa* was released, of course there was no "People" on it but it was a big success for the Supremes and right after that "I Hear a Symphony" hit number one on the charts. Then there was Thanksgiving which was always a big deal in my family, Christmas was coming up, it was almost a year since I'd met Flo at Altman's and gone to the Supremes' first *Ed Sullivan* appearance but now, by December '65 they were performing in places like the Houston Astrodome with Judy Garland, they performed in Miami at the Pompeii Room, they did endorsements for Coca-Cola and they were all over the world and all over TV. It wasn't just *Ed Sullivan*, it was the *Red Skelton Show*, the *Dean Martin Show*, the *Today Show*, the *Tonight Show*, it seemed like any time you turned on the TV, there were the Supremes doing their graceful little routines.

By now of course I was getting to be known around my new school. Kids would whisper as I walked by, "He's the one who knows the Supremes!" and I never let them forget it. The bigger the group got the more newsworthy I became because knowing the Supremes was power, I was getting to be a big star in junior high and I was just in the seventh grade. I thought, wait till I hit high school!

Naturally there were always the nonbelievers, they were the ones who in current events would be talking about the new Voting Rights Act or someone being elected the first black official in some government post and they never thought, well look at Motown, Motown's a black success story, a multimillion-dollar corporation. These kids were so snooty, they thought all of this Supremes stuff was ridiculous but I knew some of them were jealous, there would always be the one who said, "I don't believe it, I doubt it, no, no, you're lying, I don't believe it, I'll punch you in the face." And I'd give them a look I'd seen Flo use, I'd tell them, "Drop Dead."

I had my big-deal graduation camera now, it was a Brownie, the little squarish kind you'd hang round your neck and then you'd have to look down into this little glass thing you could never see the picture in and of course it never worked properly. The pictures were forever not coming out, maybe two in a roll of twelve ever came out but I had a few pictures, and even if I showed these kids one of me with the Supremes, they always suspected some kind of trick photo. "No, no, I don't believe it, they don't know you, you don't know them, you just stood next to them and let somebody take the picture quick or you begged them, but no, you were not in their room, no, they did not let you into the show, I don't believe it."

At first it used to bother me but then I said, to hell with these stupid fools, they never get downtown or anything. By now I was hanging out with a whole different bunch of kids in an older class and we were having a good time. They'd be playing all the hip music and really it was these bigger kids that showed me there was all this other music going on, they played the Temptations and the Four Tops and Martha and the Vandellas, they were into the Motown sound but not so much into the Supremes because the Supremes were by now almost too slick for them, too sophisticated. These kids liked the more danceable records—"Get Ready," "Nowhere to Run," "Going to a Go-Go"—

and as things progressed I'd even hear, "I hate the Supremes. They're too stuck up."

By now I was cutting school. Any time the Supremes were in town, if it was on a school day that was too bad, school was out, forget about it. I didn't ask my mother or anything, I just went to school in the morning, maybe the Supremes were going to be available at one o'clock so I'd go to the morning session and go to lunch and never come back, and my mother never found out because I would always tell her I was going straight down to the hotel after school was over. She did know I was skipping piano lessons for the Supremes. I had to plot out my strategy to keep myself covered, because my mother would *not* have let me cut school to go down there.

So I would go down and hang out with Flo, I'd help Greg in the dressing room, run errands and lord it over the fans. "You can't stand here," "You better be quiet," "Mr. Gordy doesn't want you fans hanging out in the lobby," "No photos please." I was being given more little jobs to do and I was getting to know all the new people that kept coming on the staff, the entourage just kept growing and changing, the second someone disappeared, someone new appeared.

One day I turned up at rehearsal and Mrs. Powell wasn't there. I said, "Where's Mrs. Powell?" and someone told me Mrs. Powell would unfortunately no longer be traveling with the Supremes. Apparently Diana had seen that Mrs. Powell got the axe, because Mrs. Powell didn't take anything from anybody, she didn't care *who* Diana Ross was or thought she was and Diana grew tired of her lectures because Miss Powell would tell her, "Miss Ross, I *know* you're not addressing *me* in that manner." And when Diana complained about a gown or something Mrs. Powell would say, "Mr. Gordy wants it done this way and this is the way it will be done," all the while speaking and presenting herself in the proper manner, though manners didn't save Mrs. Powell. Mary and Flo told me they were sad to see Mrs. Powell go, but they also said they were too old now for chaperones.

In February the Supremes came to do *Ed Sullivan* again and of course I went to meet Flo at the hotel, then I went to rehearsal and as usual I hung out with Greg while he combed wigs and gossiped about Diana. She was always good fuel for gossip. Just when you'd finished talking about her last touch of bitchiness, or the last flamboyance in her performance, or her general attitude, just when you'd worn that down she'd give you something else to work with, something else to talk about. Greg loved to say things like, "Darling, did you see what she did when she got up on that Sullivan stage? She was working that wig, she used that piece of hair that she told me to put over her eye."

Greg told me, "She insisted that I cut that wig like that and I told her, this ain't gonna look right but she said, no, I want it like a Sassoon cut that I saw in *Vogue.*" Diana would give Greg pictures she cut out of the magazines for him to copy, he said she had told him that she wanted a Rudie Gernreich look, a totally different look from Mary and Flo, and she wanted it to come over her eye so as she sang she could keep brushing the hair back out of her eye and face.

The wig was right there on the wig head and Greg told me, "Isn't that ridiculous, it looks lopsided, it looks horrible and when she put it on I thought for sure, she's gonna have a big old piece of hair over her eyes, she's gonna look like a fool."

Then Diana went up on the stage and worked that piece of hair, she kept flicking it back, Greg and I were amazed. "Wasn't she fabulous! Can you believe it! Ooh, she was right, you know that's what irks me about Diana, she's usually always right. She worked that style, oh my God! She's such a diva though." Everybody on that Ed Sullivan stage had on the same gown, the same heels, the same earrings but Diana knew how to do that little bit extra, to give herself the edge, she knew how to be the one that was somehow different because being the lead singer just wasn't enough. She was the one who had to keep pushing the hair back like it was a nuisance, like the hairstylist hadn't given her enough holding spray to hold it back or something.

That was the first time I saw Diana upstage Flo and Mary on the *Ed Sullivan Show*. They were doing "My World Is Empty Without You" and of course Diana knew the show was live, it was always rehearsed a certain way and she knew where she was supposed to be, where Flo and Mary were supposed to be, where the camera was going to be. Everything was planned out at rehearsal. Then the Supremes came out to do the live show and the camera was on all three girls, the music started up and all of a sudden, all out of the blue Diana threw that piece of hair back and raised her arms up in a big V for victory. She held them there, her arms were blocking out half of Flo's and Mary's faces and you knew she knew about it, you just knew she'd figured it all out ahead of time, she was moving herself way ahead in the group and Flo was set on fighting it. Mary just said, "Oh, you know how Diana is."

It was beginning to look like everything was planned, nothing with Motown ever happened by chance. They'd release a single one day and within a few days they'd be doing it on TV and then a week or two later that song would be the Supremes' latest hit. Everything seemed calculated, it was almost like military maneuvers, it was strategy down to the tiniest detail and like Flo said, Diana was plotting along with the rest of them.

I'd seen Diana making all kinds of changes in the Supremes' shows, just like I'd seen at the Copa. Usually it was at rehearsal. Cholly always choreographed as a unit so all three girls would be doing the same dance step and Diana would say something like, "I think it should go like this. I think the girls should be to this side of me and I should be a little over to the right. We can do the same step, that's great, but I should be a little further up, my mike should be positioned here."

So Cholly says to her, "No, Diana, I think it should stay just as it is, it looks better that way," because he's looking at it the way the audience is going to see it. Diana says okay and does it Cholly's way, and Flo's telling me, "Honey, she's gonna run and tell it, watch and see, she'll run and tell it." And I guess she ran and called Mr. Gordy in Detroit. The next thing you knew, the very next day the choreography was being done the way Diana suggested it yesterday to Cholly. Obviously Cholly had been told, "Put Diana where she wants to be." It was just like I noticed during the Copa rehearsals, except then I didn't see it all yet.

I was growing up pretty fast, I was seeing things clearer and around this time it started to be really obvious to me that Diana Ross and Berry Gordy were going together, they weren't that open about it but I always thought Diana was sweeter when Mr. Gordy was around, she seemed more relaxed, happier, and she was also nicer to me. Then I'd see them walking around holding hands, like young lovers, and Diana would be clinging onto Mr. Gordy. Flo told me Diana's dad was kind of strict, she said that must be why Diana likes Gordy, he's like a powerful father figure to her.

So in the beginning, when I first knew the Supremes people thought nothing of saying, do this Diana, because they were basically telling all the girls what to do. Wear this, stand like this, say this, dance like this, pose like this and all three girls did it. But as Diana's relationship with Mr. Gordy grew, she'd report to him and then the staff began to change their attitude and they began to get afraid of her because Mr. Gordy was the boss and Diana was becoming his protégée.

She was just like the class tattletale, you knew that she was reporting things because she'd tell us. Whatever it was, she'd simply say, "I'm going to call Mr. Gordy," and she would immediately go and pick up the phone and call, and sure enough Diana got her way, she'd be a little more out in front of the other two, her mike would be repositioned, she'd have a new speaking line, she'd have extra rehearsal time all by herself. And she'd get a little more wicked and bossy after each call.

Now the staff didn't want to tell her anymore, Diana do this. Gradually it was becoming, Miss Ross would you like to, Miss Ross how would you feel about, Miss Ross suppose we place you, Miss Ross where would you like to. And as it changed for Diana it remained the same for Flo and Mary. It was still, Flo over here, stand there, Mary over here. Flo and Mary were choreographed or harmonized to work around Diana and now it was not so much to make the group look good, it was to make Diana look good. Even I could see that.

Then of course Diana would make sure that Berry knew about anyone's behavior that wasn't strictly Supreme, and if Mr. Gordy wasn't there she'd call him to report it. Usually it was about some road manager or staff member not treating her with total respect, or it was about Flo mingling with the fans, or being late, or jumping out of the limo in the middle of the expressway. Those phone bills must have been enormous. Flo would just kind of sing out, "Diana, you know I am NOT to be played with, honey. Run and tell that to Mr. Gordy."

Mary must have seen it. I was just a kid and I saw it. Of course Flo saw it, everybody knew Flo saw it because her mouth was always going. Every time Diana got her way Flo said something like, "Look! Don't she think she's something special? She's just tooo divine. How does she rate? We're just her background and her backbone, she's becoming a star on our backs."

Mary wouldn't say anything but, "Oh, Flo, calm down." She saw it simply as her two best friends having an argument, it was Flo and Diana fighting. But for Flo it was no longer Diana, it was "Diana and Gordy," "Gordy and Diana," "Diana and Gordy."

Flo thought Mr. Gordy was much too old for Diana.

She told me so, she said she'd been interested in him but that was just a schoolgirl crush, that was way before "Where Did Our Love Go?" and it would never have got this far because Mr. Gordy was just an old man, and wasn't it too common, Miss Di-an-a Ross going with a married man. Flo would say these kind of things to me, especially when she'd had a cocktail and I knew my mother would have sent me out the room before she let me hear that stuff. Some of the time I didn't want to hear what Flo was trying to tell me.

One night after a show I was up in Flo's suite, Flo was sipping her medicine out of her crystal goblet and she was talking about astrological signs and all sorts of stuff. She told me we both were born under the same sign even though her birthday was in June and mine was in July and she said, "Baby, the planets can help you understand yourself and the other fools around you as well. Mary is a Pisces, honey, she swims in both directions, she bears watching."

I said, "What does that mean?"

"You heard the expression 'two-faced'?"

"Yeah."

"Then honey, you should understand what Flo means when she says Mary's a fish swimming in both directions."

I didn't.

She said, "Diana is an Aries, those people are pushy and self-centered. She's always going around with her nose up in the air like she's smelling something, get it? Air-ees, she was always like that, I guess I really should understand her better, even back in the projects when we were all broke she had that attitude like she was better than anybody else. Diana slept three to a bed just like at my house, honey. She ain't no better, nor did the bitch have it any better than us."

Mary told me the same kind of things, she told me about the early days in Detroit, how they would go over to Motown all the time to try and get signed, Diana was always the slick one, always the one doing the little bit extra, the one trying to help out in Berry Gordy's office. She said Diana always had on a little too much makeup, usually the wrong shade, this is how she was, what can you do?

Whereas Flo was always wanting to see that everything was fair, everything was nice, everybody was happy. She would look out the window and see the fans there, she knew they'd been there all day screaming and now it was four-thirty or five o'clock, it was dark and cold and she'd say, "That's a shame, all those fans standing out there freezing." Then she'd go around and she'd tell everyone, "I'm collecting money for the fans." Maybe she'd come up with fifteen dollars, that was a lot of money, you could get a hot chocolate for twenty-five cents. She'd tell me, "Tony, go down there and take those kids around the corner to the luncheonette, get them all hot chocolate or something, and don't let me see you picking and choosing between those fans!"

Naturally, I always picked the ones that I liked and I picked the ones with the big mouths because they could be quite vicious and you wanted them easy to handle. Flo would say, "When I say take everybody, take everybody and make sure everybody gets a cup of hot chocolate and if there's not enough money, don't be giving the donuts to these ones and then those others don't get donuts. Cut 'em in half!" She'd say, "Fair is fair, honey. You just can't be taking your friends or kids who are going to trade pictures with you. I know that goes on. Sometimes I look out the window and there's still people left down there and I know they're cold enough to want something hot to drink." She was very, very firm like that. "Don't you go getting grand on Flo."

I was already known among the fans as a real dresser. From the very beginning I always wanted to look the best when the Supremes were in town and now I was starting to notice that it worked for me, it made me popular with the adults because Berry Gordy would say to me, "Oh, you always look sharp, you always look so nice," and some of the others would tell me, "Tony, you always have the nicest clothes." They'd say, "Ooh, stand back! Let me look at you, let me see what you've got on this time. Oh! This kid's got great taste, he's got a real sense of style. Tony, you really dress nice."

So I started using it as a tool. Everything had to look that much better. I changed my style of dressing from very mod and hip to very smart and tailored, with mandatory shirt and tie because you never knew what was going to come up, where you were going to be able to go with the Supremes and I didn't want them saying, "You can't come because you don't have on proper attire." Even then I knew that a suit and tie for a man, like a black dress with a string of pearls for a woman, could take you anywhere.

There were always parties or events to attend after a show and I just tagged right along, I'd be dressed real smart and I'd go with the Supremes to a cocktail party, a big art opening, a reception. They went out as a group but this wasn't a party for let's have fun, this was party for business, to be seen and to be written about. They never stayed long because the next morning maybe they were going to be flying off somewhere, or they'd have to get up and go rehearse for the next show.

But now it was starting to appear to Florence that these people were all there to meet Diana, and Diana was being pushed by Berry Gordy or was pushing Berry Gordy to push her. The staff would tell me, "she has her ways . . ." It was becoming, I want you to meet Diana Ross, lead singer of the Supremes, and Miss Ross would love for you to come to the show, and it would make her so happy, and Miss Ross really enjoyed your last painting, your latest movie, Diana really liked this, Diana really liked that and oh, by the way, have you met Florence and Mary, the other girls?

As things progressed it seemed to always happen that when they went to parties or dinners Diana would be ready first and she and Mr. Gordy would leave first.

It was never stated, "Okay, Diana and I are going ahead, Flo and Mary can follow in fifteen minutes," but that was becoming the reality.

So Diana made her grand entrances. It looked as if she was the only Supreme to attend a function. "Isn't it nice, one of the Supremes came!" "Oh, it's the lead singer." And here's Flo and Mary rushing to get downstairs and into the limo, trailing behind Diana like accessories, with me trailing behind them—the kid in the suit with the glasses on.

Mr. Gordy would look at me and say, "Tony, I hope you're not letting your schoolwork fall behind, I hope you're doing your homework," he was very paternal. Well, with all the parties and cutting school and everything I was falling behind, and in the spring they threw me out of the IGC class for being unruly and undesirable, my mother was shocked. I was still not considered bad enough to go into the mainstream, so they put me in the SP class which was a special program, it was for kids who were reading above grade level but not for geniuses, which was fine because the students in the IGC class were really not my crowd. They sure didn't know any Temptations dance steps.

When I got demoted into the SP class, of course all the IGC kids stopped speaking to me because I was now trash, but I really didn't give a damn, I was part of a new crowd and in this crowd there were a few party people like Steven Williams, Terry Coleman, Clarence Lee, and Barry Laster who ended up being my best friend. There was a girl who'd had a baby! She'd had a baby, rumored to be from her mother's boyfriend, oooh, this was the crowd to get with.

Right across the street from the school there was a New York City bus terminal, so during the lunch break we would go in there, we'd go on the buses and if you jingled the driver's fare machine long enough change would come out and we'd get the money, we'd go to the liquor store and the man would sell us Gypsy Rose or Thunderbird, it was fifteen kids to a pint bottle but we'd come back to school drunk, they'd call our mothers, I'd get in trouble and of course most of the teachers thought it was because I hung around with a bunch of wild hooligans.

They were the ones who didn't want to eat in the lunchroom, they wanted to buy a hero sandwich and run around the streets at lunchtime, they were the ones sneaking into the Tastee Bread factory stealing pecan twirls and then selling them to the other students. They were smart, they were fun, they kept me constantly in trouble and I loved it.

In class we were always talking out of turn, cursing and giving the teacher a hard time. I'd be always talking about the Supremes, about how I knew show business, I'd be always disturbing the class, passing secret notes, talking about people, creating a big scene, standing up on the desk, and I thought nothing of it. This was my crowd, these were people who were interested in partying and having a wild time.

So things were getting to be fun in school, we formed a gang called "the notorious ones." And then Flo called. She sounded happy, she said they were going to have a whole week off and I could come stay with her in Detroit, she told me to ask my mother. She said they'd been working nonstop, they were all exhausted, and I guess a whole week of just being home in Detroit was pretty exciting for her though for me the exciting thing was going to stay with Florence Ballard, flying in an airplane and going some place I'd never been.

Of course, the moment school finished for the summer me and my mother started getting me fixed up and ready to go, this took about three weeks and all the time my mother was warning me, "Now, Anthony, don't eat too much, don't take any second helpings because you know how greedy you are and don't forget to say please and thank you."

And my stepdad was telling me, "Don't you go begging that woman for nothing." My mother's saying, "If she wants to buy you something just say no thanks."

"Yeah," my stepdad said. "You know how much that ticket must have cost her? I don't think those Supremes make that much money, not just for singing." And all this time I'm nodding and saying, "Yes mom, yes dad," and I'm thinking, get me outta here and to Motown.

So I packed my bags with a ton of new clothes and I flew to Detroit. This was the summer of '66, and I realized, Wow! I'd seen them in New York and I thought they lived high but until I went to Detroit I didn't realize how high they really lived. It was something!

Even at home, everything was taken care of for the Supremes, it was as if they were trained not to worry about a thing, don't worry your pretty talented little head over it, it's being done for you, you're too special, you're too fabulous. You want it, you've got it. You're loaded, you're a superstar, make a wish list, give it to somebody and they'll get it for you. I'm having the bathroom at my house redone, I don't like that color Cadillac, did you see those new Lincolns? You don't even have to go down to the showroom to pick out the car and sit with the sales agent and say, well maybe I can do better. No, you say, I want a car fully equipped and the showroom is called and they parade four or five cars past your door, you pick one you want and that's it, Motown will take care of the money part for you, you're a star!

You like these gowns? How do they look, do you like them, are they dazzling, are they shocking, is it a new style, am I breaking ground with this fashion? Not, how long is it going to last, can I get it cleaned. This was glamor, baby, it was here for the moment, gone forever. They were coming from nothing into incredibly fast wealth.

I saw the projects where they used to live. We drove by in Flo's Cadillac Eldorado and they looked just like my projects. They'd gone from there straight to those huge houses on Buena Vista Drive, which was in *the* fashionable section, and a lot of the Motown stars had houses in the same area. I thought, this is what it is to be a star. You live in a big, beautiful house with big fancy furniture, nice cars, everybody's beautifully dressed, fans want to go through your garbage looking for souvenirs. You never see any money pass hands, you go to a club, you order drinks, you order food. I never saw the girls go into their pocketbooks for any money.

Everybody was so pretty, everybody was so nice. I thought this was how life was for the longest time, for years and years because it looked so good, so supreme. Florence had a Yorkshire terrier. I had never seen a Yorkshire terrier before, but it was now the thing to own. Diana had a Maltese poodle. She told me that using the name "poodle" after Maltese was redundant. I was learning, it was the latest thing, you had to have your white Maltese. It was a must.

These were the things the stars had, the things they wanted. The pets to own, the way to look, the cars to drive, the shoes to wear, this is the latest rage. They had it, I saw it, and so I wanted it. When I'm grown, I'm gonna get a Cadillac, I'm gonna shop at Saks Fifth Avenue, I want to have a brick English Tudor mansion with a big awning like Flo's and I want matching crystal glassware because you're supposed to have it. Because Flo is a star and this is the way it's supposed to be, period.

Everybody crowded around them, the Supremes were home and this was big news in Detroit, everybody wanted them. The press wants them, they want to know what their black Barbie dolls have been doing. The press wants to see how Florence Ballard lives, they want to see her crystal chandeliers, her color scheme, they want to write this up in the newspapers. The girls had no rest from it, they were never just alone, just relaxing

People are in and out of your house, food and drinks for everybody, you're entertaining, wherever you are it's the place to be. Over at Mary's it's the same thing, everybody's there, it's a party. Kick off your shoes, do a routine, have some Dom Pérignon, have whatever and sometimes whoever you want.

Mary would saunter in wearing some bizarre outfit, like leopard skin and soft leather. I'd always thought of her as quiet but now I could see she was the toast of the party, the type who would jump out of the cake and hang from the crystal chandelier. Flo was a party girl too but at a different kind of party. She was the one who'd be running around making sure everybody had something to eat, something to drink, she'd be looking great and making a lot of jokes, keeping the guests satisfied whereas Mary would be striking poses, she'd be looking sexy without even trying. She was busy being a guest at her own party. And then of course there was Diana, I hardly saw Diana the whole time because she spent most of her time perfecting this and studying that, rehearsing that attitude.

I was just there for the week but for the Supremes it was nonstop. Flo was pretty happy, she didn't do a lot of bitching that week, she hardly saw Diana so they had a break from each other and Flo was looking forward to their new album, *A Go-Go*. She told me she had a lead on it, she was singing lead on "These Boots Are Made For Walking." Things were looking up.

I went back to New York, back to the projects. A few days later I was hanging around outside my building and my mother yelled down for me, Flo's on the phone. "Tony! Tony did you hear the new record, did you hear "You Can't Hurry Love"? You know what they did to Flo's voice? Can you even hear my voice on that song? You listen to it, hell, Gordy's done got the background turned down so low momma says she can't even hear my voice and she ought to know. Ain't that nothin'!"

I felt pretty sure Flo was in her medicine, she was getting real loud, all about how they could have told her but no, it was a plot, it was all done to put Diana in the spotlight, Berry and Diana were trying to take over the group and how could they do that to her, and on and on. Mary didn't even come into it, her voice was just there well behind Diana's, cooing "it's a game of give and take, oooh."

At the end of the month the Supremes came to New York to do *Ed Sullivan* again. They were working something very intricate and they needed extra time, so Phil drove them over to the CBS rehearsal studios on Eleventh Avenue and Fifty-seventh Street and of course I went with them. Right across the street from the studio was some kind of factory and I guess the guys saw the limo and asked Phil who was inside, it was a hot day and some were out there on their lunch break. I guess the word spread because when we came out from the studio all these men were hanging out the windows of the factory screaming and yelling and hollering and whistling, and some of them were calling for Flo, who had on this very sexy summer outfit, she was absolutely glittering in the summer heat.

The girls waved and everything, they all seemed very happy but then the men started chanting, Flo! Flo! Flo! Diana got in the limo, she'd had enough of the waving. Mary just followed Diana. I got in the front but Flo didn't follow. Flo strode out into the middle of Fifty-seventh Street, out in the high sun and heat of summer, she stood smack in the middle, right on the white line with the traffic whizzing by her and she threw her arms up in the air. Now the guys started throwing down all their handkerchiefs and their headbands and T-shirts, one of the hankies fell near Flo, she picked it up and started waving it at the men and all hell broke loose!

We're all sitting in the limo watching this. Phil's got the engine running and the air conditioner blowing but Diana's about to boil over, so she tells Phil, "Drive off, drive off and leave her right in the middle of the street. How common! How disgusting, standing up there making a spectacle of herself! I've never seen anything so shocking." She starts banging on the back of the seat, demanding "GO! DRIVE OFF! Do you hear me? Do you want to be fired? I said drive off, just leave her she can get a cab!'' She bangs the seat right behind me, ''Tony, get out, you can go with Flo.''

I didn't move. Phil got out of the car, I thought he was going to go get Flo but he just got out, closed the door and stood by the back door waiting for Flo to get in. Flo wouldn't get in, she kept on waving and laughing, then when she was good and ready she came back to the limo, Phil opened the back door, Flo got in, Diana didn't say a word about how common or how disgusting or how anything, she kept her demanding mouth shut.

Flo was all happy and exuberant. ''Oh, Mary, did you see some of those men, some of them were so gorgeous girrrrl! And I picked up a handkerchief and, girl, those men went wild! Oooh, did you see the muscles on that one? I thought he was gonna jump out the window. Did you hear me? I yelled, 'DON'T JUMP,' I had to dash for the car!''

Mary said, ''Yeah, it was something.'' Diana never commented.

Flo kept going, ''I had a good time! That was so much fun, why did you all get in the car so quickly?''

Diana didn't say a word, Mary just went, ''Oh girl, it was so hot.'' I wanted to turn around so bad and look at their faces in the back but I didn't dare. Flo was oblivious, she was just so excited, ''Oh I wish I had my camera. Tony where's your camera, where's your camera?''

I said, ''Oh, this thing can't work.'' I didn't want to say too much.

''Honey, you just can't see. Poor thing, with those glasses and you still can't see, all those pictures you take with the tops of everybody's heads cut off, it's too terrible.''

Flo was doing all the talking and all the giggling, and suddenly it seemed like she was all alone in that limo. There wasn't no Supreme going to sing along, and who if anybody was going to back her up when Berry Gordy got to hear about it, which of course he would after Diana put in her full report the moment she hit the hotel. There wasn't anybody going to say, hey, it was fun, it was harmless, it was innocent, it was pleasing the public but in a different way. Maybe it wasn't too Supreme but it sure made those guys feel supreme.

We all knew Mary wasn't going to say anything, just like she wasn't going to stand out on Fifty-seventh Street in some tiny outfit and drive a bunch of laborers wild. Phil wasn't going to say anything even if he wanted to, he was the chauffeur. And I couldn't say a thing because I was just the kid, I was Tony the good kid who never caused no trouble but I was learning fast, and times like this were stealing my innocence.

CHAPTER 8

———— ◆ ◆ ◆ ————

Give an Inch, Take a Mile

A*Go-Go* was a phenomenal smash album for the Supremes. It was in the days of the go-go boots craze, when everything was "a go-go" and all the restaurants and clubs were something "a go-go," like Whisky a Go-Go, you could get Fried Chicken a Go-Go, Go-Go Watches, even Wigs a Go-Go, all over Harlem they were putting up signs "a Go-Go."

So here you have *A Go-Go* with Mary Wilson doing a decent lead on a Vandellas original, "Come and Get These Memories," you have Diana Ross doing a solo without any background on "These Boots Are Made for Walking," which is the song Flo said she was supposed to be doing solo on, and you have Flo doing nothing but holding up the background. Flo has no solo, no featured spot, no nothing, and what's she going to do? She's not going to do what Motown told her to do when she asked, "Hey, what about my solo?" They told her she'd better sit down and shut up, but she wasn't going to do that.

She had all this to deal with, plus the embarrassment of everyone in Motown knowing what was going on and everyone saying, "Ain't that nothing, ain't that a shame, good as she could sing. Ain't that terrible, because Flo, damn, vocally she'd blow Diana away in a minute." She had all of this mental thing building up on her, she had to do something. Flo was a person who spoke her mind and when she was angry about something she said it, she got it off her chest, didn't keep it in like Mary. Flo didn't mope or sleep on it or brood about it. She let it out. She was one for honesty and justice and do the right thing, tell it like it is, baby.

I saw all of this stuff starting to boil up again when they released *A Go-Go* in August of '66 and the Supremes came to New York to promote the album. They did a thing one Saturday at the old Stern's department store on Forty-second Street where you could come and ask the Supremes questions and then you could line up, buy the album, and take it backstage for the girls to autograph. Of course I went, and of course when they opened the doors the fans tried to kill each other getting in so they could sit up in the front. The auditorium was packed. I guess they used to give fashion shows in this room because it had a small stage up in front, no stage curtain, just a curtain behind it and all the way down the middle, going all the way to the back of this room was a runway connected to the stage. All the seating was to the left and right of this runway.

The fans wanted the girls to come down the runway and at first the Stern's people said no for security reasons, it couldn't be done. So the Supremes sat on stage and started answering the kids' questions, very basic questions like, How do you like traveling? Are you married? Do you like New York? What do you think of the Beatles? What do you think of go-go boots? Is that why you're calling the new album *A Go-Go*? Where do you buy those long eyelashes? Is that a wig?

The girls are answering all these questions, and at some point Florence takes it upon herself to suggest, well, I think it would be fine to go down the runway. The Stern's lady seems a bit upset about this but then she tells the fans, all right, on these conditions. She warns them all, nobody is to sit on the runway, nobody is to put their hands on the runway, nobody is to reach for the girls, nobody is to pass them flowers or photos, nothing to sign, nobody is to do anything. Okay. One girl at a time.

Florence is the first one down the runway. She's dressed real nice in one of her little Jackie Kennedy pants suits with a pair of dangling earrings and she's carrying her little pocketbook all prim and proper. She walks down and some of the kids try and give her things, they try and shake her hand, she walks to the end and stays there for a while chatting with some of them, and a lot of fans start rushing to the back of the runway where Flo is. I'm sitting in the front watching this and watching Diana and Mary who are just sitting up on stage smiling, and to me it seems like Diana is looking a bit annoyed because nobody's asking her questions any more, Flo has the spotlight all to herself.

Flo stays there with the fans and she talks and talks and finally she just strolls very grandly back to the stage and she tells the girls, "See, nothing happened." So Mary comes out looking a bit scared because by this time Flo's got the fans going, these kids are not so calm any more so Mary just sort of smiles faintly and walks maybe one third of the way, she doesn't shake anybody's hand, she waves, blows a few kisses and the fans start stomping and screaming, then suddenly Mary heads back to the security of the stage.

Everybody's waiting for Diana. Everybody knows by now that Diana's the star and believe me this woman's been waiting on them too. She gets up, she just sort of stands at the front and starts smiling, she has on this huge, sweater-blouse-type concoction with batwing sleeves, and high, high spikes—nobody's ever seen a get-up like this before. Diana rolls her eyes at Flo and all of a sudden, without warning, she spreads her arms out wide and starts flying down that runway like a jet getting ready to take off. She spreads her wings and takes the entire runway, just like a perfect model would do, she makes it work overtime for her. Then she stands at the end, she gets the crowd going even more, she's reaching out and hugging people, doing that little bit extra and the fans just eat it up.

Florence is furious, really FURIOUS and immediately she jumps up, she comes down the runway, stops in the middle and gets a little crowd of her own going and I guess Diana's heard something behind her, something else besides the bedlam she's causing down at the end, because she turns around and sees Flo creating her own little bedlam and havoc. Security guys are starting to come out, they're pulling the kids back and when Diana sees all this she runs back down to where Flo is standing with her little crowd and she starts spinning in this incredible outfit with the batwing sleeves, spinning like a top.

Of course, everybody's fickle attention immediately switches from Flo to Diana, but by this time it's all out of control anyway. The crowd's gotten ugly, they're wild, they're climbing up on the runway, things are getting knocked over, chairs are flying, people are pushing and shoving, people are trying to grab albums and security's coming, they grab the girls and take them backstage, the whole thing's over.

Now everybody's trying to beat it to be the first in line for albums, somebody comes and rescues me from the middle of all this, ''he's with them,'' they take me right up over the stage and backstage, and there's the Supremes arguing in front of all these people from the store. Florence is telling Diana how bitchy she is, how she's a scene stealer, Mary's saying nothing, the road manager, Don Foster, is trying to defuse the whole situation, trying to quiet everything down, trying to get them into the chairs so they can start signing autographs but anybody can see this is just not going to work because there's too much hostility here between Diana Ross and Florence Ballard. All the store people can see this, they're all watching and even when the girls do finally sit down and sign autographs, all these people know that the Supremes are not the sweeter-than-pie goody-two-shoes girls they've been reading about.

Of course, as soon as the girls got back to the hotel Mr. Gordy got wind of what happened and of course he was upset, the whole thing being very tacky and bad for the Supremes' image. And whatever the disagreement, Stern's was not the place for Diana and Florence to air their differences, you could do that later back at the hotel, but never in public. Any Supreme knew that, but Flo thought it was already too late, it was done and in Flo's mind it was like she said, "Every time Diana does something I can't wait and stop her when we get back to the hotel because she's like a person out of control, she keeps doing and doing and doing and you give a person an inch, they take a mile." Diana was no longer the little mouse running around stealing the extra cheese, she was the cheese.

It was another nail for Flo, as Mr. Gordy liked to tell her, "You have just put another nail in your coffin," he'd say. "Reports get back to me, I'm getting tired of it." It was like a very quiet threat. Things were getting ugly and people were beginning to see it but nobody outside of Motown was ever supposed to know what was really going on with the Supremes, so security was stepped up. The girls became unavailable for some interviews, they just got kind of wrapped up and whisked from here to there and nobody was supposed to say anything to anyone on the outside, because the press was just waiting to jump at the first sign that all was not well with their little dreamgirls, the press was full of rumors.

There were a lot of rumors and many of them were accurate. I'd read things like, Florence Ballard and Berry Gordy have had a falling out, Diana Ross is going to leave and go solo, Florence Ballard is jealous about Diana Ross being given the spotlight. Motown denied them all, they just kept saying, Oh, it's just a little thing, it's all blown over, no, everybody's happy as can be.

I'd read this stuff and then Flo would call me and now she'd be asking me, what are the fans saying? And I'd ask her if this was true, if that was true. One time it was rumored that Florence Ballard was having a baby, that she had secretly gotten married, so when she called I asked her and she said, "No that's not true, that's not true, now when would I even have time to get married?"

They kept her so busy. She complained a lot about that, about how tired she was, how she got so sick sometimes. She said they had made a lot of money and she felt they didn't have to go on working every day of the month, it wasn't like they were trying to build a name for themselves. She still wanted to sing and perform and do records and appearances, travel, all that stuff but a little bit less of it, not sixty different concerts, one after another in sixty different cities and just as many days. Maybe just forty-five and take off every three or four days. But Mr. Gordy wasn't having any of it, he'd tell her, "Diana's not tired, Mary's not tired, Flo you are holding us back, you better work while you can."

Flo complained about being tired, but mainly I thought she was upset because Mary was not backing her up. She said Mary had been putting her up to do and say a lot of things, like when she asked Flo, didn't Flo agree that they needed a vacation? Flo agreed. Mary then suggested that Flo go tell Mr. Gordy. Flo went to Mr. Gordy. "We need a vacation, this is too much, we're tired, we need two weeks off, we want to go to the Caribbean and we want to go home to enjoy our houses." But when Mr. Gordy asked Mary if this was true for her too, Mary told him she was okay, she could go on another few weeks.

So Florence appeared to be the one who couldn't take it, who couldn't take all the traveling and everything else even though Mary told Flo she was tired. Diana complained she had to work even harder than the other two for the same pay, she never complained about being tired but Diana had lost pounds, she had collapsed on stage from exhaustion, and she was even more bone-thin than ever.

Which was another problem for Flo. Gordy was now

complaining that Florence was getting fat, he'd say, "Flo, you're getting heavy," and she'd snap back, "I am not getting heavy, Diana is just too thin. This is my size. The fans like it and the men like it. I stopped a whole company of men on Fifty-seventh Street, I didn't hear nobody calling for Diana."

He'd tell her, "You sing too loud," and Flo would come back with, "I can't lower my natural voice, I can't sing any softer, my voice is vibrant, this is how I sing, my whole family sings loud. Unlike some people around here, the Ballards can sing." That was her way, she got known for it. Flo didn't think it was fair the way she was being treated. It was sneaky and it was underhanded. At first she tried to speak calmly to Berry Gordy about it, but it started to get out of control.

A lot of the stuff she said was so quick and witty, for a while I thought it was real funny. Maybe Mr. Gordy would be telling her, "You know Flo, in this situation it would be advisable to," whatever he was discussing and she would say, "You know, I agree with you," which would be a big shock for everybody, "but you are just too damn short to know what you're talking about, so I won't consider it." And she'd sail out of the room having gotten her say. The woman was something, and she was not to be messed with. Even Diana knew it, who had seen it and had even been protected by it at times and I think she was scared of Flo, because she'd always quiet down immediately when Flo started in on her or on Mr. Gordy.

Flo would say things like, "I'm not sitting up here while you hold court, Berry Gordy. If anyone's going to hold court it's gonna be me, I'm the one that's a Supreme, I'm the one that's a star, don't nobody know you." Which would anger him to no end because he sort of fancied himself a celebrity, and around Motown he was known behind his back as the Fourth Supreme. Some of the other Motown people were saying, it should be Berry Gordy and the Supremes. A lot of Motown groups resented all the time he spent away from Motown on the road with the Supremes. They felt like they weren't getting proper attention and proper management, and some of them said it was because Berry Gordy was running behind that Diana Ross tramp instead of tending to company business.

It was like a big family that wins the lottery and a couple of kids get more than all the others. The Supremes were getting everything, the attention, the expensive gowns, the fancy supper club appearances, big tours, big suites, and now Mr. Gordy was with them all the time. He went all over the world with them. You couldn't help but notice the tension when he was around because he and Flo would be constantly but quietly bickering.

In September, when the Supremes flew to the Far East for a three-week tour Mr. Gordy flew with them, and I went back to school. I was starting to think about high school, which high school was I going to? I tested for the High School of Music and Art and miraculously I passed, but my mother said, "You're not going there, forget this music stuff. And anyway, soon we're moving to Queens and that school's going to be too far, and I'm going to get you away from that bunch of hooligans!"

My mother had decided that the project was starting to go downhill, and anyway the housing authority wanted to raise her rent because she had begun working as a teacher, so she and my stepfather said it was time to move. We had been driving around every Sunday looking at model apartments, we must have seen every middle-income co-op in the whole of New York City before my mother heard about some new houses they were building in Queens. Well, that was it. She was having a house built in Rosedale which was a mainly white neighborhood, real nice except for a few cross burnings they'll had there.

It was all settled and my mother insisted that she had to have everything new for the new house, we even got a brand-new, shiny Cadillac. She had to have two and a half Hollywood bathrooms with the his and hers vanities, she had to have chandeliers because now she wanted what the Supremes had. My mother took me on expeditions to furniture showrooms to compare the styles with what I'd seen at the Supremes' houses. She had to have a family room, a custom refrigerator with her name engraved on it, the whole bit. It was a big deal for my family because we were moving out of the projects and up to the upper middle class. To me it all smacked of the *Beverly Hillbillies,* except instead of black gold and Texas tea it was more like the black bourgeoisie.

Some of the other, older kids in the projects that I used to hang out with were moving away too, but they were joining the service, going to Vietnam. You'd hear, Mrs. Johnson's son got killed, you'd hear people saying all sorts of things about the war, about social consciousness. People were looking to see what was really going on, even the kids. Plus there was that whole racial climate in the wake of riots, and everybody was talking black power. I'd see white Supremes fans get dragged out of the crowd by their parents because they didn't want their kids getting caught up in this soul music business.

There was a lot going on, but to me it wasn't even a consideration. I was too young to go to Vietnam and anyway, the war had to be over soon. I was still caught up in my dream world, I was busy wondering what was the next gown Diana Ross was going to wear or how was she going to flip that wig next time. Those were my concerns, all that glittered. Of course I was wrong. The Vietnam War would end up raging on despite growing national protest—what else was I wrong about?

At the end of September, when the Supremes came back to do *Ed Sullivan* for what seemed like the fiftieth time, it stopped being so much fun. That's when Flo stopped being a funny girl. Flo came and she was sad. I wasn't hearing that great big roar of laughter. She was depressed, she was moody, she would cry. "Why are they focusing all the camera moves around Diana, why is my mike turned down so low, why did they take my song away from me, why do they have to be so sneaky, why couldn't they just tell me Flo, we're taking your song and giving it to Diana.'' I thought about that line in the song, "Funny Girl"—". . . Funny how it ain't so funny, funny girl.''

She'd cry and then in her own way she'd fight it. When they did, "You Can't Hurry Love," on *Ed Sullivan* they had on these incredible, silver-sequined gowns that blinded your eyes when the light hit them and they had these tambourines. Diana and Mary tapped their tambourines on their hips all light and ladylike but Flo, Flo had plenty of hips and she beat on that tambourine like she was singing in some Baptist choir.

Another time, of course it was live, the girls had to come out from behind these huge, gift-wrapped packages and Flo just rushed for Diana's mike because she knew it was turned up the loudest. She rushed to that mike and she belted out the background. She did what people accused Diana of doing, that little bit extra, dancing a little bit faster, turning a little bit more, taking little extra bows and everybody in the audience loved it. Well, almost everybody.

Nobody said anything about it in the dressing room while Flo was there, but the minute Flo left the room Diana seized the opportunity, "Mary! Did you see what Blondie did! She got up there at my mike, then in the middle of my song where you girls are supposed to come in with that counterpart harmony and then modulate real soft, she came in there so loud, and her singing sounded horrible, didn't it?''

And Mary said, "Oh, I don't think it was that bad, she was a little loud but maybe she was having some problems with her monitor and she couldn't hear herself.'' Then Flo came back in and it got all quiet again, but Flo knew.

One minute she'd be up, "Oh Tony, when I called you that last time I was in the Far Damn East! That's

Japan! Honey, all those people in the Far East, you should see those people, they are so damn short, they were all looking up at me.'' She said she was dressed up like a geisha girl, she showed me all these pictures of her in these kind of Chinese restaurant outfits, and pictures of the three of them having a rickshaw race. She told me about all the things she'd bought for her house, all the porcelain and raw silks. And then the next minute she'd be crying, she could change mid-sentence.

I'd fix Flo a drink, and I'd nip me one here and there too because half the time I was so nervous. Flo didn't see me. I'd go back behind the bar and pour her a drink, then while I was doing that I'd slug me down something quick. Sometimes she noticed, ''Tony, you've been drinking, come over here and let me smell your breath.''

''No, I didn't have no drink.''

''Well you're acting real giggly to me. You better not get drunk because your mother will kill me.''

So she didn't really say don't do it, and she didn't really say do it, she was like a big sister, like, I saw you sneak a drink but I'm not gonna tell. Then again, after one drink Flo was well on her way. I learned later that she had a low tolerance for alcohol.

As it went on, sometimes when she'd tell me to make her medicine I'd say, ''I'm gonna fix me a little bit,'' and she'd tell me, ''Well, you better just put a tiny capful, just for flavor—here, I better do it. Go get a soda glass and fill it all the way up with soda, I'll add the rest. And if you ever have a cold, it's good for that too.'' So now she's fixing me a drink, she doesn't know it but I'm maybe up to my third and she's still sipping her first but she's talking full speed ahead. Flo couldn't take it, she couldn't drink—I could drink her under the table.

One time up in her suite, we were both sitting there with our drinks and I was telling Flo about these strange looks I'd been getting from Diana, I told her, ''You know, I don't think she likes me.''

"You know what you better do, honey, you better stay out of her way. Why don't you think she likes you?"

"Because I just don't think she likes me. Any time I say something she makes a face. And she's told me I better not repeat anything I hear around here, she said I better mind my own business and I better keep her business to myself."

"STAY OUT OF HER WAY!" Flo says. "Stay out of her way because one time she tried to run over a little blind boy!"

I figure she's got to be kidding, she's in her medicine, who in their right mind would try to run over a blind boy?

"Tony," Flo says, "let me tell you a few things about that Diana woman. She's always been snooty and looking for a fight. One time, she got into this fury with Gladys Horton, you know, from the Marvelettes. Now Gladys, not Mary, was my absolute best friend on the road, and Diana saw her as competition. So one night, Gladys tells Diana her gown looks like a nightshirt and the two of them get into this fight over it, they're snarling like stray alley cats."

"Later on, Gladys is helping this fan, a little blind boy named Lee across the street, and Diana sees them and drives straight at Gladys and Lee with a Ford station wagon like a bat straight outta hell and Gladys pulls Lee out the way not a split second too soon. You know, honey, Diana's mother was in the car too, even her mother couldn't handle her."

I still couldn't believe Flo but she went on, "Tony, listen to Flo, there's something you should know about Diana. That woman is like a fire engine when it's got a fire to get to and it don't care what or who gets in the way. The only thing to do when you see it coming is move."

Flo added, "You know why she doesn't like you? Because you're not running behind her, fawning over her like a lot of fans and grown people around here do, and because you're good friends with me, that's why she doesn't like you. She's just plain jealous, she's a jealous woman. She's jealous of Mary for being pretty and she's jealous of me because people around here are my friends, which is more than anyone can say for her, honey.''

The Supremes left town, they appeared at the Flamingo in Las Vegas, then on to California, and back to do *Ed Sullivan* in November. It was the same except I noticed a new person in the entourage, a guy named Tommy Chapman who I was told was a kind of chauffeur and bodyguard for Mr. Gordy. He was thin, tall, like a model and at first he seemed kind of strange, maybe because he was very quiet. But Tommy was immaculate, always beautifully dressed in his long topcoats and everything. I didn't pay him much mind, he just sort of hovered around the girls and Mr. Gordy. I thought he had something to do with security, yet another guy from Motown working for Mr. Gordy.

There was another change. Flo had cut her own hair short, I thought it looked like Diana's wig. She told me she'd decided not to wear her wigs so much any more, she thought the Supremes' image was getting too plastic, she wanted to be more involved and she told me about things that were happening in Detroit and some of the other cities she'd been in, a rising unrest. She said it wasn't enough for the Supremes to do benefits for the United Negro College Fund and stuff like that. Since the Supremes were so visible, she felt that maybe people would listen to them, maybe they would be able to help the black youth of America.

I didn't know. I was into partying and having a good time. What did I know about Stokely Carmichael and all of them? But if that was what Flo wanted, that was fine. She began to teach me about the movement, the Black Power struggle. She even asked me if my parents were registered voters. She complained that the Motown people were telling her, ''Flo, you should concentrate on your weight and singing and leave the politics to people who've finished high school.''

Flo was really hurt when the people at Motown criticized her for not finishing high school. I was surprised because they always put on the press releases, "All the girls are high school graduates." Flo told me, "You know, honey, I'm not the only one at Motown that didn't finish school, but you'd think I was."

The Supremes were doing their new hit single, "You Keep Me Hanging On" on *Ed Sullivan,* on which Flo practically sang duet with Diana. Flo underscored nearly every word and you could hear her voice filling it out all the way through. I guess Diana just couldn't carry this one by herself, which was a big satisfaction for Flo. "Honey, didn't Flo give her hell on 'You Keep Me Hanging On.' I love HDH for that one, I love that song."

But after the show was over Flo told me there was this cameraman who worked in the Ed Sullivan studio and had a crush on her, and this guy had pulled her aside and told her, "Flo, every time you girls appear here, your directors tell us to follow the lead singer, don't focus too much camera time on the others and when we do, make it a group shot."

Flo said she wasn't too surprised because this happened every place they went. It was all about Diana. She said, "Mary's no help neither when it comes to us fighting for our fair share. She's too afraid of Gordy. You know, honey, he told her right to her face that she better shut up because she can't sing anyway and don't even think about complaining, she should be grateful to be in the Supremes." Flo told me, "Diana even gets her own *private* dressing room now, as if me and Mary want to look at her skinny little ass."

I had been waiting to tell Flo all about moving to Rosedale and our new house. We had just moved and my mother wanted to invite the Supremes to a December dinner as a kind of return favor for the Copa invitation. I was real excited and I told Flo, but she just said she would have to think about it, and please don't mention it to anybody else. Then the next day she said, "Baby, Flo needs a break from these people, they're getting under my nerves. But a nice dinner away from these show biz types is just what I need so we won't tell Mary or Diana, okay, because anyway those two seem to be getting as thick as thieves, they're up to something all right. But baby, I'm ready for those slick, double-dealing scamps!''

It was all set. My mother decided it was going to be a dinner for twelve, but her new dining room suite was for six and her new china was for six so something had to be done, and it just happened that my Aunt Louise, not to be outdone, had bought not only the exact same type of house as my mother but also the exact same dining suite and china. So everything matched and mom just borrowed what she needed, the suite got moved over, the china got moved over, the menu was planned and just the right mix of people was invited for "A Dinner with Flo" as my mother called it. She said it had to be formal, because Flo was coming.

When I told Flo it was going to be formal she seemed kind of disappointed, she said she was more interested in a home-cooked meal with the family but she said, "Oh well, we'll let your mother have fun. Tell her I'll be coming in full Supremes regalia and full makeup!''

The day finally came. I took the subway into the city to meet Flo at her hotel and she was beautiful as ever, she was wearing a shockingly white, full-length mink coat over a bugle-beaded cocktail dress that she called "Martha's Winter White." I thought she meant she'd borrowed it from Martha Reeves of the Vandellas, she said no, the name referred to Martha's, an exclusive Park Avenue fashion salon but I guess I got her memory going because on the way out in the limo she started telling me about the time Martha Reeves burst into the Supremes' dressing room shouting curses and ready to kick Diana in the rear. Flo laughed, "Honey, I thought I was gonna die!''

She told the whole story, me and Phil were laughing our heads off. According to Flo, Diana had stolen one of Martha's new gowns and had the design copied, after adding her own special touches of course. She'd even taken the gown to Berry Gordy to show him exactly what she wanted because after all, it wouldn't do for the Vandellas to be outdressing the Supremes.

Flo went on, "When Martha burst in, I was doing my eye makeup and I just looked up and said, "Martha, don't you come in here with none of that, 'cus you ain't hardly kicking nobody's ass in here." Martha looked ready to tear Diana limb from limb, and Diana was never one for defending herself but of course I wasn't going for it and Martha knew it and left in a hurry." As soon as Martha left, according to Flo, Diana acted all shocked and outraged. Mary just mumbled something like, "Diana, I didn't know you stole that from Martha." Flo said she told Mary, "Bitch, wake up."

Flo was having a good time. She told us all these telltale stories and we were still laughing when we pulled up in front of the house. The minute we got inside I noticed my mother had this "let the games begin" look on her face. She said the "cocktail hour" would be held in the den. Well, the house was full of relatives and a few friends who were guaranteed to spread the gossip about this whole event, everyone ooohed and aahed about Flo's white mink, and everyone said how she was just like one of the family, so natural, so open, so grand yet nice.

After cocktails came dinner with wine, everyone's tongues started loosening up and they started in on a Diana bashing spree. Flo didn't laugh much, she didn't say anything bad about Diana, and I just kept wishing they'd change the subject.

Next thing I know my mother's talking interior decorating with Flo and Flo's suddenly got the men rearranging all the furniture. All the dinner jackets and ties started coming off, and for the next three hours Flo sipped her cocktail and supervised saying, "Be open, be open, decorating is an enlightening experience."

She and my mother rearranged every room in the

entire house, I was amazed, and the next day my mother went to the engraver who did her name for the custom refrigerator and she had a small, tasteful plaque made for the foyer. It read, "Interior Design Inspiration by Miss Florence (Flo) Ballard of THE SUPREMES."

I rode with Flo back to the hotel. She kept saying what a good time she'd had, how nice my family was, how she missed her family and wished she could be home for Christmas. She talked about how refreshing it was to have the spotlight to herself for once, to be able to answer a question without Miss Bubble Eyes jumping in. She seemed kind of lonely, she said she should have thought to ask Tommy to accompany her for the evening. Then she left on tour, Christmas on the road playing the Eden Roc in Miami, while her fully decorated mansion sat waiting for her in Detroit.

CHAPTER 9

— ◆ ◆ ◆ —

Kill the Messenger

In January of '67 the Supremes were voted the number one group in America. I was real proud, but when they came to New York the same month to record and to do *Ed Sullivan* yet again, all I could see was war. There was war all around, everybody seemed to be sitting on a time bomb.

I secretly named it, Motown/Vietnam.

I walked into the dressing room and the first thing Diana said to me was, "Did your friend tell you? Did she tell you she was too drunk to go on stage with us?" I was shocked. I'd read something about Florence Ballard not appearing at some concert, "due to illness," and Diana and Mary had to go on as a duet but I'd never seen Flo drink *before* a performance, I'd never seen her really drunk, like sloshy drunk. Just a bit louder, more animated.

I saw a lot of strain. There was no more, see if Diana and Mary are going over to Saks in between performances and we'll all go together, or we're all going to do a publicity thing, let's go. Now, a lot of times when they did publicity Flo was quoted as being under the weather, Miss Ballard has been taken ill. But privately Flo was saying, "I'm not going to do anything because I'm not killing myself all day long going to thirteen different locations and they're going to ask all the questions of Diana and if they don't, then the honchos that travel on the road with us are going to make sure the interview is directed toward her." Even when they did ask Flo a question, Diana would butt in, "Oh, I can answer that for you."

Flo couldn't get a word in. On their new record, "Love Is Here and Now You're Gone," they had three little breaks for speaking parts and Flo thought, okay let Diana do the lead, we'll each do one speaking part. But that wasn't to be and Flo complained that anyway, it doesn't make any difference what I do or how loud I sing, when they mix it nobody is going to hear me.

She had always thought, Mary and I are just going to sing really loud and we'll sound good, and when Diana hits that note we'll be right under her and we'll fortify it and the harmony is going to be beautiful. And it was. But it really didn't matter because when you heard it on record they'd changed the volume and the background blended in less with Diana, more with the orchestra. So Florence and Mary were becoming orchestration rather than background singers, and it got worse and worse.

There was so much hostility there, there was a mood of tension around every movement. It was like walking on eggshells. Flo confided in me still but it was about different things, it wasn't about I'm having such a great time, I'm seeing the world, I'm going to bring you up to the house and see the beautiful things I bought. It was about hatred, and deception, how when Ed Sullivan said, "Here are the girls" and all of America looked at them they could still look pretty and all smiling together but as soon as they got in the wings it was, you bitch this, you black bitch that, you didn't do it the way it was done in rehearsal, you stepped in front of me, you sang too loud, you held your arms in front of my face. It was civil war, and Flo had everything stacked against her. To me, it just appeared to be every diva for herself.

They had stopped allowing liquor into Flo's suite. I guess Berry Gordy had come and told management,

Florence Ballard's suite is 411, there's to be no liquor delivered to 411 so if any phone calls come from that room for liquor take the order, say thank you, and never deliver it. And I guess Flo said to herself, I can't get any liquor, I need a drink, how can I get a drink? I can't go to the store, they've got security sitting on a chair outside my door, they want to know any time I leave the room, Berry Gordy's next door with Diana, he's got his door cracked, he's sticking his head out all the time, oooh, I know! I'll ask Tony.

"Tony, honey, does your mother like rum or anything? I was thinking maybe I would buy her a bottle of rum before I left town 'cause she was so nice inviting me to dinner."

"Oh yeah, Flo, my mother drinks rum, she has scotch, gin."

"Well, I was going to send you to the store to get it but, that's right, you're too young to buy it. So here's twenty dollars, ask your mother, could she buy me a fifth of Bacardi, and tell her she can keep the change."

So I went and I told my mother, and she said, "Oh God, oh certainly," and she went to the store and got a fifth of Baccardi, "oh and put it in a gift box with a ribbon, it's for my son's friend, she's in the Supremes."

Flo had given me a crisp, twenty-dollar bill, "Ma, she said you could keep the change."

"Oh, I wouldn't dream of it. Please take Miss Flo her change, tell her it's my pleasure, any time, anything else she needs, just let me know, I could shop for her."

This is what I did. I did it over and over, who knew she wasn't supposed to get a drink. When I'd get down to the hotel, of course she'd say, "Don't tell anybody 'cause these people are too damn nosy, you know how they hate me around here, everyone's getting to hate me because I speak my mind." So I'd come, I'd put on my school bookpack, who thinks anything of a fourteen-year-old kid coming in with a bookpack, "There's that boy again, ain't he so cute?" Who thinks there's two fifths in there along with the books? This was medicine for Flo's nerves because look what these people are doing to her. "Don't tell anyone I take medicine."

They all went to Detroit for their big homecoming at the Roostertail, and when they came back to New York, things were worse. Flo stayed in her suite a lot, she complained constantly of how tired she was, all the backstabbing. I guess to camouflage the fact that her eyes were all puffy from crying half the night she started wearing these dark glasses and she'd go on stage with dark, dramatic eye makeup, she asked me, "Doesn't my eye makeup look just like Elizabeth Taylor's did in *Cleopatra?*"

Flo didn't want to go out much. She wasn't interested in running around to all the different stores, she didn't even have a few minutes to hang out with the fans. There was no more taking bunches of fans around to the pizza parlor. She was now too preoccupied, too upset, too devastated. She no longer worried about who had hot chocolate, who was standing out in the freezing cold all day. It was into the studio, do what you had to do and back to the hotel suite to hold court and complain. Diana was the one who was reaching out for the fans the way Flo used to. But Flo just thought she was copying her style and it made her furious.

Now, instead of Flo telling me, take care of the fans, it was, "GET THAT NAPOLEON GORDY ON THE PHONE." "GET DIANA ON THE PHONE." And I'd call, they could usually be found in the same suite, one of them would pick up and Flo would give them a piece of her mind. Or it was "Get Mary! She's so stupid she's falling right into their trap."

Mary spent a lot of time consoling Flo. As I got to know her better I saw her always trying to calm the situation, telling Flo everything would be okay, it would all blow over. They had these long powwows and Mary would tell Flo, "Ignore them, bite your tongue, come and talk to me about it but don't immediately jump at them."

I thought this was good advice but Flo couldn't do it, she was listening but she wasn't hearing. If someone called at the last minute to say rehearsal's at three instead of two Flo would say, "Wait a goddamn minute now, I'm all fixed and ready to go at two o'clock, I know Diana just wants to get an extra hour's sleep, this is ridiculous, you got me up at this time so Diana could sleep." She was becoming paranoid, she'd create a whole story, she thought everything was directed against her. She shouted, "Tony! Get Berry Gordy on the phone, I'm going shopping!" Mary said, "Flo, you can't do that, why don't you lay back down—"

"I can't lay back down, I've got my wig on!"

"Then don't go all the way to Saks, it'll take too long. Go around here, go to some boutiques." But Flo would say, "Fuck it. They want rehearsal at three o'clock, I'll be there at four when Flo gets good and ready." She was all off by herself.

She started requesting suites with kitchens so she could cook the way she wanted and not have to leave the room. If there was no suite with kitchen available she'd cook up a mean soul food dinner in her suite on a couple of hot plates and an electric frying pan. She started traveling with a couple of pots, and some seasonings. She'd always request the best china and crystal glassware from room service and when it was all ready she'd invite a few staff people and serve up this big meal. These were her inner-circle dinners and Tommy Chapman was always there.

I noticed Tommy Chapman going around more and more with Flo. I started thinking maybe he had been brought along to sort of cool her down because she was not so focused on what Diana was doing or on what Mr. Gordy was doing when Tommy was around. Sometimes when he was in her room she'd ask me to wait in the lobby for her, she'd tell me she and Tommy had personal business to discuss.

Flo and Tommy would go for walks. Why sit in the

hotel room bitching about that Diana Ross woman on such a nice spring day, let's go stroll down Fifth Avenue, let's go to a café. They held hands, I never saw them kiss or anything like that. I tagged along. She would just tell Tommy, "Tony's going with us." I was always cutting school to be with Flo.

One day I noticed Flo taking some pills with her drink. I asked her what they were and she said they were multivitamins. I told her my mother gave me and my sister vitamins every morning along with a tablespoonful of cod liver oil and she answered, "That's good for you, baby."

I said, "But we only take one vitamin a day, you just swallowed a whole bunch."

"Well, honey, some of these are diet pills."

I remembered the way my mother would be when she was taking diet pills, she'd do things real fast, real speeded up, and she'd yell at me and my sister for no reason. It was the same with Flo. Every time I saw her she seemed more angry and sometimes she yelled at me, her outbursts scared me. I might say something simple like, "How do you feel, Flo?" and she'd scream, "Can't you see what they're doing to me? Are you crazy? They're trying to kill me, can't you see? Take off your glasses and let Flo clean them for you."

Then she'd apologize, she'd offer to buy me something, she'd start to explain how all the bickering was getting under her nerves. She'd start talking about Berry Gordy and his gambling debts, how he gambled all the time and the money he used to pay for it was really coming from the Supremes' money and she couldn't and wouldn't see her money wasted that way. She told me Diana and Mary liked to gamble too, and that Gordy had roped them into gambling so they wouldn't ask questions about where were all their earnings.

She started to complain about how the diet pills made her so nervous she couldn't help the way she acted. I told her she looked fine, she really had the best shape of all three girls, she didn't need the diet pills, and she said, "Honey, that's true but I've got Gordy on my back about losing weight and Flo's gonna show him a thing or two. At least I don't need a padded ass and tits like that Miss Ross, hear me talkin'!"

She went on to tell me about something that happened at the Twenty Grand Club in Detroit one night when she went out with Tommy Chapman. She said Tommy had been so helpful when they were in the Far East. He had helped her shop for Oriental things for her home and so one night when they were back home Tommy got the night off from Napoleon Gordy and they decided to go out on the town.

She told me, "Baby, Flo had bought a major dress, the back was to die for, I looked great honey." Tommy arrived in a limo, "only this time in the back seat," and off they went. When they got to the Twenty Grand Club, of course Flo was well known there and everyone was real nice, everyone commented on how sensational she looked and she and Tommy were having a nice romantic evening, when in walked Berry Gordy.

He walked past their table, looked at Tommy, said "Good evening, Mr. Chapman," kind of sharply, then turned to Flo and apparently said, "Diana is right, you are entirely too fat, I agree with her. You had better do something about your weight, Florence. The whole situation with your weight is ridiculous."

Flo told me that with all eyes on her, she picked up her drink and threw it in Mr. Gordy's face, "Fuck you! I don't give a damn what you or that bitch thinks." And with that she grabbed her sable coat and stormed out of the club with Tommy. She told me that was the night she decided to go on the diet pills, just to get them off her back. That's how it started, and since the diet pills put her on edge the doctor had prescribed Valium too.

I told Flo about my mother's diet pills, how she had found some that didn't make her so nervous and Flo got real interested. "Call your mother." So she talked to my mother, and my mother said she could get her some, she would tell the doctor she lost her prescription, she cooked up the whole scam. My mother called the nurse, the nurse said fine, I got on the Lexington Avenue line, went right down to Fourteenth Street, walked to the doctor's office, got this huge supply of pills for Flo and put them in my bookpack with the liquor. So there it was, diet pills, Valium, vitamins, liquor—and me running them.

Everyone had gotten into the habit of always putting her down. You're not as pretty as the other girls, you're too fat. Even Mary took me aside and asked me, "Tony, see how big Flo's gotten? Diana says she's too fat, she's squeezing into her dresses." I just said, "Mmm hmm," she looked the same size to me. If it wasn't her weight it was her haircut. They didn't like her going around without her wig, it wasn't feminine, she sang too loud, she sang too black, that's not the kind of singing we want, you didn't finish high school, you're not holding up your end of the job.

Or it was Tommy. They didn't like her hanging out with Tommy Chapman because he was a chauffeur, he was Berry Gordy's chauffeur and that was just too low for a Supreme. Flo started saying things like, "Don't be surprised if you don't see me around here much longer, honey, they're trying to push me out, they're trying to make me quit. But I ain't going, they'll have to *throw* me out."

Sometime in April Flo called to say they were coming next month to do *Ed Sullivan*, and they were also doing the Copa again. She told me all about the costumes, about how they were going to be doing an intricate medley with breakaway costume changes and then she said, "Have you heard anything in New York about the name being changed to Diana Ross and the Supremes?" I was shocked, I said, "NO!"

"Well, I'm telling you now, when we come in this time just keep your ears open for me because there's a lot of talk going around, and a lot of things are going to be changing, and you know your Auntie Diana, she's all over the place, trying to be in control of everything. Have any of the fans heard anything?"

I said, "I don't know." I didn't keep in touch with those fans.

"Well, Diana is saying she wants the name of the group changed to Diana Ross and the Supremes. What do you think?"

I didn't understand. I didn't think it was necessary and I told her so.

"Well neither do I," she said. "I don't know what Mary's going to say, but if they change it I'm not going to be singing under no Diana Ross and the Supremes." She started saying how they were harassing her, how nobody was speaking to her, she was off in one corner, she didn't know what Mary was up to, and could I get her more diet pills.

I didn't know what she meant about Mary. I only found out later that all the time she was trying to calm Flo down, Mary was being pulled back and forth between Flo and Diana. Mary was caught in the middle, and on top of that she had her own problems—she'd been told that she couldn't sing. So Mary would be in Flo's suite, then Diana would call her, "Mary, Mary where were you? Come to my room." Mary would go and Diana would tell her they had to do something about Florence, they had to get rid of Flo, how shocked she was at the way Flo was carrying on, how ridiculous, throwing a fit backstage with everyone watching, how vulgar.

I didn't know any of this until Florence came to New York to do *Ed Sullivan* and the Copa. I knew she'd missed performances but I didn't know that some other girl, Cindy Birdsong, had substituted for her at Hollywood Bowl, which was a big, important event. So when Flo came to New York she said, "Let me tell you what happened." She told me, "Honey, there was a big, important meeting up at Mr. Gordy's mansion on Outer Drive and they're trying to put a new girl in the group," of course, stupid me thought she meant they were going to add another girl to the group. She told me the girl's name was Cindy Birdsong, from Patty LaBelle and the Bluebells, she was telling me all this stuff and I was just taking it in. Later I heard Cindy's side of the story and it was about the same. Mary Wilson told the story in her book but it was slightly different. Here, according to Flo, is what really happened.

Flo and her mother arrived in Flo's Caddy for this meeting at the Gordy mansion, which was enormous—a private bowling alley, a pool house, underground tunnels through the house, the whole bit. You come into the Gordy mansion, there's a reception area which in itself is as big as a living room. Cindy Birdsong's sitting right there in plain view of Flo and her mother, she's been brought down from upstairs right before Flo arrives and Gordy's told her to sit right there and keep her mouth shut until after the meeting. So Flo and her mother come in, they look at Cindy, they have to walk right past her face and nobody speaks. Flo told me she knew it was a dirty trick. Cindy told me she was nervous as hell and she felt terrible for Flo.

Diana and Gordy are in a room off the living room, sitting there together on the piano bench. Flo and her mother go in and sit on the settee, Mary naturally arrives late and the meeting starts with Berry Gordy making a little speech about Florence causing trouble. Basically what he's telling her is, shape up or get out and I think we have to come to some terms of understanding here or you're not going to be in the group.

At which Flo's mother, Lurleen Ballard, says, "Flo wants to be in the group." She goes and touches Mary's arm—she's known Mary since Mary was just a kid. "Mary, don't you want Flo in this group? Aren't you sick of all the stuff that's been going on?" And Mary just looks at Flo, she looks at Flo's mother, "Mrs. Ballard, Florence does not want to be in this group."

Flo told me she had known the meeting was going to be about her behavior but she said she had things to talk about too, and that she had discussed it with Mary, Mary had agreed on the course they were going to take. Flo said she didn't talk about any of the things she'd wanted to, she didn't say a word in that meeting because of what Mary said. She told me, "Here I was, fighting like a dog to get an equal opportunity for everyone in the group, fighting for them to pump up the background tracks, I'm talking to Mary on the phone, talking to her in the hotels and she's on my side, we're united, Mary's not going to stand for it either, and then she sits there and she tells my mother, 'Flo doesn't want to be in this group any more.' Who told that black bitch that? Why would I create all this heartache for me if I didn't want to be in the group? I was totally, totally shocked."

Flo said she couldn't speak, she was sweating so much her pageboy wig got wet. She felt as if a million knives and gunshots had pierced her heart. By the time Berry Gordy hurriedly closed the meeting, Flo saw the clear picture. She saw who was on whose side for the first time. She said that's when she realized Mary has stabbed her in the back.

She told me, "I knew now that Diana and Gordy had got what they wanted. They had Mary on their side, Mary alone was holding all the cards in her hand. In that moment she held all the power, everybody in the room was just waiting to see which way she swam and it ended up three to one." She went on, "If I'd known that, I wouldn't have gone to that man's house. I would have told him I don't wanna be in your stinking group, take Diana Ross, take Mary Wilson and go."

Cindy told me that when Flo left, she was kind of surprised to see her and her mother walk out to the Caddy, both of them in tears with Berry Gordy's arm around them like three blind mice all hugging up each other, like they were best of friends. She said she could never understand that. Cindy didn't know what was going on, or if she was in the group or not until Gordy came back in and told Diana and Mary, "Okay, Cindy's starting rehearsal with you girls." She said Diana looked almost giddy.

On Sunday I went back down to meet Flo at Ed

Sullivan. Mr. Gordy had taken a "wait and see" attitude, one more thing and you're out, you retire peacefully. But Flo told me, "He just wants time to cover his dirty work over with roses for the public. But I'm not leaving quietly, they're going to have to fire me and I'm going to create a big mess and nobody in the world is going to like it."

Backstage she complained that her breakaway costume had been made too tight. "I swear, these people are purposefully trying to sabotage me." Mary said, "Mine fits," Diana just busied herself preparing for the show. Flo looked like she wanted to cry.

After rehearsal Flo said she wanted to treat me to a big lunch at the Stage Deli. We had a great lunch, Flo drank a few beers and she even let me have one in public, I loved her so much, I felt just great being a teenager who had a grown friend. After lunch Flo said she wanted to walk back to the hotel, it was just a few blocks away. Right across the street from the hotel we got caught by the lights and Flo said she had to get to a bathroom real quick so we stood there praying for the lights to change, but Flo couldn't hold on. "Honey," she said, "look straight ahead, don't look down, I'm not gonna make it to that ladies' room. Run to the hotel and hold an elevator for me because the fans are all gonna be in the lobby."

I did as I was told, none of the fans suspected what Flo's hurry was. Upstairs, Flo showered and changed, we both laughed our heads off. "Honey," she said, "let's forget that happened." That's the last funny thing I remember about Flo while she was in the Supremes. There wouldn't be a damn thing funny for Flo in what lay ahead, only in what remained behind.

By now rumors were flying about Flo quitting, about Diana getting star billing, about trouble in the group. Motown was still denying them and Flo was denying them too but she kept telling me, "I'm not gonna quit. If they want me out they have to throw me out and the fans aren't gonna like it one bit. It's going to be a big scandal. The whole group will fall." She said, "Anyway, Diana isn't solo material, Tommy and I have discussed it."

I was nervous and I knew they were mad at her. She was always pulling this late, late, late thing. Before that last *Ed Sullivan Show* we were in her suite and she told me, "Go downstairs and tell them I'll be down in fifteen minutes." So I go downstairs but I don't do what she's told me, I don't go outside, I can see them through the revolving doors and they're all waiting— by now when Mr. Gordy's in town there's two limos and a car—and they're all sitting there waiting for Flo. So I sit in the lobby and I figure, when she finally comes down she won't know if I told them or not.

A few minutes later Mr. Gordy comes through the revolving door into the lobby, that door must have gone round about three thousand times in a second, "Tony! Where's that Ballard bitch?" Oh God, what am I going to say? I'm too scared to say, she'll be down in fifteen minutes. I'm remembering some story I heard in school about some country where they used to kill the messenger who brought bad news and by now I'm petrified of this man but just then the elevator door opens and here she is, she looks at him right across the lobby and she shouts, "Oh, I have to get some gum, if you want to go, go."

The two limos and the car wait, she gets her gum, a couple of magazines, strolls out to the cars and announces, "I'm gonna walk." Tommy gets out, I get out, we start walking slowly, looking in store windows and stuff. Tommy doesn't say anything about hurry up, nobody says a thing about what just happened.

It was getting to be pretty much the three of us now, Flo, Tommy, and yours truly, with Diana and Mary arriving and leaving together. We'd go and look at model apartments together, Flo said it was for fun, she'd look through the newspaper and mark off all these ads, she said it didn't cost anything and she liked to get new ideas for her house but I saw her being very specific with the rental agents. I'd be listening real hard to what she was saying and she'd tell me, "Tony, you're looking straight into my mouth, you can hear my words but you can't see 'em." Then we'd go look in record shops and Flo would be putting her two cents in, just little things like, "I might do something on my own," or, "I'd like to do me an Aretha number."

Tommy started asking me questions on the side. He wanted to know, could I hear Flo, do the fans like her, don't tell anyone I asked you this but, how do you think Flo looked compared to the other two girls, do you think she's pretty, do you think she can sing?

Mr. Gordy was asking me the same kinds of questions, real casual, real matter-of-fact type of thing except they were about Diana, what are the kids outside saying about Diana, how do the fans think she looks, how do they like the way Diana dances, do they think she'd be good as a solo? Sometimes he'd trick me, like, "How do you like Flo's hair short?" And before I could answer he'd jump in, "I don't", and I knew to agree with him in a hurry.

Nobody seemed the least bit interested in Mary Wilson, nobody asked questions about her but for some reason I was beginning to feel afraid for her. She seemed very lonely and upset with what was going on. I thought she needed protection and I began to move toward her.

I felt very awkward around the Supremes now. Everyone who had once been so open became guarded and closed. Even Mary was acting secretive. On stage it was still all teeth, all smiles, all gracious, all the best of friends, and it amazed me how they could do it because about a second earlier I'd seen them standing in the wings looking so mad. Backstage the hostility was beyond all bounds, and Mr. Gordy looked like he was about to explode, he kept telling Flo, "Don't push me now," "You're going too far, Flo."

One night Mr. Gordy was in the Copa dressing room arguing with Flo and I saw him raise his hand, almost as if he was going to slap her. Immediately she screamed out, "IF YOU RAISE YOUR HAND TO

HIT ME YOU'RE GOING TO PULL BACK A BLOODY STUMP!'' Mr. Gordy just turned and left the room but Flo went right after him, she opened that dressing room door and she yelled out, where everyone could hear her, "DON'T YOU EVER WALK OUT ON ME! I'LL CUT YOU TOO SHORT TO SHIT!'' I was so nervous I had to laugh and Greg gave me the quick eye, and Diana looked at me and said, "You'll be out next." I didn't know what she was talking about, but when we got back to the hotel Flo told me, "She must mean after *she* leaves."

My friend was all out of control, and I was shocked at the way she was acting but I never thought she would leave the group or that they'd put her out. I really didn't pay it much attention. I just thought this was a shame, I thought, like Mary, "It'll all blow over." I thought the Supremes would go on like this forever, arguing and carrying on, and some of it still made me laugh. Just the way Flo put her hands on her hips and shouted and threw her mink on the floor, and the way nobody really said anything. She would just go off, "PICK UP MY MINK AND LET'S GET OUT OF THIS PLACE!" And off she'd fly, she'd fly up to her suite, I'd be scurrying after her, "Get me my MEDICINE!"

Then Flo would start drinking, she'd start crying, the fire would be going down, "Oh why are they ruining a good thing? Doesn't she have enough, why does Diana need more, more, more?" She told me they had won Mary over by telling her that Diana was leaving the group and they were only putting her name up front to get the public used to it, but Flo didn't believe it. She said she told Mary, "Mary, they've got your brain. They're going to build her up, they're going to make it Diana Ross and the Supremes on our voices, they're going to make her a solo and they're going to drop the Supremes or the Supremes is going to become another one of their B groups, like all those girl groups that are still waiting for their new gowns." Flo knew everything on a gut level.

Flo told me they were taking her group away from

her, even though she was the one instrumental in forming the Supremes on the suggestion of the Temptations (who were then known as the Primes). Flo asked her friend Mary and another girl to join, and then Paul Williams from the Primes had come along and asked if Diana could join too. Flo said she never really wanted Diana in the group—she didn't like her and Diana's voice wasn't that strong. But Paul was very friendly with Diana at the time, and since he had helped Flo a lot with her singing career, she owed him a favor and she said okay.

Flo told me, "Honey, Diana was never interested in the leads originally, she was more interested in being a model." She also told me she never wanted to sign with Motown in the first place because she'd heard they were thieves, it was Diana's idea and Flo went along with it. She said Diana had come in, taken over the group, taken over Berry Gordy, and now she was getting the name changed. She was always going after something that was somebody else's.

Flo told me about the time Diana was going out with Smokey Robinson and he was married, and about the time when Diana was going out with one of the Holland Brothers, and his wife came and tried to beat Diana up and Flo had to jump in and save her. "All the stuff I did for that bitch, all the times she was sticking her neck out, opening up her big mouth, running after somebody's boyfriend or husband, getting beat up and I would have to save her butt. Now look what she's doing to me."

Late at night, when Flo was so exhausted she could hardly stay awake, she would always say, "Tony, talk to me!" And so I would, until she finally slept. I was all up in it, I could see everybody whispering. They all knew Flo was on her way out, they knew they shouldn't stay too cozy with Flo Ballard, so they would come by her door and stick their heads in, they'd tell her, Flo I support you, you're right, this is shit that's going on but you know I can't say it publicly.

She was on the road with a whole bunch of people

but she had nobody, nobody to witness with her. She was being treated cruel but everybody had to eat, everybody had mortgages to pay and kids to feed, and you don't stand up in Berry Gordy's face and say this is not right; you may as well put a gun to your head.

CHAPTER 10

◆ ◆ ◆

Flo Asks Out

As far as anyone on the outside knew, the Copa engagement was like any other Supremes appearance only better. It was pandemonium, it was a sell-out, you couldn't beg or bribe your way in. The gowns were lavish—each time the Supremes came those gowns got more sparkling, more fabulous, and the show was incredible. Everyone left saying how brilliant the performance had been, how dazzling the girls all looked, how terrific they were together. The reviews were just overflowing with all this stuff and none of these people knew that backstage nobody was speaking to nobody.

At the end of the Copa engagement the Supremes left for a big American tour. But before they hit the road, Florence invited me to go to Las Vegas, where they were going to be performing at the Flamingo again near the beginning of July. This was going to be my birthday present, Flo was going to send me the ticket and everything and I was going to stay with her in the hotel. My mother had to think about it before letting me go, and I had to beg her. She said she didn't know, Las Vegas, that's a long flight, it's gambling, it's in the desert, it's no place for an impressionable teenager, but of course after I'd been on my best behavior for a week and I'd got a hundred on my test she had to agree. I was going. Right after school finished I was going to Las Vegas!

I had to work really hard with all my little jobs to get enough money to buy the proper summerwear with lots of dash. I had to have nice seersucker summer suits, plus my cousin James said I needed a few light-weight evening suits for the shows, I needed a panama hat, everybody in the family got involved so my aunt bought me things, my mother and grandmother bought me things, and I couldn't wait to get to hot Vegas!

I told everybody, everybody who would listen, "I'm going to Las Vegas. You ever been to Las Vegas?" knowing that they hadn't. Flo called to tell me she had cut her hair shorter, and she said, "We're going to see Elvis because he's appearing in town," we were going to see all the shows, we'd have the best tables, she created this big picture, she said I could sit next to her in the casino, I was going to meet a lot of stars be-cause Vegas was just full of nothing but stars. Viva Las Vegas!

Meanwhile the Supremes were all over America, they were in California, they were in Washington, they met President Johnson, they went to Johnny Carson's party and the reviews kept coming in great. I was so excited, and by the time school finished I was all packed and ready to go but about two days before I was due to leave, Flo called.

I was outside in front of my house holding court with a bunch of kids when my mother stuck her head out the screen door, "Anthony! It's Florence Bal-lard!" All the kids were gasping, they all ran after me, but I slammed the door and went inside to get the phone. One look at my mother's face and I knew there was trouble, she looked like someone had died or something so I picked up the phone kind of nervously and Flo sounded terrible, I knew she had been crying. She told me, "Tony, there's a lot of things going on right now, I already spoke to your mother and I told her that I don't think this would be a good time for you to come out here."

I was stunned. She went on, "I'm real sorry, I know how you've been looking forward to it and I've been looking forward to it too, but I have nothing but heartaches here. It's not a good time for me and I don't think you'd enjoy yourself, but you know I'll talk to you soon, and anyway we'll be coming to New York right after this." Then, just before she put down the phone she said, "By the way, there's a rumor around here that Cindy Birdsong's in town."

That was it, she talked for about two minutes and then she hung up and I started crying. I was so upset. I was upset not to be going and I was even more upset about the embarrassment, now I had to tell all these kids and I thought, oh no, they'll never believe me again. So I hung around my house and in the backyard, I unpacked my bags, I fought with Ramona and waited for the Supremes to come to New York. They were going to be playing the Forest Hills Tennis Stadium in Queens and maybe a couple of my friends would come along and I'd get them autographs and stuff. I just had to bide my time.

The next time Flo called I knew things weren't any better. She sounded strange, she told me she was in Detroit, she said she was at the Henry Ford Hospital in Detroit.

"Flo, you been sick?"

"Yeah, baby, I been kind of sick but I'm fine, I'm fine."

Then she started telling me this whole story. She said it happened in Las Vegas, the shows were fabulous, everybody loved them and everybody said how the Supremes were even better now than the last time they played there but something seemed funny, there was something going on behind her back and Flo didn't feel good about it. She avoided the whole dressing room scene, she kept to herself and one night after the first show she went off by herself, she figured she didn't need to change because they were supposed to wear the same costume for the second show.

So she went up to her suite at the Flamingo and was

sitting there with the radio on, doing her nails, and the man on the radio said, here's "Reflections," the new release by Diana Ross and the Supremes. Of course, nobody had said anything about no name change for "Reflections" and Flo just flipped. She went out in the hallway screaming and yelling for Berry Gordy and Diana and then she went back in her room and waited for the second show.

Right before the second show Flo comes down to wait in the wings. She's all ready to go on and suddenly three girls go parading past her toward the stage in these matching gowns, and it's Diana, Mary, and Cindy Birdsong, and Flo's gown doesn't match. Cindy's wearing one of Flo's gowns—they've changed gowns on her and she's the odd one out.

She's just taking this in when Berry Gordy comes up and he says, "Flo, don't you go up on that stage, you're fired. If you go on that stage I'm going to throw you off."

Flo didn't know what to do. One of the staff members pulled her aside and told her, "Flo, go on, Gordy ain't gonna shoot you, he ain't gonna go out on that stage and drag you off, this is Vegas. Flo, go on and tell those people out there what's going on, what they're doing to you. Those people came to see all three of you, they came to see you, not Cindy Birdsong. You're a fool not to go on. Don't let them break you, you're a grown woman."

She couldn't go on.

She said she watched Cindy Birdsong walk right past her nose in her gown with Mary Wilson and Diana Ross and she was just standing there in the wings and they're up there on that stage singing, "Baby Love," and Flo said she didn't have any fight left in her, they had won, she wanted to go home, she felt lost, she felt like she didn't have a friend in the world.

Now, I had watched them rehearse enough times and even I knew that nobody just jumps up on stage with the Supremes and starts singing with them and doing all their intricate little routines without a whole lot of training and practice. So I'm listening to all of this and I'm wondering, who trained Cindy Birdsong? Diana couldn't have trained her because by now Diana is way in front on that stage, she's not locked into any routine, she doesn't even know if the girls behind her are sashaying to the left or sashaying to the right.

I could have figured it out for myself but Flo told me. "Tony, I always knew Mary was talking out of two sides of her mouth." She told me it was Mary who was sneaking behind Flo's back, getting up early and leaving the Flamingo every day, going down the street to Caesar's Palace where Cindy Birdsong was secretly put up, and rehearsing her with Cholly Atkins. Cholly taught her the steps, Mary taught her the words, the vocal harmonies, and there she was telling her friend Flo, "Get yourself together, Flo," but she couldn't tell Flo what she was doing behind her back. Or could she have?

Flo said, "You know why they didn't fire me right away at that meeting, you know why they kept me hanging on? It's only because Cindy Birdsong was still under contract to Patti LaBelle and Mary knew that, you hear me talkin' honey, they're nothing but scheming liars, the whole bunch of them."

So Flo did the first show, Cindy did the second show, and no kind of announcement was made, but in between shows the sign on the Flamingo marquee was changed to Diana Ross and the Supremes. Berry Gordy and everyone else pretty much forgot about Flo. She went up to her room, but much later Greg told me that right after the second show Berry Gordy told someone, "Get her out of here, get her out of Vegas."

Don went up to her room and let himself in and there was Flo, sitting in the middle of her bed Indian style with her loungewear on, in a daze, drunk, in shock. She didn't know what was going on. Don said he had to wash her face and clean her up like you would a baby. He couldn't dress her. He just threw her mink coat over her, put some of her personal belongings in a carry-on bag—they'd send the rest later. He led her down to the limo with her sunglasses over her eyes, her mink coat over her pink designer lounge-wear, and a security man holding her under each arm. They got her out of Vegas, threw her on a jet, and took her straight to the hospital in Detroit. She didn't even go home first.

Flo thought she was going to create a big mess, they were going to put her out kicking and screaming and it would be a big splash, but they wore her down and she was quietly chopped. Of course, the publicity didn't say, Flo Ballard quietly fired. Rather, it said, "Flo Ballard Asks Out." But what did that mean? Did that mean, Flo was asked out by Motown, or did it mean she asked to be put out?

Flo didn't say anything publicly because she couldn't, because Motown was family and this was a family secret. There were rumors of internal strife, of Diana's romance with Berry Gordy, of professional jealousies, but they were all denied by Motown and they were denied by Flo. It was put, Florence Ballard has decided to retire from the Supremes in order to seek a quiet life and by the way, the name's been changed to Diana Ross and the Supremes.

There were rumors about a hair-pulling fight between Florence and Diana at the Flamingo Hotel, but they too were denied. Flo told everyone, "Oh no, we parted best of friends," but she had told me there had been a hair-pulling fight at the Flamingo Hotel when Flo had had enough of Diana and she just jumped her. Diana couldn't even fight, Flo just beat her up.

Flo told me all this on the phone from some private room in the Henry Ford Hospital, where she was rest-ing. I just couldn't believe it. My God, I couldn't be-lieve they did that but Flo told me, "Fuck it, fuck her, I can sing better than her."

Flo had big plans. She was a superstar, she had looks, she had money, and she had a voice. Hadn't some movie producers contacted Motown about cast-ing Flo in films after that first Copa engagement? Hell, it was well known that David Merrick wanted Flo for the all-black version of *Hello Dolly*. Like Flo was always saying, "My tomorrow looks promised."

Flo's tomorrow did look promised. She said, "Lord knows, my bread is buttered." But I remember my grandmother Vera commenting on the whole affair, "Poor Flo, don't she know tomorrow's not promised? Jesus may have promised many things, . . . 'In my father's house are many mansions,' like in the Bible, John 14: 2-3. But you know, Tony, Jesus said nothing of buttered bread."

CHAPTER 11

— ♦ ♦ ♦ —

My Wigs! My Wigs!

Flo and I must have talked on the phone for about an hour and a half. She was very upset, jumping about from one topic to another, crying because this was it—she was out of the Supremes. When I hung up that phone I was in total shock. I just stood there for about ten minutes with my mouth open and tears streaming down my face. Who in the world had ever dreamed that the Supremes would split up? You just thought it was going to be that way for ever, that the dream, the party would never end.

It was like a divorce. And with it came the news that the Supremes were now Diana Ross and the Supremes, which wasn't so shocking because by this point you didn't have to be a fan to notice that it was all about Diana.

So I didn't care too much about the name change, except I noticed it had happened just like Flo had been saying all along it was going to happen, and it wasn't the vodka coming out of the crystal decanter, it was true. Mary didn't side with her, Mary was still in the group and this Cindy Birdsong bitch was in it, and of course the very next moment I'm thinking, WHAT ABOUT ME?

I had become very used to being around the Supremes by this time. I had become very used to walking in and out of Ed Sullivan, walking in and out of lavish hotel suites, ordering what I felt like ordering from room service, mixing cocktails for Flo, mixing one for myself. I'd become very used to hopping up in a limo for three- or four-block rides from the Warwick, from the Hilton, over to some studio, the Copa, over to Ed Sullivan.

I enjoyed passing the fans waiting out in the cold, waiting in the heat for autographs, for pictures, for anything, just to get in. I enjoyed jumping out of a limo with Phil opening the door for me and me passing right through the crowds, I enjoyed a pleasant nod from Mr. Gordy, Mr. Gordy giving me comments on how good I looked, how smart I was, how was school going. I liked being the first to receive all the new records, I liked being in the know, getting postcards from Flo, letters, phone calls. It made me different, it made me special, it made me a star in my own right, if only in my own mind. And suddenly I was sure it was all over because Flo wasn't there to protect me any more. But Diana was still there and I was scared of her, though for no good reason. I remembered Flo's warning, "Stay outta her way," and I was sure Diana would be putting out my fire, probably with gasoline!

I was thinking, this is over, Flo's out, that means I'm out too, like when the President goes, out goes the Vice President and the cabinet and everyone else. Flo was out, she wouldn't be at Forest Hills, she'd been replaced by someone I'd never heard of and immediately I'm thinking, I'm going to hate this Cindy Birdsong woman.

I'm thinking, who in the world is Cindy Birdsong? What an odd name! WHAT kind of a woman has a name like that? Should I go down there when they come into town? Should I go to Forest Hills Tennis Stadium, should I try to get backstage? Will they throw me out? Who cares, I'm going down there anyway because I want to see what's going on and how DARE she! I'm gonna hate her, I'm gonna be bitchy, I'm gonna roll my eyes, I'm gonna do something to this woman because she probably can't sing any damn way! She's probably a friend of Diana Ross or worse, a cousin—that's why Flo had to go.

I decided to begin my investigation. I had it all plotted out just like in my spy days. Then I figured, maybe I'll just push her down the steps or something and she'll break her leg and then they'll have to bring Florence back and Florence will patch the whole thing up. I was on a mission. I thought, she'll probably have on one of those long gowns that are so tight they can't hardly walk in them and when they go down the steps I'll get behind her and I'll act like I stumbled and fell. I'll fall into her and this'll knock her down, I'll roll my big self over the top of her, I don't care if I get a broken arm or something because her face will be all black and blue and swollen, she'll be all messed up and just like they had to call her in to sub for Flo, they'll have to call someone in to sub for Cindy Birdsong and it'll have to be Flo because she's the only one who knows how to do it.

So I went down there and as I got near I was very nervous and very upset, I was sweating bullets. I'd never been to Forest Hills Tennis Stadium, I didn't know the ins and outs, and everyone was too busy to tell me where to go. Maybe somebody told them not to tell me, maybe they're gonna throw me out but then I ran into the conductor, Gil Askey, and he didn't seem to treat me any different, it was, "Oh hi, Tony, what's going on, come on in, this place is packed, let me get you a backstage pass," and in I waltzed with him.

So I go in with Gil and on the way he starts talking real quiet, "You know Flo's not with us no more, it was a mess! I feel so bad for Flo." He says, "We've got a new girl and you know it's not Diana any more, it's Miss Ross and you know the name was changed," he sounds so disgusted, "all I can do is take a drink and forget half of this crap ever happened." And I'm starting to wonder if a drink could make me forget, too.

The girls haven't arrived yet but I'm seeing some

new faces and right away one guy comes over to me like a gangbuster, "WHAT ARE YOU DOING HERE? WHO are you? You can't stand here!" Gil tells him, "He's all right, he's a friend of the girls, they won't like it if you put him out." This guy turns out to be Reggie Wiggins, the new assistant road manager, and he gives Gil a look like, you just play your music and mind your business, but Gil's an old-time Motowner and when he says something he doesn't care who you are, I've seen him tell off Mr. Gordy and think nothing of it, I've seen him tell Diana off, he just doesn't care. He's a musical genius, and everybody knows it.

Then this other guy, a white guy who's the new head road manager, Roger Campbell, he must have heard all the commotion because he comes over and he says, "Well, you can stay here until the girls come and then I'll see what the situation is." And I'm saying to myself, indeed you will! I thank Roger and sneer at Reggie Wiggins.

So Gil goes off talking to himself, muttering something about educated fools. He leaves me to these new guys and I'm scared but of course I don't show it, I just act mildly bitchy. I don't like this Reggie Wiggins one bit and I can tell he doesn't like me, but I know the girls are on their way because there's this whole lot of commotion. There's security people, maybe fifteen to twenty trunks full of gowns, shoes, wigs, towels, all this is coming in, and then, without warning, Diana arrives.

She's all aflutter—the lashes are going, the hands, everything is in motion, and she's trailed by three or four people all fussing around her. She breezes right past me, "Hi," it's the quickest hi I ever heard and she just keeps going, she has her very own dressing room and this whole entourage just kind of follows her away into her private world.

After Diana comes Mary. "Oh, hi Tony, how are you doing, it's good to see you." She doesn't say a word about Florence Ballard, nobody by this point has even mentioned the name Florence except Gil, Mary just says, "Tony, I want you to meet the new girl, Cindy Birdsong, Cindy this is Tony," and this woman has the nerve to tell me, "Oh, Tony! I've heard so much about you, Mary was telling me all these stories about you on the plane, that when I got to New York I was going to meet you, she told me you were good friends with Flo and I'm so pleased to meet you."

Well, I'm not thrilled, I just give her my Motown smile, all upper teeth and that's it, I go in the dressing room with them to wait while they get ready for the performance.

Next thing I know this woman just starts talking to me. Her mouth is going and going, she's very bubbly, very happy, a little like the way it was with Flo. We start talking like we've known each other forever and I'm trying to be very stern with myself, I keep telling myself, this woman is not going to break me down but the whole time Cindy's being very charming and friendly, "Oh I'm so nervous, oh this is so exciting" and I'm thinking, I'm not going to like this woman, all this time I also notice that Mary is watching me out of the corner of her eye, like, what's Tony going to say, what's he going to do?

I really don't know what to say to this Cindy. Somehow I blurt out, "Are you Diana's cousin?" And as soon as it's out I wish I hadn't because Cindy and Mary are just standing there looking completely shocked, then puzzled, and finally Cindy tells me, "No." That's all she says.

Then Mary leaves the dressing room and right away I start to like Cindy because I can see she has a real nose for gossip. The dressing room door hasn't even closed behind Mary before Cindy starts, "It's a shame about Flo isn't it, I feel so bad but I hope you don't think I had anything to do with it." I tell her, "Oh no," lying of course and telling myself, this Cindy's a sly one.

She says, "I think a lot of people that don't know me are going to think I helped put Flo out of the group and I know Flo was very popular with all the fans, but I was really surprised when they came to me to join the group." So she tells me how she didn't know anything about it, she didn't know Diana, she's definitely not related to Diana, in fact she admits that she's kind of in awe of her, she thinks she's so wonderful, so helpful with the make-up tricks and stuff and no, she didn't know Mary, she didn't know Flo, she knew of them but they weren't her friends so she was just an innocent party and as soon as Mary came back in the dressing room Cindy gave me the eye and changed the subject.

So I said to myself, this woman might not be that bad. And she was smart, she suggested, "Maybe you can help me out, give me some tips because I'm not going to try and be exactly like Flo but you know, I'm not sure of all the movements and stuff," and then she asked, "Do you think I look like Flo? You know, a lot of people say I do." And with that she suddenly held her head up like she was posing for a Hollywood still, as if she was Gloria Swanson asking Mr. de Mille if the cameras were ready to roll in Sunset Boulevard.

I said, "Well, kind of . . ."

"I think she's really pretty," Cindy said. "I'm going to try and do my makeup like her, because it'll make people feel more comfortable. I'm going to draw those dark eyebrows like she used to do. Oh, could you pass me my pocketbook?"

In that moment she seemed to me so open and sincere, she had a certain magic about her and within half an hour I adored this Cindy Birdsong. She just didn't give me a minute to dislike her, she was like a breath of fresh air and it was as if I had known her forever. She had a big, bright smile and she was just being herself, saying things like, "Oh, I'm so thrilled to be in the Supremes, it's like riding in a Caddy instead of a Ford!"

As soon as Cindy left the room I told Mary, "She's nice, that girl is so nice, she seems really happy to be in the group.'' Mary just looked at me and said, ''Honey, she's happy to be *anywhere.*''

Mary was like a different person. She seemed suddenly more talkative, and at the same time she seemed a little sullen, very sultry, she was all on edge. Even her performance that night was different. There was more hip-shaking, more eyelash-batting, more hand movements, it was like she'd become the power in the background in place of Flo, and Cindy had taken Mary's place, the one who stayed in the background, although when Cindy got up on that stage she looked something like Flo, even the way she moved was almost exactly like Flo—well, sort of, if you squinted.

Cindy had the moves down yet she seemed just a bit clumsy, her voice was just a bit off. You heard a lot more of Mary trying to do what Flo had done with her voice and not really making it, but still giving Diana a run for her money. Diana was turned up very high so she sounded like she was screeching. Later I heard her complain about how bad the sound man was, and of course he was never seen again.

It was like a battle of the voices. Diana was screeching, Mary was trying her hardest to come up from under her, and Cindy was trying to hit the high notes. You could see her getting nervous, preparing herself and thinking, in the next eight words I gotta hit that note. But then she'd flash a smile, she'd wave a hand and do a turn and keep going. I thought she was a good replacement and everyone was happy, even the people who'd really loved Flo. The guys in the band liked her and Diana was real friendly with Cindy Birdsong, she seemed to be the best of friends with her, I saw them giggling and chatting and you could tell Cindy really looked up to Diana, she just dwelled on her every word. So it seemed as if it was Cindy and Diana like it used to be Mary and Flo. Diana paid Mary no mind.

Diana Ross seemed immediately different, immediately grander. Right away I noticed things centered around her and nobody called her Diana any more, everybody called her Miss Ross. I never heard her tell anybody to call her Miss Ross, but Roger Campbell told me, "Diana prefers to be called Miss Ross," and whenever he or any other staff member spoke to me after that about any of the girls it was, "Mary is going shopping, Cindy left, Miss Ross would like you to do this. Miss Ross will be leaving the hotel at four, I don't know where Mary is, I haven't seen Cindy, Miss Ross is resting, please do not disturb her."

Diana Ross and the Supremes were riding high on the last single Flo had sung on, "Reflections." It was a smash hit, and this was the summer of '67, the place was packed, it was New York, it was a beautiful concert that started at dusk and went on into the night, the gowns sparkled under the lights, the fans went wild. No announcement was made so most of them didn't even know it wasn't Flo up there on the stage, even though to me it sounded like the songs had been speeded up a bit to get through them quickly. You heard the announcement, "Ladies and gentlemen, Diana Ross and the Supremes," and it was like nothing had changed.

But things had changed. In many ways this was a new group, it was Miss Ross, it was more glitter, it was almost a totally new staff, a larger staff, more limos, there was a banquet table backstage and flowers all over the place and nobody seemed to miss my friend. It was almost like an unspoken rule, don't even mention her name. I felt like shouting, "Doesn't anybody here remember Florence Ballard? Is everyone too scared to say the name Flo? Or too grand to remember?" But I didn't mention her name either. I missed her but I went right along with the party, and I discovered that Gil was right, a drink could make you forget. But he didn't tell me that it only helps for the moment, that memories are forever flooding back.

The very next morning bright and early I called Flo and the phone rang exactly half a time, she was waiting on the call and she just jumped right in, "Now baby, I want a detailed description of everything that

One of the last photo sessions of the original Supremes in 1967.
Around this time, Flo was under heavy attack from Berry Gordy over
her weight—but most of her fans just thought she looked shapely,
especially in her characteristic Mae West pose. *(Photo by James
Kriegsmann)*

The Supremes, in a very early publicity shot—they would soon become Berry Gordy's main interest, much to the chagrin of other Motown acts. Here they're wearing dresses like the ones Diana and her mother used to make in the early days of their career—"sleeveless!" as my grandmother would say with a raise of her eyebrows. *(Photo courtesy of Norman Stensland)*

A not widely publicized early shot of the original Supremes with a frail Diana seemingly "supported" by two vocal bricks, Florence Ballard and Mary Wilson. *(Photo courtesy of Bill Seagreaves)*

Fresh out of the projects and well into the money, Mary Wilson bought this house in the Buena Vista section of Detroit. I took this photograph of the house with Mary and her publicist standing on the steps during our stop in Detroit on her *Dreamgirl* book tour in 1986. I was amazed to see how little the house had changed, but knew that if walls could talk. . . . *(Tony Turner Collection)*

Just up the street from Mary's, this was Diana Ross's first mini-mansion after leaving the family's apartment in Detroit's Brewster Projects. Flo told me it was pure coincidence that the three girls all ended up purchasing homes on the same street— a coincidence she would come to regret. *(Tony Turner Collection)*

Located almost directly across the street from Diana's, Flo Ballard's magnificently decorated English Tudor would prove to be a good vantage point from which to monitor the comings and goings of Diana after civil war broke out between the Supremes. Even long after she had lost the house through foreclosure, Flo would trek there sometimes late at night to perform on the front steps, holding an empty liquor bottle as her makeshift microphone. *(Tony Turner Collection)*

I call this photo "Diana Ross—Twiggyized." *(RDR/Rex Features)*

A happy Flo Ballard, followed by a smiling Mary Wilson. When Flo gave me this picture she told me that her midriff-type outfit had caused yet another argument between her and Berry Gordy. She said he felt her outfit was not in keeping with the wholesome, yet demurely, sexy image of the Supremes—and then she laughed, loud and long! *(Tony Turner Collection)*

Although internal strife was raging, and Flo was in her heavy black-eye makeup, the Supremes were publicly still all smiles, striking their most ladylike pose with a couple of convention-goers. The Supremes performed at a number of conventions all around the country. *(Photo courtesy of T.T.T. Ltd.)*

A young Diana Ross photographed on a sunny day. *(Tony Turner Collection)*

Ed Sullivan with "the girls"—yet again. *(Tony Turner Collection)*

The original Supremes in July 1967, with candelabra earrings, painted-on expressions, and washed-out grins, still mobbed by admirers in the casino at the Flamingo Hotel, Las Vegas. This was to be Florence Ballard's last engagement as a Supreme. Days after this picture was taken she was forced out, and the name of the group was changed to Diana Ross and the Supremes. *(Photo Courtesy of Bill Seagreaves)*

Here I am, clowning around and doing my own little Supremes show for Diana Ross and Cindy Birdsong, in the dressing room at the Latin Casino, New Jersey. This was the night that Diana's dogs died from poisoning backstage, leading her to cancel the rest of the booked engagement. *(Tony Turner Collection)*

Berry Gordy always used to comment on how tall I was, and then he'd ask me how school was going, and did the fans think Diana Ross should leave the Supremes and go solo? Here we are outside the Empire Room on one of the rare occasions Mr. Gordy would allow himself to be photographed—I, of course, was thrilled. *(Tony Turner Collection)*

Diana Ross and the Supremes, performing the "I Am the Greatest Star" medley for the TV special, *TCB on Broadway*. This was one of the numbers which, to Mary and Cindy's disgust, didn't air on the special—it was sacrificed, reportedly in favor of numbers that featured Diana Ross more prominently, rather than the trio. *(Photo courtesy of NBC-TV: Edward M. Broussard)*

Diana doesn't look too happy with me in this picture, taken outside the star's dressing room at the Westbury Music Fair on Long Island. She had just called me into her private dressing room to give me a big lecture about how I had no class whatso- ever, because anyone with any class would know that you never say "the Sherry Netherland," you simply say, "The Sherry." *(Tony Turner Collection)*

I was extremely proud to be photographed with the beautiful Cindy Birdsong in 1969, just before she hit the stage at the Waldorf Astoria in New York. *(Tony Turner Collection)*

A fan asked Mary Wilson and me to pose for this picture, right outside Mary's suite at the Waldorf Astoria in New York where Diana Ross and the Supremes were staying and performing. By this time I had ensconced myself as a kind of unofficial personal assistant to Mary and Cindy. I was answering their phones, running errands for them, and rearranging their hotel rooms as boyfriends came and left. *(Tony Turner Collection)*

The supergroup, Diana Ross and the Supremes, captured through the lens of James Kriegsmann. His photographs of the Supremes are amongst the most famous and memorable. *(Photo by James Kriegsmann/Michael Ochs Archives)*

Diana Ross and the Supremes, all in black, at one of many conferences. Although all three of the girls are there and smiling, most of the questions were usually directed to or answered by Diana. *(Photo courtesy of T.T.T. Ltd.)*

An unusual photo opportunity—Diana Ross pictured with both her mentor and former lover, Berry Gordy, and her first husband, Bob Ellis. They often found themselves together at Diana's openings and many social events. *(Ben Mancuso/Impact Photos)*

Mary Wilson, photographed in her Angela Davis period of the early 70s, at her suite in the Sherry. *(Photo by Delcina Wilson)*

A young and jubilant Flo Ballard flashing a smile while showing off her Liz Taylor-style eye makeup. (*Photo courtesy of Doug Wright*)

A look of grief on the face of Diana Ross who, having made a dramatic and appropriately tragic entrance, sits in church during Florence Ballard's memorial service in 1976, clutching Flo's baby. Next to her, Flo's husband and Berry Gordy's one-time chauffeur, Tommy Chapman, comforts the twins. Diana never made it to the cemetery; she fled the church through a side door to avoid the angry crowds outside. (*Detroit Free Press*)

Delcina Wilson, Diana Ross, and me in happier days, at a party for Diana in New York. Amazing what another wig and another year can do. *(Ben Mancuso/Impact Photos)*

The last Supreme, Mary Wilson, posing with me while we were on tour in Canada, in 1986. Although many considered us brother-and-sister-like, within a year things would be very different between us. (Courtesy of T.T.T. Ltd.)

Here I am in the 90s, still standing—thanks Flo! *(Photo by Bill Baker for MLDIII)*

went on, did she have on my gown?'' When I told her what Cindy had on she said, ''Aha! Because they bought those gowns out of my money and I'm supposed to get those gowns back. What other gowns did you see there?''

So I started telling her about all of the gowns. She said, ''Okay, I'm supposed to get all of those gowns back because those gowns didn't come out of Motown money, they came out of the Supremes' money and Flo wants her gowns because Flo's fixing to sing.''

''Oh! What are you going to do?''

''Never mind!'' She said, ''Tell me what went on, how was Diana acting?'' So I told her how Diana had walked past me and just said ''hi'' and Flo piped in, ''Oh, that much?'' She said, ''What about Mary? What did Mary say?''

''Mary didn't say much.'' I told her some of the things Mary had said to me.

''Is that all? What did she say about me? Who talked about me?''

''Well, only Gil,'' and I told her what Gil had said.

''Bless his heart. What about the new girl?'' I told her, she said, ''Well you know honey, I'm sure she's a nice person.'' Then she wanted to know about the show, I told her it was the same, she said, ''Honey, I'm gonna get those gowns back.''

''You mean you're not coming back?'' I was still hoping.

''No honey, I'm not coming back. I'm going solo and if I ever did come back, I would *not* come back under the name Diana Ross and the Supremes. But I'm still talking to Motown and my mother says she really doesn't think they can just put me out like that, she says I must have had some kind of contract or some type of agreement and my family says they just can't put me out. Even though it's good to be rid of those people.''

She told me she had been approached a year ago about doing some solo work, which was news to me,

and she said she was going out on her own with Tommy
as her manager.

"Tommy who?" I asked.

"You know, Tommy who used to work for Berry
Gordy, you remember Tommy."

"Oh, him." I thought that was strange because I
always thought he was a chauffeur or a bodyguard.

"Yeah, Tommy's gonna be my manager." She talked
about how nice he was and how he'd been helping her
all along and he'd been telling her that she didn't have
to take all that foolishness from Gordy and Diana Ross,
that she could quit and cause a big fuss and the public
would not stand for it. Tommy was confident that he'd
be able to sell Flo as a solo and he'd been all around
with Berry Gordy, he'd been listening and learning the
entire business.

Flo was going solo and she was not spending all her
money getting a new wardrobe. She said most of those
gowns were only three months old, she wanted her
gowns, she wanted her shoes, her stage jewelry, and
everything else because it had come out of her money,
and she told me, "Flo knows how to pinch a penny."

She said Motown was trying to get her to take a low
settlement. She had signed something. She'd had a
meeting with a man from Motown right after she came
out of the hospital, when she was still in shock, still
sick and on medication for her nerves. On top of that,
Detroit was smoking from the riots. There were army
tanks in the streets, it was all debris, burnt-out cars,
burnt-out buildings. It was horrible and she'd gone to
this meeting and signed an agreement without even
knowing what she was doing. She had no attorney.
They just handed her a pen and said sign, and when it
was all over she ran out of that meeting with tears
pouring down her cheeks. But she said now she was
going to get a lawyer and have the whole thing sorted
out, including the matter of the gowns and most definitely the money.

She said she needed her money. She didn't even have
a checking account because Motown always took care

of the money, they took the money, paid the girls' bills, gave them their allowance and all she had was what was in her pocketbook when they flew her home from Vegas.

She said she'd let me know, she had a lot of business decisions to make but I should call her after the next time I saw Diana Ross and the Supremes, which I already knew was going to be at the Steel Pier in Atlantic City in two weeks. Mary, who was getting real chummy with me, had invited me to the six-day engagement. Luckily it was summer, school was out, and Mary had made arrangements for me to stay in the hotel where the band was staying.

So I took the bus down to Atlantic City, I went over to the Steel Pier, and when I got there I saw this was like an amusement park with games and candy and popcorn and a few kiddie rides and a small theater. Diana Ross and the Supremes were going to be doing about four to five twenty-minute shows a day out on this pier and I realized that the girls were sort of trapped there, there was a big mess of fans waiting outside because they knew that the Supremes would be coming in and out and it was hard to get the limo all the way down the side of the pier, through these crowds and into the backstage area.

Cindy didn't want to sit around waiting in the dressing room all that time, and neither did Diana. But Diana liked to go through the big star dramatics and go in and out five hundred times a day with the limo and the screaming fans, she'd have three or four towels wrapped around her throat, she'd bunch up, she had the big sunglasses and she'd take what seemed like an hour doing her makeup before she even set foot outside.

There were times when she wasn't going anywhere, but she'd pretend to be going, and even I could see she was testing her appeal, her power. She would come out and the fans would all mob around the door and Diana would act so shocked that anyone was there to see her, she'd sign autographs and she'd always say,

"I don't know where Mary and Cindy are, but *I'd* be just *thrilled* to sign autographs for you!''

Of course Mary and Cindy were right there in the dressing room but she'd say, "Oh, I think the other girls went off somewhere.'' Other times Diana would just come out and jump the one foot from the door into the back of the limo and the limo would take off, if you were in the way so be it, that limo would go riproaring through and everyone had to jump out the way. Cindy on the other hand wanted to eat, which was fine with me, because I liked to eat too. She said, "Well, we don't have to go out that back way, I'll just put on something casual and we'll go out through the theater. We can go out on the pier and play some games, get our fortunes told and have a few candy apples, and we'll just have a good time."

So Cindy and I would go in and out, we went further and further till eventually we got right off the Steel Pier and then we had hell getting back in because they wanted us to *pay*. Cindy told the guy, "But I'm with the Supremes," and he said, "Yeah, lady, sure," so then we had to walk all the way around the back to get to the stage entrance and we were laughing so much, we got to be good friends.

Mary was still staying very quiet about the situation. She was going about her business, doing her job, hanging out with Dionne Warwick who was also performing in Atlantic City at the time. Nobody said a word about Flo, and I didn't tell anyone I'd been speaking with her. That name was not mentioned until the day the girls got robbed.

They were staying at the Seaside Motel, two blocks off the boardwalk. We got back from the pier, the girls went off to their own rooms as usual, I went with Mary, and suddenly we heard Diana screaming, "MY WIGS! MY WIGS! OH MY GOD MY WIGS!''

Diana came out onto the balcony shrieking, and I don't know where Roger Campbell and Reggie Wiggins could have come from that quick—they just seemed to appear out of the walkway, running in response to her yells, "Pick up my WIGS! I've been ROBBED, I've been ROBBED!"

We all come running. There are white foam wig heads all over the place, Diana's standing in the middle of the bed screaming, "I've got to get out of this place! GET ME ANOTHER HOTEL!" And somebody says, "Miss Ross, your fur coats have been stolen."

All hell breaks loose. Diana turns into a wild woman, she jumps off the bed and starts spinning around like Wonder Woman, "Oh my God! Get Gordy, get Gordy, get security, I'm suing! I'M SUING!" Meanwhile everybody's calming her down, Cindy's in the room nosing around through all of Diana's business, the police come and take down their report, Diana's giving them this whole list of missing things and one of the cops says, "Now why would you girls be traveling around in the middle of August with mink coats and fox coats and sable coats?"

Immediately Diana screams, "What Is Your Badge Number! I don't see how any of that is your business, I am an INTERNATIONAL STAR!" And she gets out her pen and writes down the man's badge number, at which point Mary just leaves. I go with Mary. Cindy goes to her room, the police send somebody down with her to check under her bed and behind her door and everything because now Cindy's scared and only then does nosy Cindy realize she's been robbed too. Nothing's gone from Mary's room and I immediately pick up the phone and call Flo collect to report this bit of news.

Flo says, "Let me call Mary!" So Flo calls back, she talks to Mary for a long time, I never hear them mention anything about the show, the group or anything, then I speak with Flo again, she says, "Tony! It's a premonition! God don't like ugly I'm not saying anything about that Cindy Birdsong woman but it serves her right for taking my job. She has no business wearing my dress, honey. What type of woman is going to wear another woman's dress! Mary was spared

but God did this to those people. God don't like ugly!"
Then she tells me to keep my eyes open, to make sure
nobody breaks into Mary's room, how Mary is always
leaving her valuables lying around all over the place
and she says she'll call me next week, she has some
surprises to tell me about.

So I stayed with Mary and I started tidying up her
stuff. All her jewelry was spread around. I found her
beehive diamond ring and diamond watch just thrown
on the floor, and then I saw a telegram on the bedside
table. Mary was in the bathroom so I took a peek. I
always thought when you got a telegram it meant
someone had dropped dead but this one said, "Mary,
stick with Flo, you might be next—the Tempts."

I just put the telegram back and I never mentioned
it to Mary, but it got me thinking. This just confirmed
everything Flo had said. This could happen to you,
you could be next, Mary, the axe is waiting to swing
again. I started thinking, Flo's out, poor Mrs. Powell
is gone—a lot of people disappear around here never
to be mentioned again except in secret little telegrams
that sound just like spy stuff.

Well, I didn't think about it too long because when
I next talked to Flo she did have a surprise for me.
She said that as a kind of consolation for not going to
Vegas, she was inviting me to Detroit. She told me
Diana Ross and the Supremes were coming to perform
at a few places in town, they were going to be appearing at a big show Motown was going to be having
with a lot of different stars at a hotel in Detroit and I
should come up for that. She was going to go, her
whole family was going. She was going to sit there
and be fabulous and wear some wild outfit and just
annoy everybody to death talking about her plans, and
this sounded like fun to me.

When I got to Detroit about a week later everything
had changed and Flo wasn't going. She wasn't in that
plotting mood, she seemed mad. She said she had been
to a couple of the shows in Detroit and she hadn't been

allowed backstage, they'd completely ignored her. She also said that Mary hadn't taken any of her calls.

Nothing was the same as the last time I had visited Flo, even Detroit was different. The riots were all over but as soon as you left Flo's house on Buena Vista you could see it, it was like when the riots had happened in Harlem and I'd see people running down the street carrying the oddest stolen things. The store windows were all broken and the store gates were ripped down, it looked like the riot had just happened.

The Supremes had been at war too. Diana Ross's house still stood across the street, Mary's was still down the block, but all of that was over. Mary didn't call Flo, there was no going over to Motown, and Flo's family was on permanent guard at the door and at the window. Every time someone went in or out of Diana's house it was big news, the Ballards reported every move, "Some bitch just left," "Mary just drove down the block."

Flo looked great. She had on her at-home gown, one of about twenty and most of them had mink sleeves or sable collars. She was floating around with the big lashes and the hair all done up and she was picking up her huge French phone and arguing with Motown. She told me she wanted to get her money and forget about the whole pack of those fools. She didn't want any Supremes talk, she didn't want my news, she was just concentrating on what she had to do.

Flo said Motown was trying to cheat her, all they wanted to give her was a couple of thousand dollars a year for six years and the whole world knew she was supposed to be a millionaire, and what had happened to all the blue-chip stocks and the investments Motown always said they'd put her money in, and where were her gowns? She said she had given up trying to reach Mary, but she wanted Mary to know that they had no millions, that if Mary ever left she would find herself in the same situation, fighting for her money. She said, "Honey, one day she'll find out on her own."

Tommy was hovering around the whole time, they

were both on and off the phone all day talking to people in New York about Flo signing as a solo, but Flo said she couldn't sign 'til she had everything settled with Motown. The world was waiting, it was hot news now that Diana Ross had taken over the group and Flo was out and the public was making a big stink, which, as everyone around there kept saying, was great publicity for Flo.

As soon as the word went out and Motown made their statement people started to talk, even people who were never really interested in the Supremes, ''Oh that bitch, how could she rename a group that already exists and isn't it awful funny that one of the girls left the group at the same time?'' It didn't matter what Motown said, they said Flo left due to exhaustion, she wanted to settle down, she was tired of traveling but nobody believed it, and the press was all over Flo's front lawn, coming right up to her house without even calling, trying to get her to come out, trying to get an interview. But Flo wouldn't tell them a thing because she didn't want to talk about any rumored fights or about Diana Ross. She wanted to talk about herself, the future, her solo career, but they weren't interested in any of that.

On Sunday I went to church with Flo and everybody made a fuss of her, while badmouthing Diana Ross. Nevertheless, Flo said nothing bad in public about Diana Ross or Mary Wilson or Motown. Flo didn't need to, she seemed to have the congregation with her. The minister announced her from the pulpit, the congregation broke into applause, Flo stood up and the choir did a special song for her, it was really a big production.

Back at her house friends were knocking, family members were knocking, neighbors were knocking and they would come in and say, ''Oh! I'm so upset! Poor Flo!'' Someone else would come in, ''I'm shocked, the Supremes are at the Roostertail and you know the scab has her name up there, DIANA ROSS in all capital letters!''

Around four Flo would have her cocktail hour. Her mother would be in the kitchen preparing hors d'oeuvres, because Flo was a star, Flo was a former Supreme and God forbid Flo should do anything. Meanwhile, a whole bunch more people would be coming by saying, "Oh, Flo, I don't blame you for leaving, I don't blame you for quitting, they're gonna go down the tubes without you."

"That new girl, she doesn't know what she's doing. I saw the show, Flo, and it was *horrible*. Diana was just screaming and hollering and the other two, you couldn't even hear them."

"They're not gonna be nothing. Mary Wilson cannot sing."

"You know, Flo, it's a shame what they did to you."

And Flo would just say, "It doesn't matter honey, because I'm going to record on my own, I'm going to be a solo. I've had it with the group scene." Flo wouldn't say anything bad about Mary, she just said, "Mary'll wake up when she's good and ready," but she let them say what they wanted about Diana. And I'd just be sitting there going like a Ping-Pong ball back and forth looking into everybody's mouth with my own mouth hanging wide open. Flo would walk past me and tap me on the chin, "Close your mouth, honey, you can hear the words but you can't see them!"

The Temptations came by, the Four Tops came by, everyone came by just like you go to a house where somebody's died. There was disgust and shock and outrage but everyone was saying, "You'll show 'em Flo!"

Flo was confident, even though by the time I left nothing was settled. But I went home with the assurance that it would all soon be worked out with Motown. Flo was getting an attorney, Flo would soon be in New York, Flo would have a record out, and it was going to be a big battle between Diana Ross and the Supremes and Flo Ballard, former Supreme. She said Tommy was starting up a company to handle her because there were that many people calling and talk shows wanted her, magazines wanted her, record companies wanted her.

She kept telling everyone, "Honey, the next time you hear from me it's gonna be Flo Ballard, alone at last!" And from the way she said it and the look on her face, everybody knew exactly what she was talking about. Alone at last.

CHAPTER 12

◆ ◆ ◆

Star Supreme/ Ex-Supreme

When the New York fans found out they'd been duped, when they realized that they hadn't seen Flo up on that stage at Forest Hills, but some new Supreme called Cindy Birdsong, they were shocked. But they weren't shocked for long, because the whole thing was downplayed, and the only fuss being made seemed to be happening around Diana Ross, which of course is exactly where the fans started to focus all of their attention. One minute they'd be cursing out Diana, "Who does she think she is?" Five minutes later they were trying to catch her at the stage door, they were rushing out to buy the next record, fighting over tickets for the next show.

Diana wasn't as friendly with the fans as Mary and Cindy were, but these fans didn't really mind that Diana hardly ever stopped to give an autograph. They'd complain when Cindy or Mary stopped to give autographs and then maybe spoke to two or three people: "Hey, I was gonna get an autograph and she just jumped in the car before she got to me." Diana didn't stop to pose for one picture, nobody complained. The fans were clamoring, security guards were pushing everybody out the way, Diana would just walk the six paces to the limo, get in, and take off without so much as a howdyado unless once in a while she felt like talking. She didn't have to try any more now that she had no competition from Flo.

So why would the world be waiting for Flo to settle with Motown and come out with her solo when they had Diana Ross and the Supremes right up in front of their faces doing shows, making headlines, releasing albums, appearing on commercials for Arrid deodorant and Coca-Cola and wherever else Motown could find for them to show themselves. Everything the Supremes said was quoted, whereas Flo was quietly waiting, and I was waiting too.

School started. This was Forest Hills High School, which was supposed to be such a prestigious school, and it was the first year they were admitting blacks under a new open enrollment plan. My junior high teacher had sat me down and told me, "You know it's going to be quite a different atmosphere, it's going to be like college, the kids there will be rich kids," so me and Barry Laster, my best friend from junior high, knew this had to be the place to go. It was. The school was full of teenagers with fast cars and daddy's money. Good times seemed promised.

There were some very snooty people there, both black and white, but we immediately found the right party crowd, bourgeois but not stuck up. I memorized my lessons fast, then went to hang out in the lunchroom where we played Motown and all types of music, or in the luncheonette a few blocks away where everybody hung out, where the principal and the truant officers were always coming to chase all the teenagers back to school.

For the longest time I didn't tell anyone at Forest Hills that I knew the Supremes because I knew nobody would actually believe it. Even though I could show them pictures, I knew they wouldn't believe a word and I wanted to get my high school life off to a good start. But of course pretty soon Barry Laster told someone and they told someone else and then everybody knew, and I started holding court in the luncheonette with my pictures and everything. Soon I knew everybody—seniors, juniors, sophomores, and freshmen—and I just partied the whole time.

So September came, October came, November came, still no word from Flo but Diana Ross and the Supremes were everywhere. They were still on every TV show they could make, Diana Ross was all over, no Flo. I was talking to her on the phone more and more, running up my mother's phone bills and my mother was complaining, but on the other hand she wanted to know every single word Flo said about it and my mother was commenting, "That Diana Ross, I never could stand the woman," and, "Mary should have left with Flo, now she got stuck with that new girl."

Flo was telling me she'd hired a lawyer, Motown was holding her up, time was running out, and I could tell Flo wasn't up any more because to the world Florence Ballard was nowhere. By November it started looking really bad because by now the first record should have been out but Flo hadn't even signed yet, and Diana Ross and the Supremes had released the single "Reflections," and the *Reflections* album and *Diana Ross and the Supremes Greatest Hits*. The sleeve for this album had the name "Diana Ross" written slightly smaller than "The Supremes," but it was written in *gold* along with the words "greatest hits," so it almost read like "Diana Ross Greatest Hits." And anyway, I didn't think it ought to have been called that because it was all songs they'd recorded while Flo was in the group and the group was called the Supremes, but I guess nobody else cared because the record shot straight to number one.

Things were happening fast and furious. They were coming to town to do the *Ed Sullivan Show,* which by now was almost the *Supremes Show.* This was to be Cindy's first appearance. Flo was home in Detroit, it was coming up to the holiday season, people should have been happy, but Flo was starting to sound very strange on the phone, very depressed.

She was telling me, "You shouldn't go around with

that old Diana Ross and the Supremes because that woman is not what she seems, she's really a vicious old thing and I don't even listen to their music or anything any more. They're terrible, they're not what you think they are, they'll be a bad influence on you.'' She wanted to know what was going on, though. ''What are they doing? Tell Mary to call me. What's the matter with Mary, did Gordy break her fingers so she can't dial a phone? Tell her to give me a call.''

Of course, I couldn't wait to get back down to Ed Sullivan for Cindy's first appearance. I had to get the usual ensemble of new outfits and new coats and for a time I forgot about Flo myself because this was just so exciting. By now Diana Ross and the Supremes were staying in hotels I never even heard of before, really high-class places and Diana Ross had these huge suites whereas the girls had small suites, sometimes they just had rooms. Everything was the same, and everything was changed.

So I went down to Ed Sullivan and it seemed to be pretty much business as usual, except Flo wasn't there. I had more or less hooked myself up to Cindy, she just seemed to fit right in and she and I would do the restaurants. Then we'd go shopping, but she was not one for going up in Bergdorf Goodman and Saks Fifth Avenue and Lord and Taylor—she was going in Ohrbach's and Macy's. She had her fur, you had to have your fur, but she wore it differently. She just wore it. She had on her sunglasses and designer scarves and things like that but she didn't go out of her way to give you that star flash, she was just natural, easy-like.

We'd go shopping and she'd say, ''That's too high.'' I'd never heard a Supreme say something was too expensive, Flo wouldn't even look at the price, she'd just buy it. So this was a different type of shopping I was doing with Cindy, she'd even go down into Gimbel's basement, this girl would go in the basement where my mother would go! Cindy was just casual and friendly and she didn't put on any airs. She was excited, and nervous about wanting to be just right.

One time at a make-up counter I told Cindy, "Oh Cindy, you should get these lashes, these lashes would look good," and she answered, "No, I don't think so, those are too much like the ones Diana wears." Cindy never wanted to do anything to ruffle Diana's feathers. She would consult with her about makeup and wigs, she would listen to her, unlike Flo. Cindy never tried to compete with Diana, and Mary would watch her, she'd say, "Cindy, why don't you tell Diana what you think about that?" It looked to me in a way like Cindy wanted to go along with what Mary said, but then again she didn't want to offend Diana. Nobody wanted to offend Diana because everybody saw what happened to Flo.

I noticed a distinct separatism in the group. Diana arrived in the limo alone or with Berry Gordy, and if there was a road manager with her, you better believe he was sitting in the front with the driver, he was no longer sitting in the back. Diana would just bunch herself up like she was trying to disappear in the corner and the sunglasses were just huge and the wig was sprayed and laquered and everything centered around her, period.

Cindy and Mary seemed to be treated no different or no better than the guys in the band. No limo for Mary and Cindy, they had Reggie Wiggins driving the rental Lincoln Mark 3, and if the rental car was in the garage they just took a cab and that was that.

Diana was like a solo star, like Shirley Bassey or Johnny Mathis when they came to *Ed Sullivan*, she was always "resting" or "in rehearsal" or "at the beauty salon" because the make-up people at Ed Sullivan could no longer do *anything* for her. She went to the House of Kenneth or someone from Kenneth's came to her in between rehearsals, and when she came back you never knew what you were going to see. One time she came bouncing back in with a makeup job that looked like Hollywood gone Halloween, she looked so different, she had on padded tits and a padded ass and it was so huge that when she walked out of the room Mary just said, "Let me die. I have now seen it all."

Diana was all over the place and she was not only following directions and being handled with kid gloves, she was giving directions. In rehearsal I'd hear her tell the camera people, "I'm not standing here," "I want to enter from *this* side," and there was little they could do because she was not very sweet to anybody. I heard the people who worked at Ed Sullivan grumbling about how things weren't the same anymore, how the group had changed quite a bit since the last appearance.

The only thing that was still exactly the same was Ed Sullivan himself. He'd come in wearing his rain-or-shine coat, some suit that looked like it needed to be ironed, and he would come off the train, walk up the block, walk in the stage door, sign a few autographs, very low key. He never seemed to know quite what was going on, I wondered if he even noticed that Flo Ballard was now Cindy Birdsong.

For their November *Ed Sullivan* appearance they were doing "In and Out of Love," which was released in October but was recorded in April. So although this was a Diana Ross and the Supremes record, the record had been recorded with Florence Ballard. But that Ballard voice wasn't there any more for live performances, it wasn't holding the whole thing together and so they had Cindy lip-synching along to it on *Ed Sullivan* with Diana lip-synching way, way up front and Cindy and Mary way in the back and I wondered, why don't they do a new song? None of the fans were getting too hysterical about "In and Out of Love," you could tell they were all thinking, "This ain't that great."

I heard that they had pulled "In and Out of Love" out of the can because this was a Holland-Dozier-Holland song that had been recorded but never released. By now Holland-Dozier-Holland were not writing any more, they had just stopped and like everyone said on the inside, HDH *were* the Supremes,

they had written all of the Supremes hits, they knew
the voices, they knew the tricks to make Diana Ross
sound better in the studio than she actually sounded,
and they knew how sometimes they would have to have
Flo hitting certain notes right up under Diana to give
it the strength it needed.

The word was that HDH wanted a bigger cut of Motown, they wanted more power, more say-so, or they
were just not gonna write any more. But from what I
heard on the inside a lot of people thought that HDH
were also very unhappy with the way the whole thing
with Flo had been handled. Everybody liked Flo, and
everybody saw that what had happened to her could
happen to them too. Flo said it served those bitches
right, she said Diana Ross and the Supremes couldn't
make it without those HDH songs behind them.

Florence was like the foundation, she had a voice
that held everything together. After she left, some critics said the Supremes didn't have the same sound any
more, they were different, they weren't the same live
as on record. So on *Ed Sullivan* Diana Ross and the
Supremes almost always lip-synched the latest hits.
And a lot of the time they would record the medleys
on Thursday or Friday to get the perfect pitch, the
perfect harmony, everything perfect so that Sunday
night they wouldn't have to worry about Mary's voice
being out or Cindy being too nervous, why take that
chance when you could pay a few dollars, record it,
mix it, and let the girls move their lips.

Now the camera was focused on Diana most of the
time, her every move was traced, the angles were designed to suit her and she had her own choreography.
All the nice sways and steps that Cholly Atkins had
taught the girls were now cut down to a few little sa-
shays and a demure shimmy from Mary and Cindy,
and Diana did what she wanted, she concentrated on
herself. She was the star attraction, she was there to
fall back with Mary and Cindy at key points, to strike
the ending pose or do the cutesy turn.

I would be at the rehearsals and I'd hear the cameramen tracing Diana's every movement across the stage so that when you turned on your TV your eye would naturally wander in her direction. That's the way the shots were set up. Nothing was hidden, nothing was done behind anybody's back, this was the new program and it was done right in front of Mary, Cindy, and anybody else who was there. Berry Gordy minced no words in the things he wanted for and from Diana. He'd be sitting there watching every step and the directors would say, "Miss Ross move up, move left, move right. Mary and Cindy you girls can have a seat. Miss Ross the routine will go like this, you will begin here, you will precede down center stage left—girls please stand over here in the back and begin to come in as Miss Ross crosses in front of you."

Now Diana always came on first, and the positioning was always worked out so that when Ed called them over Diana would seem to be in a natural position for him to greet her first and foremost. Even a fool could see they were building something, and Diana wasn't idly sitting back either, I saw her work hard and when the rehearsals were over and Cindy and Mary rushed off, Diana stayed behind with Berry Gordy, with Gil Askey, they'd stay there till late going over the show and she learned everything and everybody's job.

I almost never saw Diana during the daytime, she was in the suite that she and Berry Gordy shared, which was the hugest, most lavish thing they had in the hotel. Motown now booked rooms on different floors for the girls instead of the blocks of rooms they used to book, which was a nuisance for me because I'd have to go to Mary's on the twenty-seventh floor, then come down to Cindy's on the twenty-fourth and along two or three corridors. After Flo left I started to run errands for Cindy and Mary, and they both had plenty for me to do.

So I would leave from school around one o'clock— I had the key for Mary's suite—I would go straight down to the hotel and Mary would be sound asleep, she'd probably just gotten in around six or seven from making her rounds of all the top clubs. Usually the suite looked like it was left over from a party scene, a real mess, and since none of the Motown people liked to let maids into their rooms because they had all their valuables in there, I would begin by doing what housekeeping should have done. I would empty ashtrays, collect glasses from the oddest places all over the room, put everything on a tray, and put the tray outside for housekeeping to pick up.

The message light on the phone would be on so I'd call down to the front desk, I'd take the messages— Tom Jones called, Steve McQueen called. Or the phone would ring and you never knew who it would be, it's Nancy Wilson, it's Dionne Warwick, it's Leslie Uggams, the first few times I thought, you must be kidding me, but I got used to it and I'd write the names down, putting the more important ones at the top of the list. Sometimes I'd do the same for Cindy. Both girls usually left me a note, there was always something to get from the store so I'd go running around getting these things, trying to find a grocery store in midtown Manhattan. I'd have to walk halfway across town and I'd have to lug the whole lot back to the hotel, then I'd sit down, relax, watch some TV.

Maybe the band was rehearsing for the twenty thousandth time so I'd go down there and goof off with them for a while, not for too long because I wanted to be on duty, I wanted to be helpful to the stars. Then I'd go back upstairs, do my homework real fast, maybe I'd call a few of my friends to brag, "Hi, I'm up in Mary Wilson's suite, Diana Ross is in a suite right upstairs. You don't believe me? Call me back. I'm serious, I'm at the Waldorf, call me right back."

I'd give them the number, they'd call back, "I don't believe it!" Then I'd say something like, "Come down, she's gonna be leaving at six o'clock, she's going to do a photo session, Diana Ross is gonna be leaving the hotel." I'd say, "Come to the lobby and buzz me when you get here. I'll tell them I'm going down to meet a friend of mine and then they'll talk to you because you're my friend and you'll get a picture and everything.''

Sometimes I'd tell Mary or Cindy, ''Oh, some friends of mine are downstairs, four or five guys from school and they'd really like to meet you,'' and they'd say, ''Bring them up for five minutes, let them sit in the living room and I'll come out, do a few pictures, say a few words, then they'll have to go.'' Or sometimes they'd say, ''Well, okay if they can wait until after the first show when I've got all my makeup on and everything.''

I wasn't telling Flo what Diana Ross and the Supremes were up to any more because she didn't want to know, she was sounding more and more depressed. Christmas came and went, New Year and still no settlement. Motown were dragging their feet, the people in New York were losing interest in signing Flo because people were forgetting her already, there were other things happening in the world and by now Flo just didn't want to hear all about how I'd been down here and I'd been down there to see Diana Ross and the Supremes, she was telling me, ''Tony honey, you shouldn't hang out with those people.''

So I didn't tell her, I just carried on and in January Diana Ross, Mary, and Cindy appeared on *Tarzan,* which was a weekly TV show. It was a big hit, I got all my friends to watch it. Diana Ross and the Supremes were three nuns—of course Diana was the Mother Superior, she was the lead nun. Mary had a few lines, Cindy had even less, being the low man on the totem pole. Most of the lines went to Diana Ross.

It was a big thing because the girls were wearing next to no makeup and seeing the Supremes without makeup was like seeing nuns without their habits. They were in a canoe singing things like ''Michael Row Your Boat Ashore'' and of course the canoe had to tip, all you saw was the Supremes going overboard and their dresses coming up and they're all screaming in the water, of course Diana swims to victory and saves

Mary and Cindy from drowning in a mess of menacing crocodiles. And of course they had to show Diana with her cheeks full of air fighting the current, fighting the tide in the water and you wondered if the nun's habit was going to come off her head so you could see how much hair she really had. Diana Ross was even shown swimming underwater and all the publicity went on about Diana Ross, she's such a trooper, she's a born actress, she refused to have a double, also appearing are Cindy Birdsong and Mary Wilson—and everyone said it was a triumph.

Meanwhile, Flo was in Detroit trying not to dry up and she didn't get her final agreement and settlement from Motown until February.

She called me and said she had signed, that she was worn down and she just wanted to get the whole thing over with and she wouldn't be billing herself as a former Supreme. When I asked her why, she told me that under the terms of her agreement she couldn't bill herself like that, and worse, she couldn't even mention ever having been in the Supremes, she couldn't publicly discuss the circumstances under which she left, she couldn't bring any lawsuit against Motown or anyone connected with Motown.

Flo said she didn't care, it was old history. She compared herself to Richard Nixon, "He lost and everybody thought he was down and out, and everybody thinks I'm down and out, but I'm gonna come back, I'm gonna show these people I can sing." Well, I didn't know too much about Richard Nixon back then and I certainly didn't know what was going to happen to him, but whatever Flo said, that was fine with me.

She was glad again, she was happy, she said she had gotten money from Motown, she had cut her ties, she'd been paid for her gowns, she would now be signing a solo deal in New York, and I'm thinking, this is news! Then she starts telling me maybe she'll have a record out by late March, she says she'll be coming to New York within weeks, she says, "I'm setting me up an apartment, darling," which means good times for me because I'm going to be back to my old life with Flo. She's going to be going around, she's going to be shopping, she's going to be recording so I'll be in the recording studio, I'm just going to be in full charge of all of this and when she goes back to Detroit to visit she's going to leave me the keys and I can go in and out and Flo's telling me, "You just stick with me and don't even bother going around that Diana Ross woman, that Mary Wilson or that other gal that's in the group, because those people are going nowhere, you watch!" She said, "Flo is getting ready to go through the roof."

Next thing I know Flo's married Tommy, I never even knew she liked the man that much. She came back from Hawaii—she had told me she was going on vacation but she hadn't told me where or with whom— she just called me up and announced that she had married Tommy in Hawaii. I guess she had gotten her money, gone to the bank, gone to the travel agent, dashed off with Tommy first class to Hon-O-Lulu as Flo called it, and she came back married. I just kept thinking, what? A Supreme married? It didn't sound right.

A few days later Flo and Tommy were in New York and Flo signed with ABC records. This was the beginning of March 1968, and when Flo came in this time it was a slightly different Flo from the person I'd seen eight months earlier in Detroit. She had put on weight, her makeup was heavier, she had her hair done in a blonde type of a frosted color, she wasn't an ingenue any more she was more like a classy lady. She wasn't bitching, she wasn't talking fun and party, it was business and Tommy was just hovering around her like a pot cover. He was dressed beyond belief. He was now carrying a briefcase and they had a limo picking them up at the Pierre Hotel so they could run all over town looking at sublets. Flo said, "I have no time to decorate, that's not how it's done. When you take a sublet everything is ready for you."

So the real estate agent would pick us up. Sometimes he was kept waiting endlessly in the limo for Flo to come down from her suite. She was quite grand, very Diana-ish, I thought, and Tommy was acting very bossy. I just kept my mouth shut. Most of the time they decided that the location or the building wasn't suitable and they wouldn't even look at the apartment, they just stopped the limo in front of the building, peered through the window at the doorman and the lobby, agreed that it would not do, and didn't even bother to get out of the limo.

Well, it took about three days of eight apartments a day to find something. It was on Sutton Place, and when that limo pulled up outside the building the doorman wasn't at the door, he was already out in the street almost getting knocked down, right out there with his big umbrella open to shield us from the elements. He was ready to open the limo door, ready to usher us into the lobby, ready to call the elevator for us, and as soon as you got in you knew this was the place to reside.

The elevator men wore full uniforms, and you were whisked directly up to the penthouse, the elevator door opening right into the apartment. Well, I'd never seen anything like this. Right in front of you was this vast space with a baby grand piano and a white couch and a huge aquarium. I was already thinking, good God, then I realized that this huge place with the baby grand and everything was just the reception foyer—I thought it was the living room. The place was just huge and it was packed with antique furniture and surrounded by landscaped terraces.

Flo was decked out in her mink jacket and her designer dress and she didn't say a word, she just let the man explain what was what, the three maids' rooms, the incinerator in the kitchen so you didn't have to throw your bathrobe on and go out into the hall to put the garbage out, and whatever he said she just nodded her head, just so.

They took the apartment. The furs came from Detroit, the jewelry, accounts were opened in New York, her limo idled outside almost twenty-four hours a day, and about two weeks later the Supremes came to town to do *Ed Sullivan*. This was going to be interesting. At first Flo said she and Tommy were going to go as guests, they had called and made arrangements. But right before the show they got a call back saying we're very sorry but a mistake has been made and there are no seats available for "Mrs. and Mr. Ballard." So Flo said, "Well, we'll just stay here and watch it on TV."

Of course I'm sitting there saying to myself, what should I do? Should I go to the show or should I stay at Flo's? Which is the most exciting? Flo must have read my thoughts, she told me, "Go to rehearsal, but come here to watch the show," because now she wanted to know what was going on with Diana Ross and the Supremes, she was back to wanting my little spy reports again.

I went to rehearsal, I told everybody about Flo's new apartment and Diana immediately started questioning me. She even invited me up to her suite for pizza and soda so I could tell her everything. I told her about the foyer, the incinerator, the elevator with the gates and the elevator man and everything and she said, "Well, I am sure it's not that big."

I said, "Oh, she's got three maids' rooms and she's got four couches in the living room!"

"Well, I'm sure it's not *four* couches, Tony."

I said, "I can count."

"I don't see why she should need all of that."

Well, I was sitting up in Diana's huge suite on the forty-fourth floor of the New York Hilton at Rockefeller Center and this suite was almost as lavish as Flo's apartment. *I* didn't see why *she* needed all of that. Whatever I said about Flo, Diana put it down.

Still, I told her about the fabulous views at night with all the lights of the city and she said, "Well, you know those penthouse suites get very sooty. Anyway, it's not really hers, it's no better than renting a hotel suite because it's somebody else's house so don't get too excited about it." Then she started lecturing me,

"You have to learn the difference between quality and quantity, my dear." That was that, she was through with the conversation and it was time for me to leave. "All right, I'm going to lie down, if you're not finished take some napkins and take that pizza with you." And before I could grab up my pizza properly I was at the door with hot cheese dripping.

So I went over to Flo's to watch the show and there she was, all lounged up on this huge, double-king-sized bed, I had never seen such a big bed in all my life and she had a big tray of caviar on Ritz crackers in front of her because she said, "Ritz crackers are less fattening than toast, and Flo's watching her weight." She had a magnum of Dom Pérignon champagne and the whole time she was watching the show she kept talking about how pitiful the whole thing was, she kept screaming at the screen, "MARY! WAKE UP!" "Mary, can't you see, it's all just Diana?" And when it was all over she looked at me and said, "Honey, you didn't tell me it was *this* bad. Get me another tin of Beluga caviar!"

Diana Ross and the Supremes were doing "Forever Came Today," and Flo started telling Tommy that she should get some more money from Motown because she was sure she was on that record and she was talking about royalties and things I didn't even understand but Tommy stopped her. I'd noticed a lot of times Tommy would stop her from saying things in front of me, they were becoming very secretive.

Anyway, later I brought Flo the record and I told her, "Mary says neither you nor her were on that record." Flo told me she remembered being on all those songs they'd recorded while she was in the group, she said Mary wasn't on some of them because Mary's voice didn't fit in.

She said, "Honey, I'm positive I was on that record," and she was adamant about it. Then she played it, she put it on the record player and she sang right along with it, she sounded exactly like it so I knew she'd sung on the record. Which I was glad of because

I liked it, the fans liked it, they were all saying how it seemed like Diana Ross and the Supremes were getting back to their old sound again, the old HDH sound. Little did we know that this was to be the last HDH record released by Diana Ross and the Supremes.

Flo said the Supremes had recorded so many records that were just never released or not even finished, she said she couldn't be sure exactly how many records but she knew Motown must have hundred of things on her including some solos, and she said she knew that Berry Gordy would release those records as soon as her album came out and she was a big hit on her own. She was very confident, very optimistic. All looked promised, her roller coaster was on the way up and she didn't know, I didn't know, that it was going to have to come back down again.

CHAPTER 13

—— ◆ ◆ ◆ ——

Dreams Die First

Flo was in her penthouse ready to start recording her solo album, and Diana Ross and the Supremes were coming to the Copacabana. All of this was going to be happening at the same time and I just couldn't wait for the fun to begin. It was spring, the fans were out, they were going to be out in full force at the Copa, they'd be busting to get in the lobby of the hotel and I would just be sailing in and out, dashing down from Flo's on Sutton Place or from the ABC recording studios to catch the latest piece of gossip around the Diana Ross entourage and bring it back to Flo.

Things seemed to be going great. Tommy was going off to business appointments, he was speaking to people, setting things up and talking to booking agents, he was hustling around town, the limo was at the curb when you needed it, the penthouse was gorgeous. I started making caviar-and-boiled-egg sandwiches. Flo was happy. She was positive that this would be a hit because she was a former Supreme, six months out of the group, and in the spring of '68 there was still that big cloud of mystery around her, the public still wanted to know.

Flo started recording. I went straight down to the studio and it was like a whole big production, I thought what she recorded sounded great and somebody was spending big, big money. She had this whole orchestra, this being the time when the whole string section worked together and you had the drums, the keyboard, horns and everything, just like a live performance at Lincoln Center. They were in the studio and I sat behind a kind of glass partition, there was a little area about as big as a bed where you could sit and be out of the way and see them through the glass, watching it all happen. Everybody would strike up, Flo would start singing, and it was take after take.

I noticed at some of these sessions that Flo was very nervous and tired and wary, and Tommy seemed very nasty with everybody, including Flo. She just listened and did everything he said, which kind of surprised me. So I was watching it happen but I really didn't know what was going on because Tommy was so secretive, he wasn't at all friendly and he tried to keep me from getting up into Flo's business the whole time, unsuccessfully of course.

But now Diana Ross and the Supremes were in for their Copa run so I had all that to be interested in, and I also had Reggie Wiggins to contend with because this man didn't let up on me, he was very mean and nasty to me, and I guess he had his reasons because I was a handful. I would just go marching right in and Reggie would try to stop me, "You can't come in, you think you're special. No, no, you have to wait outside like the rest of the people." But Mary or Cindy would always tell him, "Oh, he can come in," and I'd sail in feeling very happy and thinking, see, people do still like me.

So I went down to the Copa and Reggie started telling me he didn't want me opening the door, he didn't want me doing this, he didn't want me doing that, I was lucky to be there, I'd better stop trying to take control and he was scaring the shit out of me. Finally he just said, "Listen, you think you're such a cool cat, but you can go wait outside with everybody else because I'm on this job now and I heard that you just do what you want to do, but you're not doing that any more.''

Well, I wasn't going to wait outside with no fans, that would have been too embarrassing but thank God Mr. Gordy's bodyguard, Nate, came along and said, ''What are you doing out here, Tony?'' I told him what Reggie Wiggins had said, not like I was plotting or doing anything Diana-ish because Flo was always telling me, ''Don't do anything Diana-ish.'' I was just really upset. Nate didn't really say anything except, ''You're in now, you get it?'' And I went in with him right past Reggie, telling myself, you shouldn't have said anything. I thought I may have landed myself in more trouble than I'd bargained for.

I just forgot about it. The next day I saw Mr. Gordy and he came right up to me and said, ''So how you doing today, cool cat?'' Right away I knew Nate must have told him what happened with Reggie, and that's all Mr. Gordy said about it. From that day on he started calling me cool cat, and from that day to the end of his time with the Supremes, Reggie Wiggins never, ever gave me an ounce of trouble even though he still didn't like me, because if Mr. Gordy liked you you were in. That's all it took.

It was the same with Diana, even she was just a different story when Mr. Gordy was around. When he wasn't around she could be quite nasty. She didn't usually want anyone up around her suite, she would rarely let anybody in, if you had to deliver something to her from the store she would just crack the door, stick her head out, and take it in. But when Mr. Gordy was there she was just the nicest person you'd ever want to meet. He had a different effect on her. She was nicer to me, nicer to the staff, she didn't bitch or boss people around, no tantrums, she was on her best behavior.

She never paid me too much mind. But when Mr. Gordy was there and he was asking me, how's the homework, do you want some pizza, are you sure you can get back to Queens all right tonight, then she was equally nice to me and she was interested in what I had to say, interested in the schoolwork, she had time for chitchat and if Mr. Gordy wanted to buy pizza and have you come up she wanted that too. It was great.

Then the second his back was turned you got the daggers thrown at you. But whether Mr. Gordy was there or not she was always the center of everything, and in a way it was easier for her to be the center when he was there, because he wanted the same things for Diana that Diana wanted for Diana.

At the Copa, Diana had the same dressing room with the reception area and everything that the Supremes had been given on previous engagements, but this time she had it all to herself. The girls were down the hall in some small room that looked like it hadn't been used since God said Let There Be Light. It was more like a storage room than a dressing room.

I went in and there was Cindy up in her girdle and bra as if she had her slacks and blouse on, she was walking round a tiny buffet table picking through hors d'oeuvres. Mary was in her terry robe, you could see she was in a disgusted mood. They were just waiting on the whim and the whimsy of Miss Diana Ross because all the gowns were in the main dressing room with Diana, and the girls just had to wait for the gowns to arrive. They had to wait for Diana to pick the gowns for the night's show, and they had to wait for theirs to come around.

So there I was, going back and forth up and down this long, dingy hallway between Diana's dressing room and the girls' closet and Mary said, "Tony, go around to Diana to see what gown she's wearing tonight so I could at least match my nail polish. Because she always sends the gowns around so late." And she explained how she couldn't wear purple nail polish with blue sequined gowns, that just wouldn't look good.

I went to Diana's but I didn't dare ask her. Instead, I whispered to the wardrobe mistress who was fluttering around her and she didn't dare ask her either, so I had to wait quite a while and show time was now in five minutes. This is what Cindy and Mary let themselves go through. Then Diana would finally say, "Oh, we're going to wear the silver gowns tonight." So then I took those gowns around to the girls, and the girls had to scurry to get into them. Then I went back around to see if Diana was ready to leave, and she was standing there in something else because that gown didn't feel right. Besides, this one looked better with her wig. Then I had to take the other gowns around to the girls and they had to get out of the first gowns, into the second gowns, the nail polish doesn't match any more, and it's show time. What the hell.

I told all this to Flo in her Sutton Place penthouse and Flo said, "Uh-Uh! I don't want to get involved with that shit. Uh-Uh baby doll, I don't play with that shit because once Flo puts on a gown Flo goes with it and that's it."

She said, "Mary has got to learn to stand up because in the long run she will suffer. She will suffer." She told me, "Don't tell them anything about my record, baby. I won't even have them over to my penthouse," she always put it in two words like that, "I don't care who it belongs to, this pent-house belongs to me now."

She was increasingly bitchy, "I wouldn't set foot in the Copa, what would I want to go to that place for? I've been to the Copa," she said, "and when I go to the Copa, baby, it'll be for the Flo Ballard opening!"

I was running in between Flo and the girls, the girls and Diana. Cindy was less than a year in the group, everything was still new and fancy to her. Mary, who had by now fallen passionately in love with Tom Jones, was parading around with eight-by-ten pictures of him on her dresser, and eleven-by-fourteens all around her suite of her and Tom Jones, of every move they ever made, the ones she could show. She was interested in Tom Jones, she wasn't really focusing on the group as she did when Flo was in it, when it was a group group. Now it was the Diana Ross show and Mary was a background singer, but she would say sometimes, "It's not gonna be for long.'' And she said, ''Flo should have hung in, she should have listened to me because Diana is gonna be gone.'' The rumors had started already, Diana Ross was going to be going solo. The question was, when?

So it was very interesting in April of '68 at the Copa, but the Supremes' appearance was cut short because the next thing we knew Martin Luther King was assassinated. Suddenly there wasn't gonna be no show. The whole thing was a mess, everybody was screaming and crying, Harlem broke out in riots, Detroit broke out in riots, the Supremes were leaving town. They held a press conference that next day at the Copa and everybody was in black. They all looked like they were in mourning. They were leaving to go to Atlanta because they were going to be a big part of the funeral. Berry Gordy was called in to help arrange the funeral, which was going to be the biggest funeral the world had seen since the John Kennedy assassination.

So the show was rebooked for the next month. As they started talking about it I began to understand that this was the only thing to do. It would have been popularity suicide for Diana Ross and the Supremes to continue to work, being black women, after the assassination of Dr. Martin Luther King.

In fact, the Supremes were starting to get a lot of criticism from the black community. People were saying that the sound was too white, the wigs were too much, it was too much about glamor while black people were marching on Washington and getting into Afros and black power. It was beginning to seem to a lot of people that Diana Ross and the Supremes were too caught up in that Barbie doll make-believe lily-white world. (Although from what I could see, they were actually very concerned with the racial climate.)

Flo was on and off the phone, trying to reach Coretta Scott King, to send her regrets. She was stuck in New York, where she had to record her first set of songs—and at that point nobody knew which of those songs would be released. Most of the songs sounded good to me at the time but Flo didn't look like she was that pleased with any of it. She wasn't excited, she was complaining about some of the material and pretty soon even I was beginning to think that some of the songs sounded a bit on the boring side. I was starting to get into Aretha Franklin and I thought Flo should be doing more Aretha-type songs.

ABC was trying to give Flo a carbon-copy Motown sound, mainly a Diana Ross sound I thought. They had her doing these songs that sounded like a whiny Billie Holiday, and only on a few cuts did they let her go. Too much of the time it sounded like Florence Ballard fighting herself to keep her voice down. A lot of the songs, like the Beatles' "Yesterday," were just too damn sad for Flo to be singing at that point, since she was still kind of depressed after everything that had happened to her. Those kind of soft, sad songs made her sound utterly miserable.

They should have let her belt out the blues, let's be tragic, but I guess they thought, we'll make our own Supremes, so they hired some well-known people with Motown backgrounds to write and produce the songs and to play on the sessions.

But at the time I hardly listened to the music. This was going to be a record and I was in a recording studio and it was big-budget. I'd bought some friends down from high school and we sat behind the glass partition watching all these lights and buttons and huge reels of tape rolling around and wires all over the place, we were all sitting there and we weren't saying a word. It was too thrilling, this was Flo Ballard, former Supreme.

By the time Diana Ross and the Supremes came back to the Copa in May, Flo had finished recording, the release of her first single had been announced for June, and she'd started going out and performing in what she said were small clubs. She told me Cholly Atkins had helped put together a choreographed act, so I figured these clubs must be like the Copacabana. It was a couple of months before I realized what kind of places she was actually performing in.

Diana Ross and the Supremes finished out their time at the Copa, they did another *Ed Sullivan* appearance to introduce their latest single, "Some Things You Never Get Used To," which never got past number thirty on the hit parade. Then they went to do the Westbury Music Fair in Long Island, and of course I raced down there to see them.

After the show we were in the dressing room and Mary's best friend, Margie Haber, was there. Everybody knew Diana didn't like her, and neither did the guys in the band, who said, "Who's that friend of Mary's, that white girl Margie, she's kind of bossy, she's always trying to get involved in everything."

But Mary liked her, they were very good friends, and they ran all over New York when Mary was in town. Margie would usually move into the same hotel. At the time Mary needed a friend who was outside the whole Supremes thing, somebody who wouldn't always be talking about business.

So I'm backstage, and Margie comes in and asks me, "Oh Tony, what hotel are the girls staying at?" I know I can tell Margie because she's Mary's friend, so I say, "They're staying at the Sherry Netherland." Margie said, "Thanks, I'm just going outside to tell some friend of mine because Mary and I are going to drive back to the city together and I want to tell my friends so they can meet us there." At which Diana says, "Mr. Tony, can I see you for a moment, please?"

I go into Diana's private dressing room and she slams the door. "WHO told you to tell THAT woman we're at the Sherry Netherland?" Immediately I'm panicking, I tell her, "Well, that's Mary's friend and every time Mary's in New York they always go shopping together and they go out to eat and I went to Benihana with them the last time—"

"Well, you should just check before you go taking it upon yourself, MR. KNOW IT ALL, giving out people's addresses, because nobody around here died and left you boss."

I thought I was going to cry, I just said, "Well, I'm sorry."

"AND," she continued, "you have NO CLASS WHATSOEVER!"

I was just sixteen, I was trying to learn, and that's what I told her. She said, "Well, learn this, ANY-BODY with ANY CLASS knows that you NEVER say the Sherry Netherland, you always simply say, I'm at The Sherry."

"What?"

"Would you tell somebody you were at the New York Hilton at Rockefeller Center? Of course not. You'd say, I am at The Hilton. You never say I'm at the Sherry Netherland, that's why you don't know anything. You say, The Sherry."

I was shaking, I didn't know what to say so I told her, "Well, Margie's going to be riding in the limo with Mary to The Sherry."

"Is that so? Well she must be riding in your seat because there's no more room in there. Now you may go." Just like that.

Now I was really panicking, all I could think was, how the hell am I going to get back to the city? I went out and told Mary, they were having a party in the next room and Mary said, "Ignore her," that's all she said, she just went back to sipping her champagne. Then Cindy, who was always looking for a bit of gossip came over and I told her, and she said, "Don't worry, you could ride with me and Reggie," like I wanted to ride with Reggie. She said, "We're going up to Harlem, we're going to Sherman's to get us some ribs to bring back to the hotel so don't worry, you can ride with us back to the hotel and then you can get a subway back to Queens later." I thought, Flo would have sent me in a cab at the very least.

Some time later, just as suddenly as Margie had appeared on the scene she disappeared, and nobody thought to even ask, "What happened to Margie?"

Nobody was ever surprised when somebody left, or when someone new came. Around this time there was yet another new person on staff. Nobody could figure out quite what her job was, but it was said that she was a kind of secretary-assistant to Mr. Gordy. Anyway, this was someone whom Diana appeared to hate even though she claimed to be her best friend, and everyone was waiting for her to disappear too, but she didn't.

Her name was Suzanne de Passe, she was a knockout, this was the time of the mini skirts and she *wore* them, she wore the *micro* minis. She was well educated, tough, businesslike, a little snooty and she was hip, she knew the New York scene. But she was nice enough and she would turn heads everywhere she went, which did not endear her to Diana.

You could feel the electricity, the daggers thrown between Suzanne and Miss Ross. Diana would treat her rudely at times. I couldn't see what Suzanne was doing wrong, she always had a pen and paper in her hand, writing down everything, poking her nose into everything, which Reggie Wiggins and Roger Campbell certainly didn't like. They just had to dislike it quietly, because she was there by the grace of Mr. Gordy. But when Berry Gordy wasn't there Diana would stop this new girl in her tracks. Suzanne always called her Miss Ross, she was very respectful, "Miss Ross, your lunch is here," and "Miss Ross, I have made an appointment for you at the salon," and "Miss Ross, they would like you downstairs for blocking." And Diana would snap at her, "Suzanne, you are getting under my nerves, please leave the room until you are called for."

However, when Mr. Gordy came to New York, Diana couldn't be too nice to Suzanne. "Oh, she's just a bundle of energy, I always tell her that she must rest, she's always into everything, she is just so brilliant, Berry, you should be *thrilled!*" And as soon as Gordy's gone, "Suzanne, WHERE is my honey and lemon?" And Suzanne, being no fool, played her part

and let Diana do what Diana had to do. But when Mr.
Gordy was there Suzanne would get her back, she'd
freely interrupt Diana, and Mr. Gordy would stop and
listen to what Suzanne had to say, and Diana couldn't
say a thing.

So when Mr. Gordy was in town with the group it
was usually good news. He had a calming effect on
everything and now Diana Ross and the Supremes were
running all over the place doing these big, big shows.
In July they endorsed Hubert Humphrey for President
and performed at a fund-raiser for him at the Waldorf-
Astoria, and around the same time Flo invited me to
come and see her perform in Atlantic City.

School was out by now, so I took the bus down
expecting to her to be somewhere like the Steel Pier
or the Club Harlem, which was like a version of the
Copa in Atlantic City. But she wasn't there, she was
down the street the summer of '68, down the street
from the Club Harlem at some hell-hole bar on the
corner, some place called the Wonder Garden.

I was so shocked to see Flo there. This place was
full of what looked to me like tacky ladies of the evening and their low pimps. I had never seen Flo in such
a place, I had only seen her from *Ed Sullivan* on up.
But she was there, she was pregnant, she told me she
was so big because she thought she was carrying twins.
There was no entourage, nobody fussing and fluttering
over her, no suitcases or trunks filled with costumes
arriving, no glitter, and there was no Supreme air. She
was like a Supreme caught without her lashes, discovered without her wigs.

She was staying in a big suite at the Hotel Traymore
which was once, many years earlier, *the* place to stay
in Atlantic City. Her suite was as big as the suites at
the Plaza but this was not the Plaza, the place smelled
musty, the drapes were almost in shreds, roaches were
crawling here and there up the wall. Flo still had a
fabulous home in Detroit—what in God's name was
she doing here?

When I asked her what songs she was going to be

singing she just said, "I don't know." I told myself, I know pregnant women sometimes get cranky, but how could she not know what she's singing?

As it turned out she couldn't have possibly known, because although she'd arrived with some costumes, with staging, with a whole show figured out, the band in this place couldn't read music. So Flo had to wait while some half-drunk man wrote down on a piece of brown paper a list of the songs everyone in the band knew, and then Flo had to look and see which of these she knew.

I thought, maybe she just got booked into a bad gig. I had no idea that maybe she was starting to need the money. Tommy wouldn't let her go on until she got paid, she had to wait while they went to the cash register to see how many drinks they'd sold so they could pay her. I had never seen any money exchange hands at any of the Supremes' shows, it just wasn't done. There wasn't even a dressing room. Flo had to arrive from the hotel already dressed and made up and she had to wait in the manager's office perched on a beat-up old couch while they waited for the place to fill up, forget about show time. By the time they told her it was okay to start, everyone in the band was either drunk, coked up, smoked up, or a combination of all three. And I was in complete shock.

There was no lighting, just three or four white bulbs, three or four red bulbs, and a blue bulb, and the man clicked them on when they announced Florence Ballard, then when she left the stage he clicked them off and those lights made her look bad, it was horrible and people talked because she was very pregnant, she looked tired, this was not the Flo Ballard everybody remembered. One of the hookers came backstage after the show with a bottle of cheap champagne and she hugged Flo, gave her the bottle, blurted out, "Flo, you deserve better," and burst into tears.

Back at the hotel Flo cried hysterically. She started yelling at Tommy about how could he book her into a place like this, she didn't want to stay, she didn't want to go back the next night or the night after or the night after, she was just going to leave without even telling them she was leaving and I was with her the whole way but Tommy made her stay. He yanked her arm, pulled her aside, and talked with her privately so I couldn't hear, and the next thing I knew they were staying.

So here you had Flo Ballard in some hole in the damn wall, pregnant, fighting with her husband-manager who a year earlier had been a chauffeur, while a year earlier Flo had been in Vegas, she'd been gliding downstairs in a fabulous gown, thin, gorgeous, reputedly with tons of money, tons of fans just waiting for a glimpse of the elusive Miss Ballard. Twelve months later the dream was on its way out. And you had Diana Ross and the Supremes more glorious than ever, endorsing Hubert Humphrey and meeting the press in the grand ballroom of the Waldorf-Astoria where Flo had never even appeared, because after Flo left it seemed as if things only got more Supreme for Diana Ross and the Supremes.

Flo's Supreme dream was dying. Even her grand penthouse apartment was beginning to feel like Cleopatra's tomb, it wasn't fun any more because now it was a financial burden. At first the sun was always shining, but now it looked dusty and gloomy. The antique furniture looked like old junk, the drapes weren't drawn back to see the sweeping East River views. It seemed like she would soon be leaving there.

Her first single was out, it was called "It Doesn't Matter How I Say It," and it didn't go anywhere. But Flo said, "The Supremes had eleven flops honey, we had plenty of flops, they've just got to find the right sound for me." The apartment was still there, the limo was still there, Flo was still somewhat optimistic, but the bills were mounting. "They didn't know how to direct me, they didn't know the direction my voice can go, they didn't know my range, the material was not quite right, but the next one will be better because they listened to me more." And then two minutes later she would scream, "Tommy! You better DO something!"

Her future still looked assured, and she had her beautiful house in Detroit. She'd tell me, "If nothing else happens I can always go home, I'm getting ready to have my twins, I have that to look forward to. And after I get back in shape from the babies I'll start again."

Her second record was released, "Love Ain't Love." It was a better sound, it was tougher, a good up-tempo record and it did a little better, but it still didn't go anywhere because they didn't push it and after a whole year of silence, who remembered the name Florence Ballard? People knew the Supremes, they knew Diana Ross, but Flo was not allowed to mention those names. She was out by herself, up against Motown, and whatever she or Tommy tried to do to promote her, none of it, not a single thing worked.

The good booking agents wouldn't handle her. They told Tommy they'd love to but they couldn't because they'd lose an arm to Motown. Radio stations, even in Detroit wouldn't push her record because they'd lose a leg to Motown. Tommy took boxes of records and went around the DJs in Detroit and they told him, "Hey that record sounds hot, we love Flo, she's a home girl and we think there was some rotten shit that went down in that group but we can't play that. We play it and we don't get the Motown records, we don't get the Marvin Gayes, the Stevie Wonders, the Supremes. We can't touch it." They said, "Tommy, you worked with Berry Gordy, you should understand the way it works. We can't help you with this, I'll put it on at midnight, I'll give it a couple of spins but we can't pump it up like we do with the newest release by Diana Ross and the Supremes, we can't push it and we can't follow it up by saying, remember last year . . ."

Everybody wanted to but nobody would, and ABC Records didn't do anything because by now they were getting fed up with Tommy, they were fed up with the way he would walk in demanding this and demanding that, saying his wife was a Supreme, his wife had to have the best, she'd met the President, she was used to the white-glove treatment, she was a superstar. And they told him, in no uncertain terms, that his wife *had been* a Supreme.

Meantime Flo wasn't getting any thinner, and in October she called to tell me she'd given birth to twin girls, Michelle Denise and Nicole René. Flo was so proud of her girls, and I was happy for her. She wanted me to come and see them, but she was in Detroit, I was in New York, and Diana Ross and the Supremes were about to make a big splash with their first television special, *Takin' Care of Business.*

CHAPTER 14

——— ◆ ◆ ◆ ———

Flo, You Don't Have To

Diana Ross and the Supremes had released "Love Child" in September 1968, which was really their first big hit in over a year. It was as if they had found their old groove again, and the fans who'd started to slip away from them because they had a few other things to think about besides Singin' Supremes and wigs and eyelashes, came back saying that finally, here was a song they could relate to.

These fans were getting older, many of them were a couple of years older than me and they were busy wondering when they were going to get shipped out to Vietnam. They were getting into groups like Sly and the Family Stone, all the new psychedelic music, they were looking at what was going on in the world, they didn't have all that early-teen time to spend pasting pictures of the Supremes in a scrapbook anymore. There was dating to be considered, there was school, which college were you going to, there were nights spent cruising, there were drugs, there were so many other things to get involved in, and as time went on the Supremes weren't getting the huge mobs of screaming, adolescent fans waiting in the freezing cold outside Ed Sullivan. Instead, there might be eight, ten, maybe twelve diehard fanatics.

So times were changing and Berry Gordy saw that.

He saw Eldridge Cleaver and H. Rap Brown changing the way young black Americans were thinking. He saw what was happening to the Supremes' image and their record sales and he decided to give Diana Ross and the Supremes a "Love Child."

This record was so controversial, it was so different. You could relate to it because a lot of girls in high school were pregnant with a love child or you knew someone who had been sent out of town to have the baby quietly without bringing scandal to the family. The "Love Child" message was loud and clear. It wasn't for the sophisticated, moneyed audiences, it was for the teenagers who lived that story, and they bought that record. "Love Child" was a number one hit, their first since Flo left the group, and it saved their pampered necks.

Then, in a completely new twist, Diana Ross and the Supremes were paired up with the Temptations for a TV special. The Supremes were guaranteed to draw a big, older, white crowd, but the Temptations were sure to pull in a lot of the younger black and white fans who'd given up on Diana Ross and the Supremes. Motown called the show *TCB (Takin' Care of Business)*, which was what all the cool dudes of the time were saying, "Hey man, I'm takin' care of bizzness."

So it seemed like the old days again, like the Primes and the Primettes, or the days of the Motown Revues when everybody would get on the bus and tour together for weeks on end—for very little money—until they were exhausted. Everyone thought, this'll be fun, we're all stars, we're gonna be on TV together.

The Temptations thought they were going to be up there starring with Diana Ross. Mary and Cindy thought they were going to be right there working on the background, doing a one-hour TV special. They all had a rude awakening. This was the Diana Ross show, and they were all just Miss Ross's protégées and backdrops. It was all about Diana Ross, all about Diana Ross even without her wig and Ann-Margret-type falls—they had her in some scenes capitalizing on the new, natural look, widening her appeal on the backs of the Temptations and the Supremes.

Motown thought of everything, there was something for every taste. You had Diana doing Aretha's "Respect," except she wasn't really doing it because you had it as a duet, conveniently arranged in Diana's key as always with Diana singing the lighter parts while Paul Williams of the Tempts did the intricate, more soulful parts. Then you had Diana sitting tragically on the floor doing "Eleanor Rigby" for all the Beatles fans, you had the Supremes' medley of hits in case you just tuned in to hear "Stop! In the Name of Love." Then for anyone who said Diana Ross was not with the black people, you had Diana Ross trying out African dances on nationwide TV, dressed in Miriam Makeba-like outfits. These Motown people must have stayed up nights, they had everything covered, like white on rice.

Who could touch these people, they were geniuses. Berry Gordy's show had something for everybody without ever taking the focus off Diana. It was *TCB*, with the Temptations, starring Diana Ross and the Supremes—leave a space of breath, don't run those names together because Motown was now trying to make you believe that these were two separate acts, it was Diana Ross . . . And the Supremes.

Of course, I didn't see it that way at the time. I just thought this show was a big deal, I was excited and when the show came on TV I sat down with my whole family and we watched it from beginning to end with a lot of oohs and aahs and ain't that fabulous because it *was* just spectacular. They had this big, Plexiglas circular stage that somehow reminded me of the middle ring at a three-ring circus, it was raised up so you could see the musicians in the pit underneath. Who had ever seen anything like that before?

Everybody loved it, every family must have watched it and the very next day everybody was in the stores looking to buy the album. The press loved it. Now they were just waiting for Diana Ross to go solo, because how could all that talent be wasted in a pop group? You had to give her praise, she was perfect from start to finish—but who couldn't have been with such a great supporting cast?

Mary seemed more and more disgusted with the situation, and she was trying to get Cindy to be her ally, to put a cap on Diana. But she couldn't stop Diana now, nobody could, it was too late for that. Even I could see that the milk had already been spilled, you couldn't lick it back up and get it back in the pitcher. I'd hear Mary talking to Cindy, telling her not to just go along so easily with everything Diana said. "If Diana says, we're wearing silver sequins tonight, and I say we should wear the gold, bugle-beaded gowns, I think you should side with me."

She was saying the exact same things that Flo had been telling *her,* she almost became the voice of Flo. "Cindy, if we don't stick together there ain't gonna be any group." And Cindy would say, "Oh, well I didn't know," and she'd smile and say, next time, but Cindy always sided with Diana, even when she didn't want to, because Diana was the boss and Cindy knew they could be training *her* replacement down the street if she ever rocked the boat.

Mary told me, "Cindy has no backbone, she won't go up against Diana," and I thought, she's a fine one to talk. By now Mary was trying to make waves but no one was paying her any attention, no one even asked Mary what she thought because Mary Wilson's power, the power she'd had when she sat on the throne at that meeting, when everybody was waiting to see which way she'd rule, when she was the one who could tip the scale by siding with Flo and saying, hey, this shit is not going on, that power was gone in the second it took for the door to close behind Flo. That's how brief Mary's reign on Motown's power throne really was.

Flo was now in Detroit, her roller coaster seemed to be going back down again, but as far as I could see it wouldn't be going down too far. That winter *Ebony* published a big article on the "Former Supreme" at

home with her twins, and they had pictures of her rehearsing, all dolled up in a chiffon gown and the big
pearl-drop earrings, lounging in one of her famous
poses on the floor, playing takes from her album that
was soon coming out. She looked marvelous. She still
wasn't saying a thing about her departure from the
group. "They're doing their thing and Flo Ballard is
going to do hers." Her album was coming out, and it
was going to be a smash.

Just before Christmas Tommy crept into New York
to pack up the penthouse and I went down to help him.
He seemed less bossy this time, less optimistic, more
talkative, he told me about some of the problems they'd
been having trying to promote the singles, he told me
that when he married Flo, people at Motown told him,
"Hey man, why bother, you're wasting your time.
Forget it, that chick is going to be broke within a year,
she's gonna have nothing, Gordy hates her."

I didn't hear from Flo till January when she called
to tell me that ABC had shelved her album and she'd
been dropped from the label. I could hardly believe it.
The album cover had been shot by a top New York
photographer, the record had been mastered, Flo had
given me tapes of the tracks, and I'd been listening to
them—I still have them. The album had been titled,
Flo, You Don't Have To. What a title, it was just like
her, "I don't have to!"

I couldn't understand it—why wouldn't they put her
album out? Why would they spend all that money and
take a loss? Flo said the president of ABC was a golf
partner of Berry Gordy's. When she found out, she
saw the writing on the wall. The president of ABC
told her it wasn't a good idea to switch record companies. Why did he tell her that after he'd signed her?
She said, "Why did they do that, Tony? You're smart,
why did they spend all that money for orchestration,
huge string sections and everything, do two singles
and do a whole album—more than enough for an album—if they didn't want to release it? Why did they

make me waste all my money relocating to New York?''

Years later, the masters to Florence Ballard's album turned up not in the archives of ABC records, but in the Motown archives. What was Flo's album that was recorded in 1968 at ABC in New York doing in Los Angeles at Motown? The big booking agencies said Flo was too hot to handle. They told Tommy, ''They've got another girl in the background now who looks just as good and the group's doing better than ever, so I'm sorry, but we can't take this chance because if we help you, we not only lose the Supremes, we lose a lot more revenues.'' They argued that Flo was hard to work with, that she was moody, quick to fly off the handle, not serious, lazy, that she had a rumored drinking problem.

Flo said she'd been blacklisted. She accused Berry Gordy of not only trying to hold her back and trying to ruin her and not give her the money she deserved from the Supremes, but of then blackballing her future career. In January she sang at Nixon's inaugural ball and that was just about it, her future seemed to be fading right along with her money. And of course she was very, very bitter.

Despite what some people said about him, I still looked up to Berry Gordy. He was still asking me questions and they were still about Diana Ross but now it was, ''Tony, if Diana goes solo, who are you going to follow? Are you going to buy records put out by the Supremes, or are you just going to buy records put out by Diana? How will the fans react?'' I had to think, because I really didn't know.

Mr. Gordy even gave me his autograph once, which was a big surprise because Berry Gordy never gave autographs, nobody would dare ask him for his autograph or to pose for a picture. But one day, I brought down one of my huge scrapbooks so I could show Mary and Cindy how it was progressing, and they both autographed it. Diana just flipped through it quickly, but Mr. Gordy was watching and he said, "Let me see."

He started looking through it, he went page, by page, by page, and I had some pages in the book for clippings just about him so when he got to that he seemed very, very surprised that I'd included him. He started calling everybody over to look, he told them, "You see, I have articles too you know. You people think it's just about Diana Ross and the Supremes but I'm known too." Then he said, "Don't you want my autograph?" I said, "Oh yes! Definitely."

So he took out his big fountain pen and he signed it, and when I took it back I didn't stop to read it or anything. But then a couple of hours later I thought, I wonder how his handwriting looks? So I opened it up and it said, "To Anthony, my good friend. Berry Gordy." Well, when I saw "to my GOOD FRIEND" I thought, this is something! This gave me a new power, because for Berry Gordy to say those three words, it was like you'd won the million-dollar lottery.

Of course I used it, I showed it to everybody who was then living, I rushed right to Reggie Wiggins and I said, "Did you see what Mr. Gordy wrote in my book?" He just looked at it and shook his head, and I snatched it away from him. Then I showed it to all the fans and it was like I had been canonized, they looked at me in a new light, nobody even questioned it because this was considered something very powerful and I now had a whole different aura about me, I carried this aura around for the longest time.

So Diana Ross and the Supremes did "Love Child" and *TCB*, then they came out with "I'm Livin' in Shame," which was about a girl who came from the projects and got all high-society and shunned her mother, pretending her mother died in Spain because this girl had married a guy and was living high. It was so melodramatic, and when it came out everyone went to listen to it because of the provocative title. But the concensus seemed to be that the song was just plain stupid, and the star of Diana Ross and the Supremes fell off again. But the high society followers and the white middle-class crowds, who flocked to places like the Waldorf-Astoria—along with the diehard fans—remained loyal.

I was still running errands for the girls. Whenever Mary called to say she was rushing off for one of her secret rendezvous with Tom Jones, changing flights at Kennedy Airport, I'd run over there to meet her and help her get her bags from one terminal to another. By now Mary was living in Los Angeles. After the riots in Detroit Berry Gordy had moved there with the idea of getting Motown involved in the movie business, and when he moved, so did Diana, and a few other Motown insiders, although the Motown headquarters remained in Detroit.

I'd been to LA to visit Mary, where I stayed in her modern, glass ranch house in Hollywood Hills, with the kidney-shaped pool and the huge, comfortable pillows on the floor. It was clear that she was the most sought-after girl in town. She had a two-seater Mercedes Benz; I had never seen such an ugly, square car in all my life and we went everywhere in it—from Flip Wilson's over at Nicholas Canyon to Steve McQueen's, and over to Mr. Gordy's. His place was a mansion that he had bought from one of the Smothers Brothers, this thing had a moat of water around it.

Berry Gordy welcomed me, and Diana was there too. She was said to be renting a house nearby, waiting for her Beverly Hills mansion to be redone, but the romance between Diana and Mr. Gordy was no big secret by this point, the press was buzzing with rumors that Diana Ross and Berry Gordy were getting married. Some reports had Diana in Bergdorf's shopping for wedding gowns, other reports even had them secretly married for years. They didn't try to hush it up, they were widely photographed together, almost constantly. I likened them to the Captain and Tenille, or more appropriately, Ike and Tina Turner.

The only time I saw that their being a couple got to be difficult was when they were staying somewhere like the Waldorf and they were sharing a suite but no-body was supposed to know. People would come up after the show and you had to pretend that this was Diana Ross's suite when in fact it was a separate suite they'd taken just as a reception center. Mr. Gordy told me personally that nobody was to know, fans or guests or anybody, that he and Diana were sharing a suite.

By this time Berry Gordy had given me the job of greeting some of the celebrities who came to the shows and ushering them up to the after show parties. The guests would congregate, and then when one of the managers gave me the okay, I would bring the first lot of the guests up in the elevator—the most important ones. The bigger the names, the sooner they got to go up but of course it wasn't, "No, I'm taking Sammy Davis and you gotta wait right here," or, "Nina Simone gotta go up before you go up." It had to be done without saying anything, you had to just do it, to make the other person feel good that they were being pushed to the side.

By the time I brought the guests in, Diana was usually positioned lounging on a couch, the liquor was laid out, the bar was set up, the crystal was ready. Mary and Cindy were frequently missing from these gatherings. By now, it was all centered around Diana. She was a whiz at being gracious and entertaining. Very rarely did she get up from her couch, she was like a queen on a throne, perfectly perched. Everything was perfect, nothing was left to chance. Everybody who was anybody came up. You had stars, dignitaries, businessmen, boxers, anybody with a name who could get a free ride through the public relations department, or who the public relations department could get to come and see the show and have an audience with Miss Ross.

In my capacity as greeter at these parties, I always referred to Diana as Miss Ross. I didn't mind—after all, I saw her as the boss. "My name is Tony Turner, I'm helping out Diana Ross and the Supremes and Miss Ross would like me to direct you to her suite upstairs where she will be receiving you." "Miss Ross is delighted you are attending." And even if these were secondary guests who had to wait for the elevator to go up and down twenty times with the bigger names, when they finally got up in that suite and saw Diana Ross, all was forgiven because she was just very thrilled to see you and very moved that you enjoyed the show, and oh, it was simply amazing, she was so stunned when she recognized you out in the audience, she wanted to call you up on stage, she couldn't believe it. Diana always knew just enough about her guests, she knew everyone's latest play, latest show, latest painting, latest speech. This woman was no fool. Nor was I, I kept thinking, this woman's got some style, ain't nobody ever gonna beat this woman.

I heard her say the darndest things. One time, she was wearing some sort of a midi skirt, she was all in black with a turtleneck sweater and tons of chain belts around her waist and she had on these gorgeous leather boots, she was sitting on the couch with her legs up under her and just a little bit of the boot and the heel sticking out, and somebody said to her, "Oh! What magnificent boots!"

Diana said, "Yes, I got these boots in Paris. But can you believe, I actually stood on the line myself and got these boots! The line was so long and I actually had to stand there myself, I just had to have them!" She said, "You know, I was out in Paris, all alone," and with that she shot Mr. Gordy a wicked, knowing glance.

Meanwhile I was on the other side of the room, pouring somebody a drink with the glass half overflowing because I was trying so hard to hear every word Diana was saying. Diana continued on about the hassle it was to get on line, the place was mobbed, they were mobbed. God forbid a Supreme should have to wait on line, this was simply not to happen, but the boots were worth it. And everybody in the room heard the story being told, and everybody in the room thought she was just too fabulous for surviving such an experience. They all thought this was the cutest story they ever heard, and they wanted to know where this place was in Paris, "Oh Diana, it must have been too much for you!"

All this was Diana's world, and Mary and Cindy just didn't get involved. Instead, they went shopping. By now Cindy was shopping in places like Saks and Bloomingdale's, hardly in Gimbel's any more. She was still nice, but she was getting like all the other people around the group, very Supremey. Sometimes they shopped and shopped but didn't buy. Then the next day they'd say, Oh, you remember those suede pumps, what store was that in? And I'd have to remember what store I saw the hundredth pair of damn pumps in, and then they'd send me back to buy them.

Or they'd go to Georgette Klinger's for a facial, I was going there with Cindy almost every day. The first three or four times I just sat there and read *Vogue* magazines and all the ladies went in and out, the place smelled beautiful. Finally, one day I asked one of the cosmetologists, "Do you think my skin could use a facial?" She said, "Oh, it's a must!" And before anybody asked who was going to pay for anything I was ushered into a room, told to take off my shirt and glasses, they put a white gown on me, wrapped my head in a towel, laid me down on a table, looked at me through a magnifying glass and got busy on my face.

By the time I came out Cindy was waiting. She didn't say anything other than, "Oh, you had a facial, your skin looks good, you should always keep your skin up." I don't know who paid, they gave me some sample products and out I went, and every time I went back there they gave me another facial. Nobody seemed to mind.

So I hung out with Mary and Cindy and worked for them, and by now two of the fans had started doing small errands for Diana. One time during an engagement at the Waldorf Astoria in May of '69, Mr. Gordy invited the three of us up to his suite for a chat. He wanted to know, did we have any ideas about the show, and what were the fans saying? We'd been goofing around doing a Diana Ross and the Supremes number, and Mr. Gordy said, "Oh, I'd like to see you guys mimic the girls."

So we stood up and we did one number, I'd had the idea that we should do something he wrote so we went way back and we did "Buttered Popcorn." He thought it was so great and so comical, he seemed to be so amazed and he said that the next night, which was closing night, he was going to have everybody up to the suite to watch us do some more songs. We were shocked, we thought he was only kidding, but we said, "Well, we know the whole show."

So we rehearsed, and sure enough after the second show the next night, like around one in the morning after all the guests had gone, Mr. Gordy called us over and said he wasn't going to start the show until everybody was there. Mary came, Cindy came, all the staff came, but Diana seemed reluctant to come out. She was in the bedroom and Mr. Gordy had to send Nate into there to tell her to come out. We waited, everybody waited, finally the message came back that Diana was tired and had taken off her wig and makeup. Mr. Gordy just looked at Nate and said, "Tell Miss Ross I said to come out here now. Tell her to put her wig back on and come out."

Nobody said a word. Nate went and about five minutes later, which seemed like fifty-five minutes, Diana came into the room as if she were sleepwalking. She looked so tired and so tiny in that big terrycloth robe. She had taken off all her makeup and you could see she'd thrown the wig back on her head because it was all lopsided. She came in, sat down, she didn't smile, she didn't frown, and Gordy told us, "Okay, now you can begin."

We did the whole show. We did the medleys, the hits, the ballads, the show tunes, and everybody clapped after each number. Mr. Gordy thought it was hysterical, he laughed and then he said, "Plus they know the songs I wrote too!'' So after we did the whole show we had to do those other songs. We did the staging, the routines, the turns, the twists, it was like a comedy hour. I think everybody else was kind of bored but Mr. Gordy liked it so much he invited us all to go to the Latin Casino in Cherry Hill, New Jersey, where Diana Ross and the Supremes were going to be performing a few days later. There was going to be a photographer there and he wanted to get a picture of us. He said we could stay at the Rickshaw Inn, that we should call our parents to get permission and he would send a car for us.

So I called my mother from a phone booth at the Waldorf and before I could get a word in she said she had received a call that my father had died. This was my natural father, not my stepfather. My parents had divorced when I was about two and I had only seen him a few times since then—in the beginning he used to take me to visit his mother, my grandmother Minnie, but when she died he just didn't come to pick me up any more.

I hardly knew the man, it was like telling me, ''Oh, the mailman died'' or something. For some reason my mother sounded all upset, I could hear it in her voice and I figured, well, maybe this was her first boyfriend. I said, ''So what do you want me to do?'' Then I said, ''Anyway, Mr. Gordy wants me to go to New Jersey this coming weekend,'' and my mother flew into a *rage*.

''WHAT! You can't go to New Jersey! You have to go to your father's funeral.'' She was screaming. ''Get your fresh self home RIGHT NOW, Anthony!''

I shouted, ''I am Not going to that man's funeral, I hardly even know him. I'm going to the Latin Casino and I'm staying at the Rickshaw Inn. Overnight.''

I dug down deep but I didn't know why, and she kept arguing, it was the hugest fight and in the end I just hung up the phone, and went about my business. I felt very sure of myself. I was fifteen going on sixteen, I was at the Waldorf, Diana Ross and Berry

Gordy were on the twenty-fifth floor, Mary was on the twenty-sixth floor, Cindy was on the twenty-seventh, and I kept telling myself, I have my business to do, it's my father's fault he'd forgotten.

I was all caught up in my own dream. I just kept thinking, I haven't seen the man since I was five years old, what am I supposed to do? So my mother was furious but I didn't care.

We went to Cherry Hill, watched the show, and then Mr. Gordy brought the whole crew back to Diana's dressing suite to see us. This dressing suite was like a palace, it was huge and once again Mr. Gordy had to insist that Diana come out from the inner dressing room to see us perform. Mary and Cindy shared a small cubbyhole of a dressing area on the other side of the building. They came right away. Cindy arrived in a robe, Mary had on this sensational black leather outfit with tight, tight pants and she was holding Jason, her Yorkshire terrier, in her arms like he was a newborn baby. By this time Mary and Diana were both traveling with their dogs. Diana had a Yorkshire called Little Bit and a Maltese called Tiffany. They were rarely on a leash, and if you tried to pet them they'd yap at your ankles.

So everybody came in and we were about to perform when Mary started complaining about the strobe light being in the wrong place during the song "Reflections" in the first show. She stood there with her hands on her hips and launched into what must have been a ten-minute speech, which even to me sounded like a whole lot of nothing, nothing connected with anything else. Everyone looked at her in shock, nobody spoke. Finally Mary finished her speech with Walter Cronkite's "and that's the way it was," announced that she was going for a hamburger because she had the munchies, turned to Reggie, and said, "WHY ARE YOU STILL STANDING HERE? Get the car!" And she left in a hurry like a real diva. No one in the room said a thing, we all just glanced around at each other, afraid to speak, until Mr. Gordy broke the ice. He had a very puzzled look on his face and he just said, "Does anybody know what the hell that woman was talking about?" No one answered him, he shook his head, "That's a stupid woman, THAT IS A STUPID WOMAN." And we continued with our little performance.

By the time the pictures had been taken it was time for the Supremes' second show, so we were escorted out. But they never got to finish that show, and I never got to sleep at the Rickshaw Inn that night, because near the end all this screaming broke out, all this hollering and it was coming from backstage.

Mr. Gordy and everybody at the Motown table, including me, jumped up and flew backstage. It was all confusion. Diana was screaming and screaming, "MY DOGS ARE DEAD!" They were calling the hospital, they were calling the doctor, Diana was bitching, Mr. Gordy said nothing. Diana was giving the orders, "Pack Up! We're leaving! I'm suing this place and we're never coming back!"

The staff started packing up and the owners were going crazy because how could this woman just up and leave right in the middle of a two-week engagement that had been sold out for months, this was unheard of and they were saying it was all Diana's fault the dogs ate poison, and then they said, "Couldn't the Supremes go on without her?" Everyone looked at them like, are you crazy? The Supremes go on without Diana Ross? Get Serious!

CHAPTER 15

◆ ◆ ◆

Who Discovered
These Boys?

I remember in the fall of 1969 Berry Gordy asking me, "Tony, how do you find time to do your homework? Let me see, you must be about ready to graduate soon."

Little did he know that I was by now in the twelfth grade for the second time, I was what you'd call a Super Senior because I had taken so much time off trying to get involved in all the Supremes' business any way I could. I had been busy riding to performances all around the East Coast, hopping planes to Los Angeles so I could turn up unannounced at Mary's house for her impromptu parties, or to drop by at Berry Gordy's Bel-Air mansion. And at school I was a total social butterfly, I thought there was no life after high school.

I was now arriving at school every day in style, driving up in my shiny new Corvette Stingray—my one major indulgence after I got over the surprise of discovering that my natural father hadn't forgotten me after all. After the funeral his widow, Diane Oliver-Turner had contacted me with instructions to be present for the opening of my father's safe deposit box. So I went down to this surprisingly prestigious midtown Manhattan bank, and when I got there I met Diane Oliver-Turner, an attorney, and a New York state inspector, all looking very serious and very shocked that a teenager would show up all by himself for such an important event.

I had to show all kinds of identification, including my birth certificate, to prove that Roland Turner was really my natural father. Diane, who was white, seemed very cold and distant, and demanded to see the birth certificate. I told her, "Listen, lady, the bank officials, the attorney, and the inspector from New York State have all looked at my papers and found them official and in order." I turned to the men, whose faces had gone completely pale, and I said, "Now open the box."

Well, there wasn't much at all in that box, but what it did hold for me would prove to be a foundation for my future. There was a long letter from a father to a son he had neglected. There were also two insurance policies, one that his wife knew about and a large one that was secreted away at another location, and the last will and testament of my grandmother, Minnie Turner, which directed me to a trust fund and account at yet another bank. This one was on Park Avenue near the Waldorf. I had passed it so many times on my Supremes errands, never dreaming that one day I would have business inside that would provide insights into my father's and grandmother's plans for me.

The insurance company informed me that the face value of the policies would double since my father's death had been accidental—he'd died in an automobile accident. The trust officer at the bank told me that the principal amount of the trust had grown considerably, and so as the sole heir I was now, suddenly and to my complete surprise, one mildly well-off teenager.

Of course when I didn't graduate in June my mother was in complete tears—trust funds or no trust funds, this was just an outrage. I had already been accepted by several colleges, but I couldn't go because I hadn't graduated. It didn't bother me, however, because most of the people I hung out with had also failed, about sixty percent of the senior class had returned to sit up in the lunchroom for another year, and I was just thrilled to be back in school with my brand-new car parked outside. I wasn't ready to leave such good friendships or, of course, my own sphere of fame and influence. High school provided me with my own stage, the lunchroom proved to be the ideal spot for my own little talk show, and as speculation soared over Diana Ross's solo career, those talk shows just grew more and more lively.

By now, in the fall of '69, the tensions in the group were mounting, I could see it clearly and nobody seemed to be very happy. Nobody was talking about anything or to anyone. Diana and Mary and Cindy weren't discussing Diana's leaving because Mary would rather not deal with it, she seemed to have buried her head in the sand and Cindy wasn't rocking no boats, while Diana's attitude was, it ain't none of your business, I'm getting up out of this mess. Berry Gordy wasn't saying much either except, Diana Ross is a star because she acts like one.

Mary and Cindy were now almost not moving at all onstage, they were way back and they just stood there smiling painfully while Diana went wherever she wanted to go trailing a long, golden microphone cord. And it seemed like Mary and Cindy now realized just how much Motown and Diana and Berry Gordy didn't need them. They saw it the night Diana's dogs died. There was no Supremes without Diana, those girls just wouldn't have a job without her, and, everyone seemed to agree, nor would anybody else.

It was even as though Diana Ross and the Supremes were responsible for the success of the Temptations, with such widely seen productions as *TCB* and *G.I.T. on Broadway*. Whereas, of course, the Temptations were already stars. But you always felt somehow that Diana had carried all of Motown to worldwide fame on her frail, hardworking back. And it would be the same with the Jackson Five—at least, that was the initial plan.

So tensions were high and everyone was just waiting

for Diana Ross to cut her ties and go solo, but it looked like that wasn't going to happen until the group had another hit. Everyone was saying, she's going solo, she's going solo, the press was full of it, but the Supremes were dying and Motown was desperately trying to hide the fact. Diana couldn't just up and go solo, the timing had to be perfect, it all had to look nice and amicable.

Diana Ross and the Supremes were still playing Vegas, Forest Hills, and of course *Ed Sullivan*—and you still couldn't get a ticket. But that gold record, that platinum album wasn't there and Motown didn't want Diana leaving the Supremes in limbo with a string of flops behind them, because that just wouldn't look good.

Motown had tried just about everything to win the fans back. After "Living in Shame" they put out "The Composer," and "No Matter What Sign You Are," which nobody much liked. But the girls were confident they would get a hit. The old music was changing, the style was changing, and the company thought these were the kinds of songs people wanted to listen to. I would tell Mary that I didn't like a particular new record, and she'd argue that it was a new sound, really different, and really quite interesting. She always looked at the positive end of things but some of that stuff was horrible, she had to know it and the albums were getting increasingly pitiful.

Then, sometime in the summer when everyone was rushing off to Woodstock, Motown tried to change that glamorous Supremes image to fit in with the new hippie looks, and the girls started performing in street clothes. It was shocking. They performed in whatever they felt like wearing on stage, with everybody wearing different outfits—Cindy in a print dress, Diana in a sleeveless designer jumpsuit with a feather boa, Mary in black pants and some long-fringed Woodstock-type vest. I found it very distracting. When they did Vegas or the Waldorf or the other supper clubs they still wore glittering gowns, but for the small tours upstate they just didn't bother any more. The dance routines, the poses, the attitudes, all seemed lost without the usual glitz.

So I spoke right up. "The show looks terrible without the gowns, and people are complaining about spending their money and not seeing the glamorous outfits." Diana gave me a look that said, if we wanted your opinion we'd have asked you. Mary told me she felt "uncomfortable performing without the gowns," after all they were a big part of the image. Cindy said she wasn't too bothered, she could go either way, she was just looking forward to Diana leaving.

So I could only assume that this new stylistic direction was all up to Miss Ross. She was trying to be more hip and current, to experiment, and I guess she thought this was a look to try out at the smaller gigs, but thank God it didn't last too long. It didn't last because it didn't work, and by the end of that summer Diana Ross and the Supremes were still on shaky ground. There was still no hit. In fact, some of the Motown people were saying that the group had come full circle and were back to being the no-hit Supremes.

Panic set in. It wasn't just the Supremes who were slipping, the whole of Motown was showing the down side of the business, and fans were wondering if Motown was really such a big, happy family after all. By now the company was in and out of court with David Ruffin of the Tempts, and with Holland-Dozier-Holland, and the word was out that Eddie Kendrick was none too happy about the way things were being handled, that he wanted to leave the Tempts to go solo. Martha Reeves was another unhappy Motown artist now that the Vandellas weren't pumping out any hits, and even the Four Tops were having trouble. What the hell was happening to the Sound of Young America?

So Motown was sweating because they had to produce a big hit to save Diana's career. Diana was waiting, she was completely off by herself, and as Cindy said, she was "really under the gun." Cindy and Mary were waiting on her, they knew they were just being used to keep Diana afloat until that hit record came along. Then *Look* magazine did a cover story on Diana "The Supreme Supreme." It was the first Diana solo article, and the last issue of *Look*.

By now she had appeared without the Supremes as a kind of comical Snow White on Dinah Shore's TV special "Like Hep," followed some time later by another no-Supremes TV appearance on Rowan and Martin's Laugh-In. The press was just full of news about how many offers Diana Ross was getting for movies, Broadway shows, TV shows, but of course she couldn't accept any offers while she was with the Supremes, and she couldn't just quit the Supremes until they had a hit, so in the meantime everyone was just holding their tongues, holding her back, and the prevailing moods were getting darker and darker.

Finally, just when I thought I was about to suffocate from the phony, strained atmosphere that surrounded Diana Ross and the Supremes, they found their hit, "Some Day We'll Be Together." It was an old song, first recorded by Johnnie and Jackie about ten years earlier, so it hadn't been written for the Supremes—in fact it was supposed to be put out on Diana's first solo album, possibly her first single, but I guess they saw its potential so they put it out under the Diana Ross and the Supremes name and, by the grace of God, cleared the way for Diana's ladylike exit from a desperate situation.

When I listened to this record I couldn't figure out why I could hear four or five voices in the background, male and female. Only later did I find out that one of the male voices was Johnnie Bristol leading Diana through the song, and the other voices were session back-up singers. Cindy and Mary weren't even on the record, they hadn't been anywhere near the studio. In fact Mary, and according to Mary she and Cindy, had been on only a few records since Flo left in 1967— they hadn't been on "Love Child." It was all the work of session singers.

I thought, that Gordy, you gotta hand it to him, what

foresight this man has. He sold us product that wasn't what the label said it was, and we loved it. We just didn't know that what we were hearing was pure Diana Ross starting about the time the group's name got changed. Berry Gordy had been selling us Diana Ross for two years, testing his market, and by the time Diana went solo the public was accustomed to her voice without Cindy, Mary, or "that Ballard bitch."

"Someday" was released as Diana Ross and the Supremes' final single, and the second it looked like a hit Motown made their big announcement, the Farewell Concert of Diana Ross and the Supremes, January 14, 1970, Las Vegas. Motown immediately started planning the farewell because it had to be a big thing, it had to be a bon voyage and a launching pad for Diana's solo career. The publicity had to be right, everybody who was anybody in show business had to be there—this was going to be an important historical entertainment event so the talk and the plans started right away.

A few days later Diana Ross, superstar, played hostess, mentor, and impresario when she brought the Jackson Five to New York. They were going to debut on *Ed Sullivan,* and naturally I got myself all tangled up in it.

Motown had launched a big publicity thing about how Diana Ross had discovered the Jackson Five, that she had found them in some obscure little club and brought them to the attention of Mr. Berry Gordy. And he pronounced these kids great and put them under contract, then sent them on the road. Diana was going to introduce them on *Ed Sullivan* and host their debut on Hollywood Palace. She was going to be the one who carried them to fame on her back like a fairy godmother. That's how it came out. It wasn't Diana Ross and the Supremes had discovered, it was Diana, Diana, Diana.

Of course, ever since that day everybody and their mother claims to have discovered the Jackson Five, and back then everybody at Motown knew it was not

Diana Ross or the Supremes. Maybe it was Gladys Knight, maybe it was Bobby Taylor and the Vancouvers. But Diana was the Motown prima donna who needed the good publicity, so she took the honors.

Diana breezed into town with Suzanne de Passe and some new staff that I didn't know, who were working with the Jackson Five. The Jacksons' parents were there, they seemed to be a close-knit, happy family and the Jackson Five themselves were very excited. I didn't know where these boys had come from, nor did I much care. As far as I was concerned, I was there because it was all about Diana. Who cared what went on with these children?

It was almost like they were from another planet. I just kept thinking, where in the world did they get their clothes from, their outfits were so loud, so gauche and horrible. But the boys were not young star brats, in fact they were very unaffected and nice, especially Michael. Marlon was off to himself but Jermaine, Jackie, and Tito, the three older ones, were more outgoing, wilder. I pretty much focused on Jermaine as the one I thought would emerge as the star.

When I first met Michael he was a quiet young kid offering me a bag of peanuts. I didn't pay him much mind until later. Diana introduced us, "Tony, this is Michael, he's the lead singer." I said, "Oh hi, how are you?" He said, "Oh hi, how are you? Nice to meet you," and then he just stood around staring at Diana and I went over to Jermaine and Jackie because they were my own age and they wanted to know what was happening in New York, this was one of their first visits to the city.

They were all staying at the Warwick Hotel. Motown had gotten them a bunch of rooms together and Michael would wander in and out of the rooms. I'd be playing cards and Monopoly with the other brothers. Michael really didn't get involved in much of that and I, wanting to appear very worldly and grown, didn't pay him much attention. He was just very, very quiet and stayed around his mother a lot.

But when Michael hit the stage he came alive. When he got to the *Ed Sullivan* studio he only needed to be told once what to do. The other brothers needed to be reminded, no you come this way, you do this, you do that. You didn't have to tell Michael anything, you told him once and he did it and he was flawless, on his mark, he was perfect, even then he was dancing like crazy. He stood out from the very beginning, and the older brothers knew their place and worked together very well as a unit.

Michael seemed to be the one most infatuated with Diana at the time, pretty much the same as I had been with Flo, and although Diana paid Michael more attention she didn't seem to favor any one of them. She was the star of Motown and she was on a publicity thing with the Jackson Five that was going to enhance her own image. She was going to be seated in the *Ed Sullivan* audience for their first appearance, somebody was going to announce that she had discovered them, she would very grandly stand and wave, and the Jacksons would perform. Mary told me that this type of thing had been going on in other cities too, that Diana had hosted a big party for them in Los Angeles, and at a club called the Daisy in Beverly Hills.

This was company business, Motown's idea of piggybacking. The idea was to get the public saying, "Oooh, wasn't that so nice, a great big superstar like her—look how she helped these unknown boys, she put them on the road, she's not that bad, she helps people, isn't she lovely." Diana needed this kind of publicity and Motown needed a new supergroup.

But Diana really wasn't too enthused about it. She'd have to work even harder, and she didn't seem all buddy-buddy with the Jacksons or anything. To me, her attitude seemed like, I'm in town with these kids, I've got to make some public appearances with them, Tony, see if you can help me out for once. Take these guys off my hands. You're always hanging around us getting into things that aren't any of your business, now get up in this.

She was all too thrilled to speak to me now because she needed me for something—I was their age, I knew all the stores, I knew what was happening, so I was told to take them around, take them shopping, show them the sights. But I was warned in no uncertain terms to behave myself! Well, needless to say these kids didn't shop Henri Bendel's or Bergdorf Goodman, that wasn't in Motown's budget for the Jackson Five— yet. So off to Alexander's on Fifty-ninth Street I went trucking with these five guys and some weary-looking management type from Motown—he handled the money. We went to the young men's department, "The Tomorrow Shop," and the Jackson Five proceeded to go through that place like a whirlwind, picking up things and oohing and aahing over everything like boys let loose on a wild spending spree in a toy store. One of the brothers said, "Tony, aren't you going to buy anything? Our treat." I said I thought Diana wouldn't like it and they said, "She's nice to us, Diana won't mind." After they'd coaxed me and agreed to take any blame I dived into the spree, admittedly with some restraint. They were so nice to me. I didn't care *who* discovered these boys.

I'd never seen so much energy. These guys sure knew how to spend money! I was shocked because I was coming from a Miss Powell school of thought, and you just did not walk into a store, even if you were only in Alexander's, and behave like that, run- ning through the clothes racks like hooligans and be- ing so very gauche, and then as soon as they got out the store they just couldn't wait to put on their new clothes.

I tried hard to be appalled, but really I had great fun and then we went driving around in a limo looking up at the Empire State Building and stuff like that, I even showed them where Flo and I had met. Then they did their show and became an immediate sensation, and a couple of weeks later Diana hosted their debut on the Hollywood Palace, I thought it was interesting that Diana's script focused on Michael as "a great

young star'' and billed them as Michael Jackson and
the Jackson Five. I thought, maybe she couldn't help
it, being so used to seeing her own name always pre-
ceding the Supremes. At that time Michael wasn't separate and apart from the group. In fact, hardly anybody
had heard of the Jackson Five. But, of course, they
went through the roof overnight.

The next big *Ed Sullivan* event was the last appearance on the show by Diana Ross and the Supremes,
December 21, 1969. The press was by now buzzing
with speculation about the details of the split. Who
was the new Supreme to be? There were readers' polls,
''Who Should Replace Diana?'' There was a lot of
talk about the future solo career of Miss Ross, and
there had also been a big story that focused for once
not on Diana, but on Cindy ''the shapely singer star''
and her boyfriend, Charles Hewlitt.

I was immediately suspicious. I didn't like this man
Charles. He was very quiet, he stayed to himself, and
I never knew much about him because he never said
much. He was supposed to be a businessman, a salesman in the dental supply business, but all I knew was
that he liked the finer things in life. Cindy told me he
had just turned up in her dressing room one day, got
himself hooked up with her, and after that whenever
the Supremes were appearing someplace really hot or
extravagant he was always there. I don't know when
he found time to be selling anything or where he got
all the money to trail behind them. I thought this man
needed further investigation, and I was not alone.

Cindy decided to center her whole foolish self
around him. She was always talking about Charles this,
Charles that, and she would send me out to buy expensive gifts for him. But I was still kind of suspicious
of him, and when Cindy Birdsong was kidnapped in
early December from her Beverly Hills apartment, I
became even more so.

She was with Charles and another, unidentified man
when it happened. As she told it, Cindy and the two
men returned to her apartment, found an intruder in-

side, the intruder made Cindy tie up the two men, then he forced Cindy down to the garage, into the car, and he started driving. Charles managed to untie himself, too late to do anything of course.

Meanwhile Cindy, alone with her abductor, managed to unlock the car door and jump out onto the California freeway. When I heard about this I kept thinking, now ain't that peculiar? What kind of a botch-up kidnap was this? The man didn't even handcuff Cindy in the car. But Cindy couldn't give the police a proper description of her abductor, even though she was sitting right next to him in the car.

The whole thing seemed fishy to me, but this was big news. It made every newspaper and wire service and for the first time Cindy's real age was mentioned, which shocked a lot of people because she was a few years older than Diana and Mary. This was around the time of the Manson murders, so everyone was especially on edge. How could a Supreme be living with such lax security?

Motown managed to weather the incident and the publicity, while still busily promoting Diana Ross's future career. They were planning her split from the group every step of the way down to the finest details, and of course I wasn't going to miss any of it. So when Diana Ross and the Supremes came for their last *Ed Sullivan* appearance I skipped school, jumped in my car, and went on down to the hotel.

I went straight to Mary's suite, and as soon as I got inside Mary said, "I want you to meet Delcina Wilson, she's going to be hanging out with us today, and Delcina, this is Tony. You two should meet." She added. "Delcina lives here in New York," and immediately I asked myself, where on earth did this girl come from? I've never seen her around, I've never heard mention of her, I don't know if she's some relative of Mary's or not, and she seems to be around my age, maybe two or three years older—who *is* she?

Delcina was tall, dark, beautiful, and completely loaded with camera equipment. I later found out that

she was not related to Mary. She considered herself
the consummate Supremes' photographer, and had
been chasing them around just as I had. Somehow we
had never before crossed paths, and she remained a
mystery for some time.

She seemed to take to me right away, but I immediately hated her. She had this bossy, superior attitude,
and she was dressed very expensive. I was kind of
taken aback by her. She had that attitude like, don't
play with me, don't try and pull anything over on me,
don't even think about telling me any hogwash because I know what's happening here. She was no
stranger to Diana and Cindy either. Everybody seemed
to know her except me, I just knew I didn't like her.

So we went on our regular day—rehearsals, in and
out, up and down, there was the excitement of this
being the last *Ed Sullivan* performance, the new gold,
beaded gowns that had been specially designed, the
staging of the show, the fans, the press, the air of good
riddance and the whole time this Delcina Wilson girl
was being pushy and giving an attitude like she's the
one running the show and everyone else can just stay
out of her way.

The girls had to go for some additional rehearsal
over at the CBS rehearsal studio on West Fifty-seventh
Street. Cindy and Mary wanted to talk privately in
their limo, so Delcina and I were told to go with Reggie in the rented Lincoln, which didn't thrill me or
her. But we jumped in, and at the last minute Reggie
jumped out because they needed him inside so I was
left alone to drive with this Delcina girl. That's when
she started dishing dirt about the girls, and I would
say our friendship was formed in the ten minutes it
took to get from Ed Sullivan to the CBS studio, because I realized, this girl likes a bit of news!

After that we quickly became the best of friends.
She was a big Flo fan and we spent the rest of that
day hanging out together, dishing dirt together, watching the show together. And that show must have been
designed for our kind of gossip, it was the most perfect

visual ending to the way things had been going for the Supremes since I first saw them when I was twelve and they were all bunched around one mike doing "Come See About Me," and everybody back at the projects wanted to talk about Diana and her little bit extra.

Well, she had gone far on that little bit and she was still doing and getting it, except now all of that extra stuff was carefully choreographed, carefully doled out, it was all out in the open and nobody had to be told that Diana was the shooting star headed for eternity with a dream that would soon include only her, alone at last.

They came out for the final number after Ed Sullivan made his unmoving parting speech, and they started walking on this ramp toward the audience, lip-synching "Someday We'll Be Together." Then at a certain point way back on the ramp Mary and Cindy paused, one on the left and one on the right, and they remained glued in that position while Diana very dramatically strutted farther, and farther, and farther away from the Supremes and directly into the camera, so that when you looked at it on the screen Diana now appeared to be three or four city blocks ahead of them, she no longer needed them and Mary and Cindy had faded like dying bridesmaids into the background.

It was not an equal split or a happy split, but it was a relief. Backstage after the show they were not all hugging together, nobody was wishing farewell, it was tragic. There was no love lost, and there was no phony pretending to be emotional among themselves. It was a big thing for the press, but it was no big thing for the girls.

The public's support really came out for the Supremes because everybody seemed assured, "Oh yeah, the Supremes, they're gonna be great! But that Diana Ross girl, what can she do alone without the Supremes? Can she go it as a solo?" Some even thought she was going to flop.

But Berry Gordy knew she wouldn't fail. Her act

was already booked into all the top clubs, sight unseen. And backstage at *Ed Sullivan* you could see that Diana could not be bothered with Mary or Cindy. She was concentrating on herself, anxious to get the upcoming farewell performance behind her and clear up those last obligations to the Supremes. She was excited and she was sure she would go out and make it on her own, she was already into rehearsal with her solo show and it was going to be a big extravaganza, whereas the Supremes were going to basically keep the same old tried-and-true show they'd been doing with Diana.

Mary and Cindy seemed relieved. Mary said she was looking forward to running the group democratically and they had decided that everything would be put to the vote, everybody would be given equal say, she thought everybody would get to sing lead now although there was a new lead singer. They had bookings set up too, and they'd started on a new album. They seemed quietly thrilled. Nobody was making any big noise about the future New Supremes.

Berry Gordy was not talking Supremes. He was talking pure Diana, he kept referring to her as if she was an ensconced deity and Diana herself was all talk about her big opening that was coming up in Miami, she was telling everybody about her several costumes, she was going to do something brand new, she was having four background singers, dancers, a full orchestra, eight complete costume changes some of which would be done right on stage, she was even going to change her wig a few times!

The Supremes had never done any costume changes in their live shows, but now Diana was telling everyone how she was going to have minks, diamonds, sequins, pants, dresses, whatever worked with the song and no costume change would take longer than a minute, it was going to be breathtaking. She was going to need a ramp on stage, she was having a special tent designed to be part of the stage for her costume changes. This sounded like it was going to be some production.

Nobody stopped to say, this is the last *Ed Sullivan* girls, remember when we first came on this show? Remember those little chiffon dresses we wore? Remember how nervous we were? Nobody even said, Remember Flo? Nobody let on what they knew, what they felt, what they thought.

But I was remembering it, thinking that from December of 1964 to December of 1969 had been a very fast time, a lot had happened and I was certainly a long way from where I was when I first walked into B. Altman's hoping the doorman wouldn't throw me out on my ear and I first saw Flo standing there looking every inch like anyone's dreamgirl, and just a bit like my Aunt Estelle.

That was a long time ago, a long way off for me now. I was a totally different person with experiences that I never would have dreamed I was going to have. And I guess it was a long way off for Diana Ross and the Supremes too. Right now they were just thinking about next week, the upcoming farewell concert, and all the hullabaloo of these big changes. Maybe, just maybe after all of that, Mary and Diana would remember Flo Ballard.

CHAPTER 16

◆ ◆ ◆

Forget the Fuckin' Routine

As soon as the farewell concert was announced, Jean Terrell was named to replace Diana Ross. The gossip started immediately: "Jean Terrell? Who in the world has ever heard of Jean Terrell?" Her only claim to fame was that she was the sister of a former heavyweight boxing champion, Ernie Terrell. Hardly anyone even knew that she'd been singing in Ernie's group, The Heavyweights, or that Ernie even had a group. And as soon as they'd finished wondering why Jean, they started asking, "Why isn't Florence Ballard replacing Diana Ross?"

I had talked with Flo on the phone a few times during this period and as far as I knew things still looked good. She never gave any reports of any problems and I figured well, she has the kids, the house, her husband, she doesn't need the money, she's going to settle down for a while and maybe when the kids are one or two years older she's going to start up again. She could see what was happening to Diana Ross and the Supremes, she knew they were dying from a lack of hits and she told me, "Although I still feel something for them in a way—it serves those bitches right."

So of course as soon as the news about the farewell came out I was immediately on my private line to Flo and she told me she was definitely going, she said she

257

hadn't been invited by Motown but she didn't have to be. She'd tried to get in touch with Mary and even Diana, but no one ever returned her calls. So I told Mary about Flo's plans and Mary said she didn't think it was a good idea for her to come.

It didn't matter, Flo had decided she was going anyway. She had been a part of it, she was the creator of the Supremes, she'd picked the name, and she was on her way to Las Vegas. Flo told me that Mary Wilson had once again failed to stand up for her old friend. Mary had not even suggested Flo as a candidate to replace Diana. Flo said Mary was too scared to invite her to Vegas for the farewell or even to return any of her calls. She said Mary was probably remembering a big scene that had happened one time up at Berry Gordy's mansion about a year and a half earlier.

She told me the story about one of Gordy's big Motown staff soirées out by his pool house. Of course Flo wasn't invited, but Mary kept on hammering at her to go along uninvited and Flo said she thought it was a bad idea but she went anyway. She got all dressed up and turned up with Mary, and she said that when they arrived, "Tony, you could have heard a pin drop on a bunch of goose feathers—after the gasps had died down." She told me, "Honey, it was like when Moses parted the Red Sea," everyone moved aside for her to glide by. They were all glad to see her, but nobody could appear too thrilled because Berry Gordy and Diana Ross were watching.

Flo said she stayed clear of Berry Gordy, and he made no attempt to acknowledge her existence. He was stretched out on a chaise longue, Diana was stretched out on the next chaise. They had their court jesters around them, so Flo and Mary sauntered over to the other side of the pool, to the bar area, and soon enough Diana started to make little trips over.

Flo said every time Diana came over the whole place got kind of quiet. The first time, she came over and asked Flo how she was doing. Flo said, "Pretty good, and you?" Diana went back to Berry Gordy and they started whispering. Five minutes later she was back, she'd heard that Flo's two singles flopped. How had her career been going since? Flo answered, "Fine." Diana went back and whispered to Gordy, everyone else went back to their conversations with an eye and an ear open in Flo's direction.

Five minutes later Diana's back again, commenting on Flo's weight, and isn't that the dress Flo bought four or five years ago when she sang background for Diana, and how amazing that the dress still fits.

"Yeah," Flo's getting louder, "and by the way, Diana, ain't that the same wig?"

Every time Diana comes over she gets bitchier, Flo gets louder, the place stops moving, and all eyes turn. Flo's slugging cocktails, she's warming up now, Diana comes over to talk about Flo's weight again, and when she leaves Flo finally turns to Mary and screams, "IF THAT FUCKIN' BITCH COMES OVER HERE ONE MORE TIME I'M GONNA KICK HER BLACK ASS."

Everyone stops breathing, all eyes swing from Flo over to Diana and Gordy, and the next thing you hear is Berry Gordy's only slightly raised voice saying, "Who Brought That Woman Here?" He's shooting daggers at Mary, "Whoever brought that woman here better get her *out* of *my house!*"

Flo told me, "Tony, I went to get up off the bar stool and my foot missed the place where the floor should have been. I almost went down but I got myself back together and I stormed out, Mary came right behind me but I know Mary's just scared to death of Berry Gordy, she's scared for her own financial future because that Gordy's drilled it into her head that she can't sing any more." She said, "Why doesn't Mary become the lead singer? Mary can sing, they just brainwashed her. I would have gone in the background with Cindy and let Mary sing lead, but Mary's just a puppet now, she can't do a thing. She's at their mercy, she played their game. But honey, I couldn't pay the price."

In the end Flo said she didn't really blame Mary, she blamed Motown. "Baby, I'm gonna go to the farewell invited or not because it's a public show. I'm gonna go, I'm gonna look great and I'll make the press, I'll make publicity for myself and maybe one or two reporters will want to interview me because there's plenty that needs to be told. Maybe some record company will want to see what *I* can do."

Flo said she was going to go with a cheerful attitude, she was going to be on her best behavior. She'd been very depressed lately but she had been having some therapy sessions and had laid a lot of those old problems to rest. And even though she wasn't in the group, it seemed to me as if Flo felt the same sense of freedom that Mary and Cindy were feeling now that Diana was on her way out. Maybe she was wondering if she'd been wrong in the way she handled the whole situation with Diana, if she'd been wrong in thinking that Diana would never leave.

Anyway, she was going to farewell and Delcina was going too. She was calling me every night, my mother always said, "It's that crazy girl again" and I'd take the call in the private apartment I'd had built in my mother's basement with some of my inheritance. We'd talk on the phone three or four hours about everything and anything concerning the group and Delcina started asking me, "Aren't you going to Vegas?" I said, "No, I need the money for college, I have about three hundred and something dollars for mad money and that's not enough." She said, "I heard Flo's coming and you know you can't miss this, baby!" I said, "I can't go."

I just didn't want to blow the money to go hopping off to Las Vegas where I had never been, where Flo had promised to take me but couldn't because she got thrown out of the goddamn group. So I wanted to but I couldn't and one day Delcina called and said, "You're going to Vegas! You can go with me, I'll take care of everything."

I said to myself, now wait a minute! I don't even know this fool girl that good, how is she going to pay my way? I asked her, "Do you *know* how much money that would cost?" She told me, "Don't you worry. I have plenty of money, I'll be able to pay your way with plenty to spare. A boyfriend of mine is going to be flying out there." She said, "Anyway, let's go out to dine and you'll meet him. I'll send a car for you."

The next day not only does she send a car but she comes to my house in a big black Rolls-Royce. I'm thinking, Great God! And my mother's watching out the window, asking, "Who's this girl?" I tell her, "I don't know, I met her through Mary." So I jump in the Rolls and we go to this really elegant restaurant called La Côte Basque and she's known here, they usher us to her favorite table and call her "Miss Wilson," and before we're even seated she's demanding Dom Perignon and caviar. We start eating, I haven't seen no boyfriend but she starts informing me that he's coming, he's a big-time racketeer.

"Oh my God!"

She says, "Yeah, he's in the Mafia," she says it just like, my husband is a dentist, my lover is a jeweler.

"What!"

She says, "Yeah, you know, La Cosa Nostra."

Just at that moment I see Jacqueline Kennedy and escort come into the restaurant and I do a double, "Oh my God!"

She says, "Now don't worry, when he comes you just act natural. He'll like you."

Almost on cue the boyfriend comes sauntering in and he's got the look, he's got the dark glasses, the jewelry, the long cashmere coat, the hat and everything. As the Dom Perignon and the evening progress Delcina starts talking to him about Vegas, wouldn't it be a good idea if Tony came along, Tony could keep her company, she goes on and on until the boyfriend tells me, just as if it were his own idea and it's the only thing in the world to do, he tells me I should accompany them to Las Vegas.

He says I'm so charming, so amusing, so provocative yet innocent and anyway he has business in Vegas so I'll be company for Delcina. He says it's the perfect thing because he'll be busy and he's really not interested in that show business type of a deal. So Delcina and I say, fine, of course the boyfriend's going to pay for everything and we're going to stay in his usual suite at Caesar's Palace instead of at the Frontier where the girls will be staying, because Delcina would rather be near Flo. We figure Flo's going to create quite a stir just by showing up.

A few days later Delcina calls and tells me, "Meet me for lunch, then we'll do Bloomingdale's. We have to have a new wardrobe for the trip." I've already noticed that Delcina's another big fashion plate. Well, I'm still in high school but I only have three classes, I start school at seven and I'm through by ten so we meet for lunch, then we start doing Bloomie's. We're in the cosmetics department, she's having her face made up, she's buying different lipsticks, a dozen of these, she must have that, she's demanding and getting and it's perfectly clear to anyone that you don't mess with this girl. If she wants something, you find it or else!

She's shopping like a Supreme and I tell her, "Well, I only took three hundred dollars out of my account." She says, "Oh no, your money's no good. Simply put it away. I'm going to buy everything, get everything you need. Get goo-gobs of cologne. Get shoes, Italian. Get everything, 'cause we're going in style!" She tells me she has nine thousand, six hundred dollars, in cash, in twenties! She says her boyfriend threw it at her this morning—for shopping! And I'm trying to stop my mouth from hanging open as I start buying.

We must have bought up half of Bloomingdale's. After she'd done spending the ninety-six hundred dollars she just started writing checks. I'm thinking, this girl can shop! She's *worse* than a Supreme! We came out of there loaded. This was the third trip, and of course there was a limo at the curb waiting because this girl went nowhere without a limousine, there seemed to be no end to this boyfriend's money, even the black Rolls was his and in the middle of all this she told me she wanted to go to F.A.O. Schwartz to buy some gifts for her daughter. Well, this girl couldn't have been much more than nineteen but she had a five-year-old daughter.

Delcina was amazing, there was no end to it. A few days later she decided we needed new luggage. She got another fistful of fifties from the boyfriend and we hopped in the limo to Fifth Avenue, over to Mark Cross to buy luggage. She said she had the tickets, we were of course flying first class, and I should call Flo to find out when she was arriving so Delcina could send a car for her.

So a couple of days before we were due to leave I called Flo. She was still coming, she had made the air and hotel reservations, she'd found a seamstress who was copying some Bill Blass gowns for her out of *Vogue* and *Town and Country,* she was having two special wigs made up, she was going to look stunning. She said, "Honey, I have a whole new trousseau!" I thought that was something out of a wedding, but it sounded good. She said she was arriving two days early and leaving two days late so she could really milk the press, and she had enough money to be seen around town. She didn't gamble much, but she was having her furs cleaned so she could take them out to the heat of Vegas, and since the casino would be air-conditioned, furs would be appropriate. She had it all mapped out.

The day comes, Delcina pulls up right in front of my door in that big black Rolls, I come out with my four-piece set of Mark Cross luggage, my mother comes out and Delcina, who's never met my mother says, "Hello, Eleanor, what's going on? Girl, you look just like Della Reese!" I don't even look at my mother's face. The driver, who looks like a hitman, opens the door, I jump right in and off we go, first class American Airlines to Vegas. Her boyfriend was coming separately by private chartered jet.

We arrive at Caesar's and Delcina immediately starts, "Get me this. Get us that. I can't be bothered to check in. Give me three keys. Bring our suitcases and don't you dare scratch them, they're from Mark Cross, my dear.'' The suite's beyond belief in its lavishness, I cannot believe how huge it is and she's telling the bellboy, ''Get this bar stocked up. I requested a case of Dom Pérignon be in place upon my arrival. Get everything done up in here, I'm a regular.'' This girl is something.

She tells me, ''Call downstairs and see where Flo's at. If she doesn't like her room she can move in here.'' I call. No Flo, she hasn't checked in. Delcina calls Mary, ''Mary we're here. We're coming over.'' We limo down the street to the Frontier Hotel where the Supremes are staying, and as soon as we enter the lobby she shouts at the desk clerk, ''Where's Berry Gordy and Diana Ross?'' When the clerk won't give her their room number she says, ''This is ridiculous. Let's check out backstage before we go up to Mother Mary's.'' The girl doesn't care what she says, she seems to have the attitude of Diana Ross and the spunk of Florence Ballard all mixed in together and I'm thinking, what a combo.

We go backstage, someone says, ''Can I help you?'' I start explaining that I'm Tony, I'm here for Mary, I'm here for Diana, you know, for the farewell show and it's okay for me to be back here, you can call and check if you want. Delcina just says, ''DO YOU KNOW WHO I AM? Look, just show us to the dressing room or GET OUTTA MY WAY!'' Then she turns to me, ''Who the hell does Miss Thing think he is?'' No one's backstage. We call Mary from there and she says she'll be down in an hour, we can go out for an early dinner.

I call back to Caesar's and Flo still hasn't checked in so Delcina says, ''Let's gamble!'' We go to the casino and wherever we go everybody makes adjustments for her. She's telling me, don't speak to this one and speak to that one and curse this one out. Even the dealers in the casino know her—I still don't know exactly who this girl is but of course they give her the best treatment the place has to offer. She takes over a table, starts playing craps, and tells me, "Blow on these dice, baby." She's winning left and right and then she says, "Go call Detroit. See what's happened to Flo Ballard. I'm on a winning streak here."

So I dash to dial Flo's number and to my surprise she picks up, she's crying, she sounds like she might be drunk. She screams, "I'M NOT COMING." I ask her, "What happened?" She tells me everything was set, everything was ready to go, but it was just not to be. She gave Tommy the money to pick everything up, he was going to pick up the tickets for her and Tommy first class, he was going to pick up the furs from the cleaner, the gowns from the seamstress, the wigs, she said she had handed him thousands of dollars to pay everybody for all of this stuff but she felt it was somehow not meant to be.

Flo hadn't seen Tommy in four days. He took the money and she had no idea where he was. She said, "There's no more money, Tony." She was still sobbing, she said all her charge cards were completely charged up between Tommy and that attorney who was supposed to be taking care of her business, she had no way of getting to Vegas, no cash on hand. She said she'd even thought of taking the Greyhound bus. I told her "No, don't you dare take the bus." I said I was going to talk to Mary, I was going to talk to Delcina, and we'd get her to Vegas. Flo hung up.

I raced back to Delcina. I hardly had time to wonder how come Flo could be broke or to think that she could have meant broke forever, because in the meantime Delcina had won twelve thousand dollars and it sent me into shock. She said, "Let's get out of here, we've done this place." While Delcina cashed in her chips I told her what had happened to Flo and she said, "Here's two thousand for you," just like that. Then she said, "We'll call Flo." So we called Flo back and we said we would buy her a ticket, she should come, we had plenty of money. But Flo was too hysterical by now and she said, "Forget it. It was not meant to be," and hung right up again.

Delcina said, "What's taking Mary so long? Let's go up, let's tell Mary." We hadn't told Mary that Flo was coming because it was meant to be a big surprise, but now we thought we had to tell her what happened, thinking for sure she would call Flo and say, don't worry, I'll pay your fare, you can pick up some dresses out here. But all Mary said was, "Well, perhaps everything worked out for the best." I looked at Delcina and Delcina looked at me, it was the same look I'd seen pass between Flo and Mary when they were upset with Diana. And then we knew there was no need to discuss it any further with Mary, and we thought maybe the rumors were right about Berry Gordy sending Flo a message to tell her, don't come, don't spoil everything. We called Flo again, we knew she *had* to come. Her mother answered and said no, it was too late, Flo was unavailable.

Well, now that Flo wasn't going to be staying at Caesar's Palace Delcina decided that the whole idea of us staying there was out of the question, we had to immediately move to the Frontier Hotel which is where the show was. So she went to the front desk and demanded a suite. They told her the hotel was fully booked, no way in the world could she get a suite, not even a couple of rooms. She proceeded to fly into a complete rage, a total ranting and raving fit, demanding to see the manager, screaming like a wild woman, demanding that someone simply be asked out!

I was visibly startled and she told me, "Calm *down*. Wait right here, I'll be out." They rushed her into the manager's office with her waving the ten grand and I waited outside. About ten minutes later, which seemed like ten hours to me, she came out. "We're moving." So I said, "Oh, we have to go pack." She said, "No we don't! They've already called Caesar's, they're packing our stuff up right now, it'll be here shortly. Here's your key to our suite, darling." I thought, this girl knows how to do things! I must learn from her!

Meanwhile I was thinking, where's the boyfriend? When he finally showed up, discovered we were not at Caesar's and found us at the Frontier, he just dropped his bags, changed his clothes, and disappeared. Delcina said, "Don't pay him no mind," she didn't care. Delcina changed her clothes and we headed for the casino once more.

On the night of the show we went backstage, where the tensions and bitchiness were barely covered. It was a mob scene with all the stars, all the Motown people, everyone was nervous. They were going to record the final parts of a live album that night, having already recorded everything for the past three nights, and the show wasn't 'til midnight—everybody was calling it "the bewitching hour." We called Flo again, she was still unavailable.

Backstage wasn't the big party I thought they'd have on a night like this, it was just a lot of people and a sense of relief in the air. I noticed that everyone knew Delcina, everyone seemed to like her. Mary was there steadily sipping champagne, steadily sipping, steadily sipping and surprise surprise, her old friend Margie had turned up, "like a bad penny" Delcina said.

Diana hadn't been seen all day. She was up in her suite in complete seclusion. Cindy was going around the huge buffet table eating everything that wasn't nailed down, plus she was chomping away on the box of chocolates Charles had sent like there was no tomorrow. Delcina thought nothing of telling her, "CINDY! GIRRL! Don't EAT like that, consider your WAISTLINE!" I thought I was bad, but this girl was ferocious!

By show time Mary was in my opinion getting decidedly and determinedly quite bold, saying, "I'm not going to let Diana outdo me or push me to the side or upstage me, not tonight." She was telling Cindy, "Sing out loud and sing out clear, if Diana picks up her mike, if she deviates from the routine, forget the fuckin' routine, if she does something she doesn't normally do like ad lib forever or go out in the audience, you pick up your mike and you do the same.''

She tells her, ''This is the last time we're ever going to be on stage with her, and she's going to go all out. Trust me, I've known her a long time, maybe too long. She's got the press here, she's got the stars, she's got Gordy's family, and she's going to think nothing of it. She's going to do just like Gordy always tells her, 'forget the other girls, go for yourself.' Cindy, tonight, go for *yourself*, 'cause girl, I'm going for mine.'' And I'm thinking to myself, Mary, girl you should have felt that way years ago.

Well, when they hit that stage that's exactly what they did, they went for themselves. The place was packed, you'd have had to have been Twiggy to get through those tables. Diana Ross and the Supremes were working that stage that last go-round and the whole thing was just like a Supreme free-for-all. It was like a three-ring circus, you couldn't watch the whole thing, you had to keep switching from girl to girl because this was not a trio any more, it wasn't even Diana Ross and the Supremes, it was every woman, every would-be diva for herself.

Cindy was the only one who kind of stayed where she should have been. She did a little extra but not too much. Diana upstaged them something terrible, she had tons of cord, she was just all over the place. She was hamming it up with the audience, singing ''My Man'' directly to Berry Gordy, she was sitting on the floor, sitting on the edge of the stage, going up a staircase, she was out in the audience, she was sitting on people's laps, she was having people sing along with her. She was parading through the audience telling some of the Motown women, ''Oooh, you could have been one of the Supremes! You could have been a Supreme!'' It was like, anyone could have been a Supreme but nobody could have been Diana. The Supremes didn't even matter at this point.

Mary was half singing, half screaming at the top of her lungs because her mike was turned down so low, and by the time the show was halfway through she sounded all hoarse and off-key, she was going on and on and on in no apparent tune with anybody else. They did show songs, they did psychedelic stuff like "Aquarius" that went on for ever, they did old Supremes' hits like, "Baby Love," and "Stop! In the Name of Love," they did "Love Child" and they ended with "Someday We'll Be Together," but none of those hits sounded quite like anything people expected. Diana Ross and the Supremes were finally finishing, it was time to wake up.

It was definitely the end of an era. The girls got gold watches, flowers, Ed Sullivan had sent a telegram, a big banner was hoisted that said "GOOD LUCK TO DIANA" in huge letters and then in smaller letters, "And Continued Success To The Supremes." Nothing had changed.

Then they brought Jean Terrell up on stage and I thought, she's sort of plain, she's tall, she's gawky, she's not the most feminine thing I've seen. Mary and Cindy were standing there with hair cascading from these Gibson girl-style wigs with falls attached, and Diana had her usual big Diana Ross special with the hair flicking over her eye. But this Jean Terrell had on the tiniest, shortest, pixie grandmother wig and I told myself, I don't think she looks right for the part!

She was towering over Mary and Cindy in some little, plain, polyester-type number with a little jacket that looked like it was off the rack at some bargain cocktail dress store (although it wasn't), and Mary, Cindy, and Diana were standing right next to her in their black velvet, full-length Bob Mackie gowns. It was like standing your neighbor up next to some glamorous stars, and I figured, why didn't anybody at Motown think, we're gonna put her up on stage, we're gonna unveil her to the world tonight, let's get her a dazzling gown and let's get some hair on this woman's head!

Of course, there was a huge party afterward which was more like a mob scene trying to look like a party, and I was introduced to Jean. Close up she looked a lot better. She seemed nice but kind of withdrawn. I thought she was shy because of all the excitement, all the press coming at her left and right, she seemed overwhelmed by it all. As for Delcina's boyfriend, he didn't appear until the next day. He rolled in, said he had business to take care of, and rolled out again, but I noticed that all the Motown people seemed to know him, even the band knew him, although he certainly wasn't there to see the show or hang out with the stars. Delcina paid him very little attention, he just gave her money if she ever ran out, which she hardly ever did.

It was all over. We left town like we came with Delcina and I flying first class, limo, the whole bit and the boyfriend on another private jet. By the time we left Vegas we must have called Flo about twenty times, Delcina was on and off the phone talking to Flo and her mother like she had known them for fifty years, demanding that Flo just get on a plane, first-class ticket, limo would meet her, telling her we'd take her shopping, get her some outfits, and she would go to Georgette Klinger for a facial, someone would come to the suite and do her hair and makeup, Delcina would take care of it all and on and on, but Flo was too upset. She wasn't coming. She was missing the big farewell, missing her big comeback, and she sounded all worn out.

You could tell she'd been crying, you could hear her kids in the background, Tommy hadn't showed up yet, and I just felt sad because this was not the way I had ever thought it would turn out, with the original Supremes going on three separate roller coasters headed in three separate directions, and Flo's going so far and violently down.

The farewell show was all over, and everything yet nothing had changed. Diana and Berry Gordy went off to the blackjack tables to gamble big money on their movie-star dreams, Mary escaped to her suite with her friend Margie and sat up till dawn toasting the bright, free future, Cindy partied the night away, and Flo was left in Detroit, broke, drunk, and beat.

Someone had shot her moon. And I couldn't understand what had happened to her dream, until I knew her nightmare.

CHAPTER 17

◆ ◆ ◆

"Don't Quote the Obvious"

It was 1970 and the big farewell was over. Diana Ross and the Supremes were now officially what they had actually been since the summer of 1967, the summer when Flo was suddenly ditched in Vegas—they were back to being called just the Supremes. For the longest time they had been two acts managed as two separate entities, with Diana Ross doing her solo act and the Supremes tagging along behind as her background adornment. Maybe it started back in the summer of '65 at the Copa, when Gordy took "People" away from Flo and presented it to Diana.

But to me a whole different time was now beginning. The sixties were over, I was finally coming up to graduation, and I couldn't wait, I'd had enough, I was by now applying to colleges in New York. I had never even considered going out of town because New York was where the action was, to me New York was parties and music and clubs and Supremes business, and that's what life was. I thought, the new Supremes are coming in, they're going to get a big introduction on *Ed Sullivan*, it's going to be fabulous. It took me the longest time to realize that the Supremes had become just a Motown name and a Motown-made image, with a succession of divas coming and going while Mary Wilson fought valiantly to hold it all together.

The first time I saw the New Supremes was in February, a month after the farewell, when they came to do their first *Ed Sullivan* appearance without Diana. Mary had telephoned me to ask if I could bring my car because they wanted to do some running around. Now why on earth would they want to use my car when they had a limo sitting outside the theater? But I didn't think about it too much. I decided to borrow my father's car because my Corvette wasn't big enough to fit me and three Supremes.

It was a snowy Saturday night in New York City, the traffic was a mess, and I was just going to be late. By now the whole thing was no big deal—I hadn't even tried to rush there for the rehearsal or anything. But from the moment I got there I was surprised because there was no limo waiting outside, there were no fans waiting by the door. I went inside, the girls were already getting packed up and ready to leave for the day and immediately it seemed like I had slipped back in time, back to the first time six years earlier when I had bravely marched my nosy self into the *Ed Sullivan* studios with my head full of spy tricks. There was nobody fussing around the girls, nobody helping them get packed up or hurrying them along.

Berry Gordy wasn't there, no tons of staff, no Gil Askey the musical conductor, no hairdresser, no wardrobe mistress, no make-up artist other than the ones employed by Ed Sullivan. They had a skeleton crew, just like the first time they had appeared on *Ed Sullivan*. That first time it was all so fabulous to me, and now I thought, oh my God, where's the limo? Where's the entourage?

Roger Campbell was nowhere to be seen. Reggie Wiggins was there, now promoted to head road manager. Reggie seemed different, not so arrogant or bossy, he seemed genuinely relaxed. Even in those five minutes before I left with the girls he was actually being friendly and I figured, well maybe the pressure's eased off now that Diana isn't around.

Mary said they wanted to go look at some new wigs,

so we piled into my father's car. We went around to the wig shop, which was staying open late for the Supremes, and they had this whole big selection of wigs layed out for the girls. Right away Jean Terrell started complaining that the prices were too outrageous, but I was looking at the tiny, acrylic-type wig she had on and, believe me, she needed a wig and she needed it quick.

She tried on wig after wig, none of which pleased her, and Mary was giving suggestions, being very accommodating almost to the point of phoniness. On the other hand, I was telling Jean, "Girl, that wig don't look right on you, that color is not for you. Try this one, try something a bit more Diahann Carrollish."

Meanwhile Mary was shooting me the evil eye like, don't keep putting your two cents in. "Oh, Tony, don't be so picky, let Jean decide. She's the one that's got to wear the wig."

"Well, *I* know the look," I informed her.

Just at this point I heard a big commotion, a big banging on the door downstairs, and then all this screaming and I was thinking, I hope this place isn't getting ready to be robbed. So I took a peek and there was Delcina Wilson standing at the door screaming, "Tony, will you tell THIS BITCH to let me in before I knock her down!" And before I could say a word she just pushed the saleswoman out the way and marched upstairs. She came in like a complete whirlwind, took one look at Jean, and immediately said, "Wrong. Wrong. Wrong. That wig is definitely wrong da'ling. You need more hair, you're a big girl!"

Nobody said anything. Then the hairstylist spoke up, "Yes, yes, I think she's right. Let me show you something a little fuller." And after much coaxing from me, Delcina, Mary, and Cindy, and after much looking at the price tags and Mary telling her not to worry about it, Motown would pay for everything, Jean finally picked a wig—which was none too soon because it was getting late and we had to meet Cholly Atkins for extra rehearsal downtown.

We went driving off through the snow. I was trying to go fast but not too fast because I had the New Supremes in my step-dad's brand-new Caddy. When we got there I was in for another surprise because this was no big-time CBS-type rehearsal studio, but rather an old, old loft-type building with a narrow, narrow staircase that was very steep and when we finally got to the top the studio actually turned out to be somebody's apartment.

I thought, is *this* where the girls are supposed to rehearse their new song that they're going to be performing *tomorrow* on *Ed Sullivan?* I was also kind of surprised that they didn't have this all rehearsed already, I figured maybe Cholly had made some last-minute changes. But as they started running through their new song, "Up the Ladder To the Roof," I could see that Jean was having a bit of trouble getting the movements to flow as gracefully as Cholly thought they should.

She was trying to fit in, but then again she kept saying how uncomfortable she was with some of the steps. And I said to myself, *this* girl is just like Diana, the same stubbornness, the same medicine but in another bottle.

Delcina and I were perched in the corner looking shocked. We couldn't believe what we were hearing. Mary was jumping to help, trying to see that everything went nice and smooth, trying to play the peacemaker all over again, and finally she told Cholly, "Let me show Jean what you mean." So Cholly took a break and came over to talk with Delcina and me while Mary, who thought she knew what Cholly meant but didn't, tried to help Jean along with Cindy, who also thought she knew what he meant but didn't.

Cholly came over and asked me, "Have you heard from Flo?" Well, after the farewell fiasco I had only talked to Flo briefly a couple of times, I didn't think it would be proper to go into a lot of detail with her about how fabulous the show was, how everybody was there, how it went on and on and everything and

Cholly said, "I think you should call her for a chat because she's run into some difficulties."

I told him, "Well I know she was having some difficulties between her and Tommy."

"It's more than that," he said. "You should call her because she needs people who love her. You should talk to her, things are changing rapidly for her."

I thought nothing more about it, I thought maybe things were changing for the better, and just at this point we looked back and saw that Mary and Cindy had shown Jean something that was not what it should have been. Cholly went over and did the best he could, but everyone was tired and it was decided that rehearsal would continue in the morning.

As we all left, Mary almost killed herself coming down those steep steps in her maxi-length coat. Had I not been in front of her she would have gone down the whole flight. Immediately she started saying the oddest thing, "Tony, if I fell down at this point and ruined my face Gordy would *kill* me. Gordy would absolutely kill me. Cholly, you gotta find a better rehearsal studio, some place with an elevator."

Cholly didn't say a word.

Back at the hotel Mary showed me the new album, which was yet another surprise. The gowns they were wearing on the cover were the same gowns that Diana Ross and the Supremes had worn. I guess I looked kind of shocked because Mary said, "Well, Tony, we gotta work with what we have."

For once Delcina didn't comment, but the moment we left there she said, "How shocking, no new gowns! The girls have come down a step!" I was still taking it all in. I thought, maybe tomorrow the limo will be there, Berry Gordy will be there, the entourage will be there.

The next day Delcina and I went to catch the one o'clock dress rehearsal at Ed Sullivan and arrived to find the girls wearing the new wigs and the old Diana Ross and the Supremes gowns. Motown had not bought new gowns for the new group's debut. Mary had squeezed herself into Diana's old gown because Jean, who was bigger and taller had to squeeze—and I do mean squeeze—into Mary's old gown, and despite the adjustments that had been made, the gown looked like it might burst at any moment. What an injustice!

I looked to Delcina because I didn't know whether to laugh or cry. It was so comical, but at the same time the whole thing was pitiful. Mary said they would be getting new gowns, this was only temporary. As it turned out there would be very few new costumes bought for the Supremes—they would continue to squeeze into all of those old gowns for years.

The dress rehearsal went fine, the show went fine, I thought it was actually very good and Jean had a style all of her own, she didn't try to copy Diana. She was pure voice, she didn't have the mannerisms or the theatrics. Jean had this attitude like, I'm a professional, I'm a singer, I'm pure voice, I don't need Diana's extra flimflam. I am *not* the Ross girl.

Cindy and Mary sounded great on background, I guess I wasn't used to hearing their voices on most of those Diana Ross and the Supremes records because this sound was now surprising. The background voices were turned up again like they had been for all those early Supremes hits, the harmonies were back, and it made me sit up and listen.

Even so, the Motown honchos and the expected entourage never showed up. All you had was Ed Sullivan saying his usual, "Ladies and Gentlemen, the Supremes," and then the girls sang their new release. It was like riding in limousines and Cadillacs all your life with maybe two other limos trailing behind you and Hertz rental trucks arriving ahead of you with trunks full of costumes, and then suddenly you're in a Ford with a couple of suitcases each. It was too sudden, and when it was all over I asked Mary, "Where's everybody?"

"Don't quote the obvious," was all she answered.

The Supremes left town without the usual broohaha, it was very subdued but Mary said she enjoyed it this way. "People have to grow, people have to change, you have to be open to new ideas." I was appalled, I was dismayed, to me this was not what the Supremes were all about.

As soon as they were gone Delcina said, "Let's see what Diana's up to."

So she made the arrangements—Diana was going to be opening her new solo tour in Miami at the Fontainebleau Hotel which for Delcina was like saying Diana was going to be at Bonwit Teller at two o'clock. Traveling, airfare, hotels, all of this meant nothing to her. She said, "We simply must go," and by this time I didn't even question where the money was coming from. Delcina said everything would be taken care of, and as usual it was.

We flew down first class and of course Delcina had a limo waiting at the airport in Miami, we raced off to the Fontainebleau Hotel and found Diana surrounded by staff and costumes and fresh flowers and press and everything you'd expect plus more. Gil Askey was with her, she had two people taking care of costumes, she had tight security, make-up people, hairdressers. And Berry Gordy was standing guard.

Diana was unusually friendly and relaxed. She was a solo star and she didn't have to worry about the other girls or about stepping on anybody's toes or having people say how rude or nasty she was. She was grander than ever, and as soon as we saw the thousands of dollars' worth of Bob Mackie costumes and we saw the all-white audience and the huge red velvet tent up on stage with two women stationed inside to rip the costumes off her, the dancers, the background singers, we knew this show was going to be something to talk about.

Even so it was startling. The show opened with Diana singing from the wings, you saw no one, all you heard was the first verse of "Don't Rain on My Parade" booming over the loudspeakers. But when you saw her come out it was another thing. She burst out on that stage and all you saw was this tiny little face and long eyelashes under the hugest, huger-than-Angela Davis Afro wig, and you're saying, my God, how is this woman balancing that Afro on top of her head and then the spotlight widens around her and you notice the gown. My God the woman is wearing the African liberation colors of red, black, and green.

She had been accused of being too white, too pop, too this, too that, and here she was in this African-style sarong dripping and glittering in red, black, and green sequins and bugle beads, and she was singing a Barbra Streisand tune. The whole thing was stunning.

Just about the first words Diana spoke on stage were, "Welcome to the Let's-See-If-Diana-Ross-Can-Make-It-On-Her-Own Show," and the audience cracked up. She had great background singers, the same group that had backed her up in the studio when she was Diana Ross and the Supremes, except now they were called the Black Berries instead of the Andantes. She had two male dancers, and after the opening number she disappeared into her red tent, threw off her African regalia, and popped back out in another startling outfit. I don't know how many times she changed costumes, some of the changes were done right on the stage with the two dancers undressing her while the spotlight was just on her face.

She sang show tunes, her own new material, but no Supremes tunes except for one mandatory, teary-eyed medley. This was a completely new show, a new concept, and it was sensational, one of the most dazzling things I had ever seen. How that woman did that stuff two times a day with all the wigs and costumes was beyond me. I thought there was no limit at this point, I thought she would never top this show. But of course she did, over and over again.

We knew that Diana had been in the studio much more than the Supremes had been, we knew she had been testing out several different producers, that they had even gone to non-Motowner Bones Howe, a big pop producer. It seemed that Berry Gordy had begun forsaking his own producers and writers, experimenting with outsiders and trying to come up with a hit for Diana. Diana had told me she was going to be releasing an album called *Time and Love*, written by Laura Nyro and produced by Bones. She and Gordy were very high on it. I don't know what happened with all that material, because it never saw the light of day. By the time Diana's first solo recording was released she was doing something completely different, something tried and true—she was doing some Ashford and Simpson material.

But Diana's first release, "Reach Out and Touch (Somebody's Hand)" didn't turn out to be the big hit it was supposed to be, never climbing past number twenty on the pop charts. The black-tie-and-furs crowd paid to see Diana's shows in places like the Waldorf in New York, but the younger crowd rushed out to buy the New Supremes' records. The Supremes got hit after hit, but their show didn't really change.

I went back down to Miami a few weeks later to catch their first show—not at the Fontainebleau, but one step down at the Deauville Hotel. For their show, the Supremes wore the gowns they had worn on the TV special, *G.I.T. on Broadway*. There were no costume changes, no dancers, still no big staff and still no Berry Gordy, but it was a very good show.

We spent our days in Miami lounging around the pool. Margie Haber had surprisingly reappeared and was sticking to Mary like a Siamese twin, they were talking non-stop about Tom Jones, how relieved Mary was that she was finished with him and all that she had been through.

One afternoon I went up to Mary's suite that she shared with Jean, and I was quite surprised to see Mary and Reggie sitting there listening to the Temptations' "Cloud Nine" and smoking a joint. This was something altogether new, but Mary was very casual, very matter-of-fact and she offered me some. "I don't even know how to smoke," I said.

She said, "Try it," and I immediately choked to death. At which Mary commented, "You didn't inhale it properly. Well, don't tell anybody I smoke." I said okay, and that was that.

Times were changing, life around the Supremes was changing, but they didn't want to change their image. After Diana's solo tour people started asking, when are the Supremes gonna ditch those wigs and appear in naturals? *Soul* magazine asked Mary in an interview and she said she didn't think Afros or Afro wigs looked good with beaded gowns. People were stunned by her statement. The fans were now college kids and senior high school kids, and they were no longer letting their mothers straighten and relax their hair, these kids wanted to stay current. And sure enough on the back cover of the New Supremes' second album, *New Ways but Love Stays*, there was a sensational picture of the girls in black turtlenecks, no sequins, no gowns, and what looked like their own hair in Afros.

They tried it and that was that, no big fuss was made. The album did well and "Stoned Love," which was the single off that album, went to number one on the R & B charts and earned them another gold, but you'd hardly have guessed that they were selling more records than Diana because Motown wasn't putting any publicity behind the New Supremes—everything was stacked up behind Diana Ross, of course.

Diana was getting the TV specials and the movies and she was playing in the top spots, while the Supremes were slipping to B group—even C group— status. Mary didn't even want to hear about what Diana was up to, and of course Diana couldn't be bothered with any Supremes news. The Supremes were dead and gone as far as she was concerned, she never even mentioned them, and nobody ever mentioned Flo until one day the notorious, fabulous Gregg the hairdresser reappeared on Mary's staff.

I hadn't seen Gregg since Flo was put out of the group and we soon got back to dishing dirt about the girls. One night he told me he'd gotten fired because Diana was jealous of him, Diana couldn't stand to see him get more attention than she did. He said,

"That woman's lack of self-confidence was unbelievable, she was jealous of anyone that got any attention be it man, woman, or child."

But he had to agree that Diana's solo show was not to be beat, that she seemed to be more relaxed and natural since she left the Supremes, and that life around the Supremes was definitely more pleasant since Diana left. In fact life was so pleasant, so casual, so loose, there was nobody watching every move, it almost seemed like there was no real management at all and pretty soon the whole thing started turning into a big mess of confusion.

Nobody was really concentrating on Supremes business, it was all dogs, boyfriends, girlfriends. During their first appearance at the Copa in the spring of 1970, Tom Jones was in town doing the last three days of his Waldorf, Empire Room engagement so Mary, who'd obviously forgotten those conversations she had with Margie by the pool in Miami, decided to stay at the Waldorf. Meanwhile Cindy and her boyfriend, Charles, had secretly pushed their two beds together at the Sherry where she and Jean were staying.

These are the things the Supremes were focusing on. After Tom Jones left town, I helped Mary move to the Sherry. Then Mary got a telegram from Tom Jones. She read it, tore it up, and threw it in the garbage and of course I couldn't resist asking her, "What did he say?"

"Same old story." That's all she told me, and that's the last I heard of Mary's Tom Jones affair.

So I was dashing down from classes every day to spend the afternoon stuck in Cindy's room waiting for a phone call from the bank to confirm that her mortgage had been approved for her Benedict Canyon dreamhome, next door to Diahann Carroll's, and who should call but Cindy's mother, to say she was coming in to see the show that night.

Now I had to immediately start separating beds, moving furniture, and getting Charles' clothes out of Cindy's room at the Sherry to another room Cindy had found for him. Then, when Cindy's mother left, the beds went back together and the two of them started cooking these huge meals in Cindy's room.

Cindy sent me out to Macy's to buy hotplates, pots and pans, and some obscure spices that Charles had to have. It took me two days to round up all of this stuff, Charles made this whole big production on two hotplates, and it was the worst-tasting crap we had ever eaten. Then Cindy made me embarrass myself taking all this used equipment back to Macy's because she didn't want to be bothered traveling with it and she wanted her money back.

Naturally the whole situation was just food for gossip between me and Delcina. By now we were like twins, we went everywhere together, and before long the Supremes' crew were calling us "The Mob." It was Delcina and Tony, Tony and Delcina, "Here they come, get out the way they're comin' through!" We bought matching floor-length fur coats at B. Altman's. That shopping trip was the first time I'd been back since the day I met Flo, and it really didn't seem so grand any more.

I was now driving to college all bunched up in my fur coat and sunglassses like a Motown star. Delcina was calling me at home and saying, "Come on, we're flying out for the Supremes' show." I would have to explain that I couldn't get out of class, and where would I leave my car? How was I supposed to get to the airport? She said, "Bitch, leave that damn car home. I'm sending a limo for you!"

Sure enough the limo would be there waiting for me right in front of the school and off we'd go every weekend to wherever the Supremes were.

Once, Delcina called up, "We're going to Mary's." I said, "I can't go to no Mary's."

"Tell your mother you're coming over my house." So I was supposed to be over at Delcina's house weekends and we'd be in L.A. We never called to say we were coming, we flew first class and Delcina would tell the airline people, "I trust that you're sitting nobody next to us because we want double seats. He wants two seats and I want two seats, we need our beauty rest.''

When we got to LA the limo was waiting and we went up to Mary's. She wasn't expecting us, we just knocked. She opened the door, ''Hi, what are you all doin'?'' Just like we lived around the corner.

''We've come out here for a weekend of fun and frolic,'' said Delcina.

''Good Lord, what are you all gonna get into now?''

Berry Gordy and Diana Ross were hardly ever out of the news. After Diana went solo their romantic relationship just got to be more of a newsworthy item and everyone was forever asking, when would they be getting married? Berry Gordy would answer that he wanted to but she didn't, other reports would say that Diana wanted to but Berry didn't.

Motown people told me it was impossible, Diana and Gordy couldn't dream of getting married at this point because everyone would say, he's only pushing her because she's his wife. I thought that was pretty stupid. Even I knew you could make a bedroom decision without a marriage certificate, and having watched the way the New Supremes were being handled I was pretty sure the whole thing was indeed a bedroom, and not a boardroom, decision. It seemed like Berry Gordy had become Diana Ross's biggest fan. He idolized her, and the next thing you knew Diana had married someone else.

She married a man named Robert Silberstein a.k.a. Bob Ellis, and apparently shocked not only the public but Motown too because nobody had ever expected Diana to marry anybody but Berry Gordy, however long it took, and everybody had always expected Diana to have a great big wedding. She got married very quickly, very quietly, it was so sudden she didn't invite her mother, she didn't even invite Berry Gordy. She was married in January of 1971, and by August she was an adoring mother. Of course, the rumors flew.

Cindy and Charles Hewlett had been married the

previous June, and by March of 1972 Cindy was pregnant and ready to leave the Supremes. She was replaced by Lynda Lawrence. Although the Supremes would be voted the top female vocal group for 1972 in a *Soul* magazine readers' poll, they were really going nowhere, being booked into less and less prestigious places. Motown continued to deprive them of the attention they deserved.

But could Motown have done anything else? They couldn't have Diana Ross, who'd been billed as the Motown prima donna since 1966, out there on her own, and have the Supremes neck and neck, and have the Supremes surpass her. How would that have looked?

So the press releases were not put out for the Supremes, the tour schedule was not published, the TV appearances began to get more obscure. Diana made her debut as a movie star in *Lady Sings the Blues,* she did her big nightclub shows, the new Supremes never appeared in the same places as Diana Ross.

Diana never mentioned the Supremes and I never once saw Berry Gordy with the Supremes, he was always with Diana. After Diana got married it just became a trio instead of a duo. The first time I saw them after she got married was at a Waldorf appearance and to me it seemed like nothing had changed, her husband was almost an accessory. It was still Diana and Berry Gordy decending the staircase together, coming down to go to the Empire room, meeting the people afterward, and Diana would say, "Oh, have you met my husband? He's down over there talking to somebody." Diana still looked to Berry Gordy for everything, and whatever she wanted she got.

Sometimes Gordy would ask me, "How's Mary? How's she doing?" I'd tell him, "Oh yeah, she's in Vegas, she's fine." And he'd say, "Oh good, give her my regards." That was all, it was like talking about a person he never really knew.

By the time the Supremes, with Lynda Lawrence now in place of Cindy, came to do the Copa in June of 1972 there was more bickering in the group than there ever was in the beginning. Mary was no longer telling me, "Oh, don't mind Jean, you know how she is," because Mary had by now decided to take full control and be a Diana-ish type of character, and Jean Terrell was not having it, she was telling Mary, "Honey, you can't even sing, how are you gonna make all the decisions and tell me what to do."

Mary was saying, "I am the Original Supreme, I started the group." It seemed like everybody had at one time or another started that group. She even claimed, *"I* picked the name."

"Well, you're not the lead singer," Jean told her, "and whatever hit we get, however big or small, is coming off of my voice so I'm not listening to you." Then she added, "Just because you've been here the longest, maybe you've been here *too* long."

Jean and Lynda both had great voices and they teamed up together, they wanted to get away from the old Supremes image, to do something more R & B, but Mary wanted to stay locked into that faded image. So you had Jean and Lynda on this side of the fence, Mary on the other side, everybody was just a bit too grand in one way or another and I'd had enough.

So when I met the Three Degrees at the Copa just before the Supremes were due to start their engagement it was like a breath of fresh air. Of course, I went there ready to laugh at them, I thought it was just too ridiculous for a group like them to be appearing somewhere like the Copa.

I went to the opening night and the moment the Three Degrees came out I was just in total laughter over those polyester hotpants they had on and those big, cheap wigs. But when they opened their mouths I was floored, that show was sensational. The voices, the harmonies were unbelievable. It was far better than anything the Supremes had ever done.

Later, when I went into the dressing room, I was appalled to see one of the Three Degrees was sweeping the floor. You would never see a Supreme sweeping a dressing room floor. A Supreme would tell somebody to call somebody to call somebody else to find out who's in charge of floor-sweeping who would then get this person and bring them in to sweep. When I mentioned what I'd observed to their manager, Richard Barrett, he said, "Oh please, don't come around my girls giving them those diva Supreme ideas."

Richard Barrett insisted I come to the show every night. I got sick, he sent a limo for me. The next thing I knew he'd offered me a job as his personal assistant. I told him I would definitely think about it. I had by now tried college for about a year. I figured, the Supremes weren't going anywhere, especially with Motown's paltry assistance.

The Three Degrees closed at the Copa, and the Supremes opened. During the engagement Jean and Mary had some type of argument and Jean flew back to L.A. Mary Wilson was told by somebody at Motown, do NOT go on that stage tonight without Jean, don't work tonight—and they flew in Cindy Birdsong.

The next night Mary Wilson, Lynda Lawrence, and a pregnant Cindy Birdsong went on stage with Lynda doing all the leads. Then Jean came back, and Cindy went to visit her mother in New Jersey. Meanwhile Lynda, Mary, and Jean got into another fight, and Mary decided *she* wasn't going on.

Jean and Lynda now can't find Cindy because she's in New Jersey making pies with her mother, so Motown tells Lynda and Jean to go on without Mary, which further infuriates Mary because they didn't let her go on without Jean.

Lynda and Jean go on without Mary. Cindy is finally located and told to get back to New York City and never leave until the engagement is over but the next night Mary's thought better of it and Mary, Lynda, and Jean go on, with Cindy sitting pregnant eating Chinese food, ringside at the Copa. Meanwhile Jules Podell, the owner of the Copacabana, is livid and doesn't want to hear from those Supremes ever again, vowing that this will be their last engagement at the Copa.

And it was.

The Supremes left town, I immediately called Richard Barrett and told him I would take the position with the Three Degrees, and that's what I did. It was a very pleasurable experience. A few months after I started with the group I moved out of my family's house into a Fifth Avenue duplex co-op that I bought with the money from my trust fund.

I stayed with the Three Degrees while the Supremes became a revolving door and turned from a B group into a C group. Lynda and Jean left in 1973, the dynamic singer Scherrie Payne joined, and Cindy came back to the group. Mary got married to a man named Pedro Ferrer.

Mary fired the Supremes' manager and gave Pedro the job, and if Gordy hadn't already washed his hands of the Supremes, he did then, because no one but Mary liked Pedro. Cindy didn't trust him, Mary now thought she was Diana Ross and she was running the group her way, which was actually Pedro's way, and Pedro decided Cindy had to go.

I ended up staying with the Three Degrees until they made big money and started to act worse than the Supremes ever did. It looked like more of the same. Same shit, different group, and I decided to retire and try another field.

I got a great job almost by chance, almost in the same way that I had met Florence Ballard. I sold the duplex and went looking for a house in Long Island. I had been dreaming of an English Tudor just like Flo's, all brick, with the canopy, the stained-glass windows, and the fireplace and lush landscape. I must have been dreaming about it ever since the day I first pulled up in front of Flo's picture-perfect Tudor on Buena Vista, and that's what I bought, just about the same time as Flo was losing hers. Except I didn't know it. I didn't know her dream was dying so fast.

CHAPTER 18

◆ ◆ ◆

The-Twins-Gotta-
Eat

Looking back now, Cholly didn't say any more to me about Flo after the time in the rehearsal studio. Nobody ever said anything about Flo. I called her a few times, she told me her nerves and her blood pressure were bad, and she asked after Mary. The first time it hit me that things for Flo were not what they had once been was when Delcina and I went down to Detroit in 1970. We had gone to Detroit with Mary who still had her house down the street from Flo's. She had family living in it at the time, and stayed there whenever she visited Detroit.

The first thing I thought was, Flo's house looks like it needs some work. The carpet needed shampooing, the place needed a paint job, a few things were broken, the furniture was dirty. The place had lost its glamor. Everything wasn't crisp and shiny and silvery, it was looking like a house that had fallen on hard times.

We stayed in Detroit four or five days, hanging out with Flo. Every time we left the house Delcina and I would look at each other, both of us wondering about Flo's mental state, because she kept drifting off in and out of conversations, unable to stay on the subject.

Tommy wasn't there. We were told he was working on the road with a group, so that sounded good, the man was working and it looked like somebody needed the money. The Caddy needed a new transmission, it could drive but it couldn't back up out of the driveway so you had to give Flo a push to get the Caddy out onto the street.

"Flo," I said, "why don't you park your car in front of your house, why do you keep pulling it in? Just leave it in front so you don't have to worry about backing it up."

"Oh, I never thought of that," she said. "I'm so used to putting it in the driveway." Just like she was used to spending money. It was a habit she never questioned, and if there was nobody around to push the car out, she was stuck. She said sometimes she would put the car in reverse, stick her foot out the door, and push it back with her foot.

I screamed, "A Supreme? This should never happen to a Supreme!"

"Oh, Tony," she said, "you don't know what I've been through. You don't know the half of it. I've been in a lot of tight jams here lately." But she still had the house, she still had the Caddy, the twins were running riot all over the house, and they were still dressed beautifully. Flo changed them head to toe five or six times a day and they had closets full of outfits from Lord & Taylor. So I figured maybe she was down to her last hundred thousand or so.

I just thought, Flo's got to get back to work. She said she was on a diet and that with Tommy working for a group now, he'd be making connections, letting influential people know that his wife, Flo Ballard, was one of the Supremes. But he never did. He didn't last long with the group either.

Flo had become quite full-figured and her clothes weren't fitting like they used to. She was still made up, but the eyelash glue was thick and sloppily applied. She looked all painted up, really tragic, like an old Kewpie doll on a stick, everything exaggerated. "Flo, your cheeks look kinda red," I told her.

"Honey, I have no money for rouge, I put Elizabeth

Arden's red lipstick on my cheeks." And all I thought was, Oh! What an amazing idea! What a good beauty trick!

One night we were sitting around talking and Flo said, "Tony, do you remember a long time ago I told you how I once had a crush on Gordy?" And she started on this long story about how she had really been deeply in love with Gordy. Flo told me that once, on tour in London in 1965, Diana had very matter-of-factly announced to her, "He's my man now."

Flo said she very sweetly asked Diana, "Which man of many are you referring to, my dear?"

"Berry." That was Diana's short reply.

I couldn't believe what she was telling me, I just thought about all the things she'd said about Gordy, always telling me that he was a dirty old man, he was this, he was that, he was too old for Diana, he was too short, and what does Diana see in him?

"Flo, I never thought you really liked him that much. Look at how you used to yell at him and curse him out and everything."

"Honey, love is confusin'. Love HURTS," she said. And then she drifted off and started talking about something else.

Later I remembered a thing Mary had told me about a huge oil painting Gordy had hanging over the fireplace in his grand living room, a painting of Gordy all dressed up as Napoleon, with the hand in the jacket and everything. I said, "Flo, remember when you used to say to Gordy, 'Who the hell do you think you are? Napoleon?' Mary says he had a painting up at the house like that."

"Yeah, honey, ain't that sick," she said. "That man actually has a Napoleon complex. I guess Diana has one in her house as Mary Antoinette or something! You know? Because she has that attitude like, let them eat cake!"

"The *hell* with them," she said, "everybody else is starving, the group is being pushed aside. The things they're doing to Mary and the group, I would never have stood for that.''

Flo was still fighting, but now she was fighting to survive, not to sing, and I didn't know it. Another time we were in the kitchen, Flo was making potato salad, and she said, "You know, I'm gonna do something, anything, because the twins gotta eat. I won't let my girls suffer!''

Flo was trying to reopen her case against Motown on the grounds that she hadn't gotten her fair share. She didn't tell me she was broke, that her lawyer had swindled her through various means. She didn't mention any of that, she just said that she and her brother, Billy Ballard, were looking for new attorneys to represent her. She seemed a little secretive about it.

Flo was sitting up there in that kitchen making potato salad and she said, "Yeah, I might be suing because I didn't get my right money and I don't mean no harm to Mary or anyone else but I'm going to have to implicate them as soon as I get a tough lawyer who can handle it. I'm going to have to implicate them in the suit. But they know what they did, and I'm gonna sue them and get my money because it's awful funny that my money is getting kind of low.''

When I told this to Mary she immediately said, "Tony, don't pay Flo no mind.''

I said, "Flo's down there talking about she's gonna get even and she's suing because she didn't get her right money.''

"Oh really?'' said Mary. "Well, you shouldn't pay anything that Flo says any attention, don't get involved with Flo because she's talking crazy and making wild, unfounded accusations, and someone is bound to get hurt.''

But Delcina and I had a big conference and we decided that the reason Mary was being so nonchalant about the whole thing and looking so terrified at the same time was because now the whole filth and the ugliness of what had actually happened to Flo was going to come out.

Mary kept repeating, "Flo got her money, it was all very basic—what's her problem?"

"Well, the house don't look that good," I told her. "The house looks like it needs redecorating and painting and plastering and new wallpaper and the carpet is worn out and dirty."

Mary said, "Well, Tony, you know Flo. Sometimes she can pinch a penny and she probably just doesn't want to spend." The Flo I knew had always been very generous and lavish.

Flo was very close-mouthed about a lot of things during that trip. It seemed like she had been running around talking to one attorney after another and they all said the case was too hot, or they didn't show up for the appointment, or they returned Flo's retainer, or they just couldn't do it. She even mentioned that she was going to be contacting Julian Bond, who was then a Georgia state senator active in the civil rights movement. I wondered, now what does politics and the civil rights movement have to do with Flo making a record? Delcina and I were thinking very basic, we were thinking, Flo needs to get a record out, get some gowns, and get back on the road where she belongs.

I went back to New York, and Flo started calling me regularly. Each time she called she was unfolding the story piece by piece by piece. I was listening, but I guess I wasn't hearing her cry. Because she'd say things like, "A taste of honey is worse than none at all, and I had it and I lost it but I'm gonna get my money, and everybody knows that they didn't pay me my right money, Mary knows it, Diana knows it, Gordy knows it, they all know I was maliciously put out of that group, the whole thing is coming out along with all of Berry Gordy's dirty laundry."

She said she was suing not only Motown but also Diana, Mary, and Cindy for conspiracy to do her out of her money. She had contacted the FBI, the state of Michigan's attorney general, the IRS, the county court, congressmen, banks, she was talking subpoenas, she was talking Motown and Mafia and all this stuff and I just wasn't hearing. I guess I was so brainwashed by the whole Supremes image and the glory of it all that I couldn't understand her rambling.

The old Hitsville building on West Grand Boulevard got turned into a museum, the big new downtown Detroit office building that Motown had poured all that money into renovating stood empty. The only people left were the ones who were no longer part of the organization, the hangers-on who couldn't make the plane fare, and ex-Supreme Flo Ballard. I went to see her, and now she was selling her jewelry and her furniture. Her excuse was "Well, I'm thinking of redecorating, and the kids have torn this up so I'm gonna sell it and I'm gonna get something else."

She was selling furniture, lamps, dresses, "Oh, this will never fit me again." She was having a big tag sale and there wasn't anything new coming in. Tommy was definitely not around, and she'd sit talking about the old days.

Flo would sit and tell me how Diana used to flirt with every and any man around Motown that she thought could do her some good, she said, "Some of those men used to laugh behind her back. They'd come to me and say, Flo, when you gonna get off your high horse and throw yourself at me, you stacked baby." And she threw her head back and laughed that contagious Flo laugh, then suddenly added remorsefully, "Honey, some of those men were just too fresh."

She told me about Mary and how Mary used to come and cry on her shoulder after Marvin Gaye married Berry Gordy's older sister, Anna. Then she'd tell me, "You make sure Mary watches out for that evil Gordy man," then she'd wander back to her lawsuit, the Supremes conspiracy, the twins-gotta-eat theory.

She said, "Honey, everyone could see it was them who was up against me. Cholly tried to help me but what could he do, sometimes I was so sick I could hardly move and then to make things worse they would purposefully add or speed up the day's schedule. And Mary just seemed to go along with it, then she began to avoid me along with Diana and Gordy, and that really hurt."

Mary never talked about Flo and I never saw her over at Flo's house when she was in Detroit, so I would tell her, Flo's selling her furniture, Flo's selling her jewelry, poor Flo, she's gained so much weight, poor Flo, she should be singing, poor Flo this, poor Flo that until I guess Mary got tired of me and my poor Flos and one day she just turned to me and shouted, "Tony, you know I can't go around trying to save Flo, because Flo spent her money, she mismanaged it. So what should I do about it?"

That was basically it until Flo called me on the phone one day and asked me to testify. "Tony, you know I got that big case coming up and you know you could tell how they used to treat me when I was in the group, how they used to dog me, how they used to do all those terrible things to me and play tricks on me. You know, people used to put stuff in my drink."

She said, "Yeah, people used to put stuff in my drink to make me drowsy, they used to tell me rehearsal was at two when it was really at twelve so it would look like I was late. They used to trick me, they tried to sabotage me. They tried to brainwash me. They tried to get control of my mind. Tony, you gotta testify for me so you can tell them what you saw because I need witnesses." I guess she figured, well Tony can't be touched by Motown, he can't be blacklisted, and he was there, he can testify. Then she said, "I should ask Mary. But Mary won't testify for me."

When I asked Mary about that, she got very stern and said, "Flo did not ever ask me to testify for her, nor should you testify for Flo. You should not get tangled up in it, stay out of it. Because today Flo is suing and tomorrow she won't be. You know how Flo changes her mind."

I would have testified, but not too long after that Flo called and said, "Baby, I decided I'm gonna take a different approach in this case." That's all. She said she'd call me back and the next time I heard from her it was like she'd never spoken to me about any of this ever before. She was trying to reconstruct an itinerary of all the appearances she had made with the Supremes so it could be figured how much she should have been paid because the bank would not release any records, and Motown wouldn't release the performance contracts.

She said, "Honey, all the fans you know, call them and ask where or when they saw us perform, what clubs, look through your scrapbooks, send me copies of the dates that you have, ask the other fans to send you copies of what they have and then mail it all to me."

She was perfectly clear in what she wanted, and between me and maybe twenty people we were able to come up with a halfway decent outline for Flo. She was asking people all over the world too, and they were willing to help her.

Flo continued to flip back and forth between lucid and wild talk. "Tony, you know they never gave me back my eye makeup either. Tony, when you go down there you look in that big steamer trunk that Mary has, some of my false eyelashes were left in there too and some of my pancake makeup and stuff, because I saw a photo of Mary and she had on my shade. I know she still has my makeup in there. But I didn't get my money and I'm suing for my money."

She believed in the conspiracy against her. I think she realized that she'd played into their hands by not staying calm, maybe she should not have cursed Berry Gordy out, maybe she should not have said, fuck them, I'll make a big scene and get thrown out. Maybe she should have played their game because now here she was with nothing left but her kids and a husband who came and went. She was a battered woman, mentally and physically. Yet at this point she never said a bad word against Tommy.

Sometimes when I saw Flo she had bruise marks on her, it seemed like she was forever falling down the stairs or tripping over things. Once, I asked her about a new black eye. She told me she fell and hit her eye on the doorknob. I went along with it and then told the story to Delcina who said, "Don't be so stupid! Wake up! What was she doing, peeking through a peekhole?"

I said, "Well, she could have been walking and she could have gotten near the door, she could have tripped and fallen and when she came down her eye was near the doorknob."

Delcina said, "Flo did not fall."

And I thought about when I saw Tommy rough up Flo when she wanted to walk out of the Wonder Garden in Atlantic City, I thought, maybe she didn't fall down all those other times.

Then in 1973 Flo called up all out of breath and she said, "Tony, guess what happened! Guess what happened!" I said, "What? Then she started crying, she was furious, she said, "That man was *crazy!*"

I said, "Who? Tommy?"

"No, that lawyer, he shot himself!"

I said, "What happened? You drove him crazy?"

She said, "No! wait, wait! He got shot. In court," and she told me the whole story of how her new lawyer was in court with another case and he went crazy, he pulled a gun to shoot the judge and the guard then shot her lawyer, and now her affairs were all in turmoil because after two years on her case this lawyer looked like he was getting somewhere, he wasn't scared of Motown, he wasn't scared of Gordy, he was her ray of hope and now he was dead.

Some wild and unusual shit was always happening to Flo. In the end she lost the suit, she said they told her some crazy things. She said they told her she could bring a case of mental and emotional distress against Motown in a lower court, but in the suit about the money she would have to give back all the money that Motown had given her before they would void her agreement with Motown. And of course she couldn't give that money back because it was spent.

I thought, now if you were supposed to get a million

dollars and somebody gave you $160,000, why would you have to give back the $160,000 to see if you were going to get the million? It didn't sound like good sense to me. I called Flo and asked her, ''Why do you have to give back money if you didn't get enough money?''

Nobody could believe that's what the judge had ordered, because it didn't make any sense. It was a tangled mess, and Flo was sounding very confused and disorganized, she was running helter-skelter and it was tearing her mind up. By now she had three kids to feed, she had this huge house to heat, and worse, she had gone from gutter to glitter and was now flat broke. But who knew.

I went there and sat with her and the kids in Flo's master bedroom, warmed by a little electric heater. We sat there with our coats on, Flo in full makeup wearing a tattered white mink that was too small to reach around her and a muumuu cleverly wrapped as a turban around her head, and I thought, the woman is strong. One time I went to Flo's house and there was nothing left, no furniture, the place was almost bare. Flo was so far gone, she was sitting on an old wooden rocking chair rocking back and forth. She barely spoke.

She'd sold the white Louis XVI furniture and the crystal chandeliers and the marble tables and the seventeen-foot velvet couch that they had to break the wall open to get in, and she was just sitting there peeling potatoes and letting the peelings drop on newspaper spread all around her feet on the floor. She said she was making french fries.

And this was the first time I really took a good look at her, but it was way too late then. She took this big turkey roasting pan and put it across the back burner and the front burner, filled it with lard, and that's all she had to eat—french fries for her and the kids, and me. She had bought Kool-Aid, but it wasn't the presweetened kind and she didn't have any sugar in the house, she had no salt, no pepper, no ketchup. All she had was the red brick house.

And I said to myself, poor Flo's flipped. I thought, can you blame her? Maybe her mind has left her, she don't care about furniture, she don't care about eating off fancy dishes, don't say anything embarrassing like, Flo what happened to your china? The thing that we who love her have to do is try to help her get herself together.

Ever optimistic, I suggested maybe she could still get back in the group. By this time Cindy had come and gone and Jean and Lynda Lawrence were getting ready to go, maybe Florence could make a triumphant return because it didn't seem like Berry Gordy cared who was in the group at this point. I even told Mary when I saw her, "Mary, you should send Flo to a fat farm, send her to Elizabeth Arden, get her all fixed up and do her triumphant return. That's what the group needs right now, a good shot in the arm, a burst of publicity."

Mary said, "No, that won't work," and that was basically it because Mary knew more than I did. Her cousin Josephine lived up the street from Flo in Mary's old house and Flo was over there a lot, and I didn't know it then but Josephine would call Mary and tell her, Flo looks like hell, Flo and the kids ain't got nothing to eat or any clothes.

But Mary didn't go into it, she just said, "I don't want Florence back in the group, I'm looking for a new direction now." She said, "I've got my own problems, I can't start feeling sorry for Flo now."

That was the last time I went to Flo's house when she was living there. I found out with everybody else that Flo was really and truly destitute, and had been since the day in 1969 when her lawyer, Baun, called and told her, Good morning, you're broke.

It was February 1975. I had just bought my new house that was almost a carbon copy of Flo's, and I was lying on the carpet looking at television. The news came on—"Coming up, former Supreme, flat broke, living on welfare," with a little picture of Florence

Ballard. I could not believe it. I jumped up and I called Flo's number in Detroit. It was disconnected. I called a friend of mine in Detroit who said, "Did you hear? It's true, she's on the cover of *Jet.*"

I hung up and raced to get a copy of *Jet,* and there she was on the cover in front of that house. The first thing in my mind was, why in the world would she pose for a picture like this. *Who* is doing her publicity?

I still didn't get it. Who would let poor Flo stand up with what looks like two black eyes form a bad make-up job, and a tattered raccoon hooded coat that had seen better days? Who would let her pose like that, standing in the snow in front of her house with the torn canvas awning and boards across the stained-glass windows?

And that was just the cover. I started looking at the pictures they had of her inside the magazine, how huge she had gotten in six months. She had some big cast on her leg and she was gazing up at a picture of herself when she was young and in the money and in the group—I thought the whole thing was horrible.

Then I read it, the whole story of how she's on welfare, she's getting Aid for Dependent Children, she's lost the house through foreclosure and they're trying to sell it, she's living with her three kids and her mother in a two-bedroom apartment, and on and on. And I thought, now it all makes sense.

It took me about a week to locate Flo, and it was the saddest thing. We talked on the phone, that's when she came out with everything, with Tommy, how no-good he was, how he used to beat her, how he used her. Then the standard Diana Ross-Berry Gordy story, how they had bought off the judge, how she had been struggling for all these years, how her brother Billy had done everything he could to help her, how for the longest time they couldn't get a lawyer to touch the case and everybody sympathized with her, everybody said she had a good case but nobody wanted to help.

I went to Detroit and sure enough Flo was living with her mother in a little apartment. She looked sad, she didn't care, she no longer needed the black eye-liner and the dark eye makeup because her eyes had big, dark circles under them from crying and drinking and wandering the streets at night. We sat up and got drunk and talked, and about one in the morning Flo decided that she was going for a drive.

So we're both drunk and we get up in the old Cadillac which by now has rope holding the passenger door closed so you have to slide in through the other door. We drive around, we're playing *Diana Ross and the Supremes Greatest Hits* on the eight-track, she's doing lead, I'm giving her hell on background.

Flo says, "Let's go over my house and break in."

Sounds good to me. We start driving over to the old house, and she's telling me she tried to borrow money to get the house back because they told her if she got the five or seven thousand she owed she could go back in there. She tells me she went to Diana to borrow the money because she'd had a lot of job offers since her story broke, she would be able to repay it and Diana told Flo to go and sign the papers in some office in Detroit.

Flo said, when she got to the office she was surprised to find Diana there with some lawyer-types and Diana had a lot of papers for her to sign. Flo didn't mind signing them but Diana wanted her to sign some papers that were blank, they didn't have a word on them and these people were telling her, "Don't worry, just go ahead and sign these." Flo said she wasn't going to sign no blank papers, she said by this point she had been through so much, she had been ripped off and ruined and she was not trusting anyone any more, she was not signing, she said there were a lot of strings attached, one being that she could never tell anybody where she got the money.

So we're driving through the night, it's snowing, it's cold, it's pitch-black, and we get to this wreck of a house. Flo pulls out two candles from the trunk, she goes round the back of the house, and the next thing I know she's opening up the front door.

Well, even with that little bit of candle I can see that the whole house is in shambles, there's ice on the floor, doors are hanging off their hinges, wallpaper is peeling off the wall, it's freezing cold and Flo decides we're going to look through the house, and decide what she's going to do with it if she gets it back. The Eldorado's still running outside because once you turn it off it won't start up again, and we're walking around the place like we're looking at a house for the first time, like when we looked at Flo's penthouse with the real estate man except this time we're seeing it by the light of a candle stump. And Flo's saying, "I think I'm gonna do the whole thing in Parisien Blue."

We must have spent about three hours decorating the house room by room, and as the sun came up we were sitting on the floor singing "Baby Love," "I Hear a Symphony," Flo did all the dance routines but she wouldn't sing any song past "Reflections."

We went back to that house every night while I was in Detroit. Some nights Flo took the kids. She would wake them up, put slippers on their feet, put their coats over their pajamas, pile them in the back seat, and take them to their old house. Some nights she would do a show. The kids would sit on the steps, I would announce her, and she'd make a grand entrance out the front door. She would stand on the porch with the crystal decanter for a microphone and do the whole show, opening with "Put on a Happy Face." She did the medleys, she did "People," and she closed with "Mame." Then I would clap, the kids would clap, Flo would do her bows, rush backstage into the house, and we would go home.

Once she belted out those songs so loud she woke up the neighbors and then they invited us in. We all had bacon and eggs at five in the morning and the lady started telling me, poor Flo, people should stick by her and on and on and suddenly Flo jumped up screaming, "I DON'T NEED NO MOTHER FUCKIN' BODY TO STICK BY ME! I'M FLO BAL-

LARD! I'M A SUPREME. LET ME OUTTA HERE
I GOTTA SHOW TO DO!'' It was heartbreaking.

I did what I could to help Flo and by now there were
other people trying to help too. One of the first to
come by after the news broke was Eddie Kendrick,
and some of the other Motowners and neighbors and
fans would come knocking on her door, ''Here, give
Flo this money.''

''You want to see her? She's right here.''

''No, I don't want to see her. Just tell her I was by
when she's feeling better. Just out of friendship, we
grew up together, out of respect.'' Mary on the other
hand, who by now was married and had moved into
her huge mansion in Hancock Park with the white
stretch Mercedes Benz 600 and the vintage Silver
Cloud Rolls-Royce in the drive, she told me, mimick-
ing her Latin husband, ''It's not my problem.''

It was horribly sad. Flo was now a broken woman,
a woman who had a great voice, who had been gorgeous, whom people loved. But she didn't know how
to play Motown's game of politics. Maybe she had just
awakened from her dream, maybe she had just realized
that there were no perfect houses with perfect dreamgirls and perfectly dreamy guys inside, maybe she saw
that this was not Levittown and she was not Miss
America, and nothing was ever fair and it was too late.
She was just thirty-one and it looked like life for her
was over.

Once, when she and I were looking through her
scrapbooks, she said, ''Baby, I believe that it's written
down somewhere, Diana and Mary get everything, Flo
gets nothing.'' Then she launched into singing,
''. . . them that's got will get, them that's not will
lose, so the Bible says and I believe that it still is news,
your papa may have, your mama may have, but honey
God bless the child that got his own.''

She went on, ''You tell me why Diana acts that way.
It's a sickness honey, simply a sickness, she thinks it's
all about her. Tony, that whole Supremes thing is a
total sickness.'' She would talk to me very seriously, al-

most like she was warning me to look carefully. "You have to realize that you've grown up real good, you've made good for yourself and you got a nice house, nice car, nice clothes, nice job, and you're moving in the direction of what you always said you wanted to be, a road manager. And sometimes things turn out, but things are not always what they seem, not even death."

I thought she'd had too much to drink and that maybe I had too because I was listening, turning the old, chipped crystal goblet around and around in my hand and trying to figure out what she was telling me. She said, "Some people in and around the Supremes are very evil, but they take a glamorous form." I couldn't understand that, evil with glamorous form but she went on, "Just like a pretty dress on an evil person doesn't make them a pretty person."

She said, "Remember, dirt is dirt. Roses are my favorite flower and they're beautiful, but they grow in dirt and even though the dirt may be covered over with roses that doesn't make the dirt pretty, it's the roses that are pretty. This is what you must remember, hear Flo talkin'."

And then all of a sudden, after all of this Flo calls up one day in October of '75 and says, "Baby, I'm making a comeback!"

I said, "What do you mean you're making a comeback?"

"Honey, I'm planning a big show. I'm gonna be in New York, I'm gonna have singers, I've got it all planned out. Oh, by the way I moved."

I said, "Where did you move to?" The woman was broke.

"Oh chil', I'm in the money honey, you gotta come up. I've got a beautiful place, I've got this big house, everything is new, oh, the carpet's amazing and honey, I'm the first person in Detroit with a brand-new Cadillac Seville. They rode it off the assembly line for me. You *have* to come up."

Sure enough, Flo was back up in the money again

and I figured it was a lot of money because she had bought a big house with furniture just like the old days, everything was gorgeous, she was dressed lovely, the new car was in the driveway, and Tommy was back. He came back when the money came back. He was all up in the silk robes again, saying my wife this and my wife that, every other thing was, my wife.

I was happy for Flo. I didn't care where she got the money from, she said she had gotten it from a suit, the woman was a bed of suits and she didn't tell me which one, she just said, "I gotta keep it hush-hush, very hush-hush." Then a few days later she started putting out this story that she got money from a suit after she fell down and broke her ankle in front of some supermarket. Next thing, someone came over and said, "Flo girl, I heard you hit the numbers, babe."

Finally a good friend of Flo's told me that the money came from Berry Gordy because he felt bad about everything and it was just too ugly to have Flo going around Detroit like that with those kids about to catch pneumonia. Flo later claimed that's where she got the money from, and from what I saw she must have known it was coming because if she put the check in the bank Monday, by Tuesday she was shopping and by Wednesday she was all set up.

The wigs were all lined up, the outfits, the makeup, everything was just so, just like it was 1967 all over again and she told me that what had happened to her would never happen again because she was taking care of her own money and she was paying cash for everything. So they could never again take her house from her and her children because she owed nobody nothing.

She was going into rehearsal with a girl and a guy doing background and she was either going to do this and go on the road because people were interested, or she was going to do a book. She said the book was finished, she had written it herself, she said, "I wrote the whole thing longhand, honey, in six spiral-bound notebooks.'' It was going to be called *Flo, My Story*, and she said Doubleday was interested in publishing it. She said, "It's hot stuff, baby, you have no idea what went on."

It seemed like Flo had changed overnight back to the person she had once been. Her lawsuits looked like a bunch of dead ends but now she was saying, "Forget it. I got some money, I got a house for my kids, let's leave it." So I left it. Once again the future looked promised and her bread for the moment appeared to be buttered. This was finally her time.

CHAPTER 19

◆ ◆ ◆

Flo, My Story

I called Florence on Valentine's Day, 1976, and she was talking very up. She was in the middle of rehearsing down in her basement studio, but she took a break to talk to me and she played a tape over the phone of what she hoped would be her new record. She was very excited. She put the phone by the speaker and it sounded really, really good, really current. It was like a fast Aretha Franklin-style number.

"Flo, things are looking good, what are you gonna do?" I asked.

"Well, I'm still deciding," she told me. "I'm either gonna go with the book and get my name back out and then start singing. Or I'm going to leave the book and forget all that bitterness, not drag all that stuff back up, and go with my career, and then if my career doesn't take off I can still go back to the book, *Flo, My Story.*"

"You should do both," I told her. "This is not the time to be taking chances. If you've got someone interested in the book, then go with the book *and* go with the singing career."

She was so busy, the phone was ringing again, she was on a new diet but she wasn't going to worry herself trying for that bone-thin sixties look. She said, "Look at Aretha and Roberta Flack, they're not that thin.'' She said she was taking high-blood-pressure medication and not drinking, she was taking care of her skin, thinking of even frosting her hair again. ''I still look pretty good for a former Supreme, and my pipes are in excellent condition.''

So she sounded fine, she had changed almost overnight back into the old Flo, so I wasn't worried. I was going off to Europe for a while and I'd call her when I returned.

Before I got back home I called her from Philadelphia where I'd stopped over at Richard Barrett's Gladwyne estate. I told her that maybe Richard could help her get a deal with Philadelphia International Records and she sounded very interested. I said, ''That tape you played me, you should send me a copy.'' And she said, ''Well, I'm going out to the Kentucky Fried Chicken to get some food because I don't feel like cooking tonight and on the way back I'll pick up some tapes and make a copy, but make sure my tape doesn't get into the wrong hands!'' I said I'd call her from home the next day.

The next day I got home to my house, I walked in the door, put my bags down in the living room, and the phone in the kitchen rang.

It was a friend of mine named Grier who also knew Flo very well, and he said, ''What are you doing?

''Nothing.''

''Are you home alone?''

''No, the housekeeper's here.''

''Good. Did you hear?''

I said, ''Hear what?''

''Flo is dead.'' Just like that, he didn't prepare me or anything.

I screamed, ''What!

''Flo is Dead, Tony. She was rushed to the hospital—''

I said, ''But I spoke to Flo yesterday, she was going to get chicken. What happened? She got knocked down or something?''

He said, ''Tony, Flo was rushed to the emergency

room and she died a few hours later. Tommy called
me up, he was trying to call your house and you
weren't there, and he wants you to call him right away.
Hang up the phone and call Tommy immediately, then
call me right back."

I was just standing there, I still had on my coat and
gloves, and I started to dial the phone. Tommy picked
up immediately, he must have been sitting on top of it
and I said, "Tommy, what's happened?"

"My wife is dead! My wife is dead!" he moaned.

"What happened?" I was too shocked to cry, I was
just trying to figure it out, something seemed wrong
with the story, this wasn't what was supposed to happen.

Tommy said, "I was working, I came home, and
they'd taken her to the hospital. She fell on the floor
in the living room and she was paralyzed, they think
she had a stroke but they're going to do an autopsy."
He said the kids and Flo's sister called the ambulance
when they found her. She was alive, but talking in
slurred speech when she got to the hospital and they
started working on her and it looked like she was going to be all right. Next thing she had another seizure
right in the hospital and she died. They said her body
was filled with blood clots, and one of the blood clots
had shot directly up to her heart.

I could hear people in the background screaming
and crying, and Tommy said, "You gotta get up here,
you gotta help me," I thought he meant, help him with
the funeral plans. It was about ten at night by now and
I told Tommy I'd try to catch the eleven-fifteen flight
to Detroit.

I called the airport and couldn't get a flight out 'til
seven the next morning. So I called Tommy right back,
I was still standing in the same spot in the kitchen with
my coat and gloves on and he said, "There's plenty of
people here, don't worry. I'll send somebody to pick
you up at the airport and you can stay in the house."

"Well, I don't think I should stay at the house with
all the family and the confusion and everything."

He said, "Oh no, you must stay at the house! You have to see the house! My wife did more to it since you were here and it's so gorgeous, and my wife is gone, she left me and the house is a mansion—oh, you know what you could do for me when you get up here, you could help me find a maid." And I said to myself, wait now, this man is crazy, he's delirious.

I called Grier back. We stayed on the phone till three in the morning and he was drinking on his end, I was drinking on my end, we were both crying and remembering things about Flo and then I was trying to pack, I had a phone cord that could reach around the world so I was talking and crying and packing all at the same time, and when I got to Detroit the next day I went right over to the house.

Tommy grabbed me, hugged me, almost knocked me down, and then he started showing me Flo's latest acquisitions. He said, "We didn't have these lamps the last time you were here, look at these lamps! Flo had these specially made up from Oriental ginger jars. Look how thick this carpet is! Is this carpet not up to your ankles?"

The man was just going on and on and on. Then he took me in a corner, he said, "You know, Flo's family doesn't like me, you know what I'm saying? They're just trying to take over everything but I told them, I'm the husband and what I say goes. Because they want to run the funeral one way, and I told them, I'm not running it that way, I'm doing what I want to do. And you know, I spoke on the phone with Berry Gordy and I told him, you better do the right thing." Tommy said, "because you know all about that money she got, you know about that, right Tony? Well she spent a lot of that money on this new house and everything for the kids, so we don't have much cash left but Motown is paying for the whole funeral, and I want nothing but the best for my wife."

He told me, "I picked out this huge casket, it's going to be open from head to toe, and she's gonna have on a satin robe, her best friend is coming to do her makeup and her hair, and she's gonna look just like she did when she was in the Supremes.'' He said, ''Because you know, sometimes when people die suddenly like that, their face goes back to when they were young, and the undertaker's going to fix her so she looks very stylish, just like a Supreme, all laid out.''

''Tommy, are you burying her in an old Supreme gown?'' I was appalled. ''No, I thought of that but she couldn't fit in none of the old gowns. But I'm gonna bury her in a satin gown with little satin slippers, and I'm having Rolls-Royces and vintage cars come in.'' It was like somebody planning a wedding reception. He went on, ''There's gonna be tons of food and everything, I'm having nothing but the best.''

There was already tons of food all over the house and people were lining up, the place was packed, you could hardly move. You had to take the phone off the hook just to give yourself a rest. Fans and onlookers were standing outside, Motown people were coming in to pay their sympathies, relatives were coming, friends were coming, you wouldn't have believed that a few months ago nobody wanted to see this woman.

Then there were all the calls back and forth with Motown. Diana Ross was coming in and things had to be planned to accommodate her, Mary was on her way from L.A., and then at the last minute the funeral had to be rushed forward a day to accommodate all the stars who wanted to come and couldn't make it on a Saturday.

We went to the funeral home. The moment we got there Tommy had to faint and scream and cry, he threw himself on top of Flo in the casket and had to be pried loose. The place was in turmoil, everyone was falling out and being revived and fainting again. It was a mob scene.

They had to keep the funeral home open till very late that night because Flo was on public display, and everyone was waiting on line, everyone was going back to the end of the line to get a second look, they were all pushing forward to get a look at the stars who were being ushered in, and there was Flo lying there in state, in her flowing satin robe and her Supremes eyelashes.

She looked beautiful, like she was in bed with pillows propped up behind her. She actually looked like her old self—regal, grand, younger, and softer—she looked at peace.

Mary arrived. I was surprised because after everything she'd said to me about Flo, she appeared to be in more shock than Flo's family. She came in like a walking zombie and when she saw Flo she broke down completely. Later I saw her back at the house, Tommy was carrying on, every time things calmed down he'd start them up again with a big scream, and I heard Mary tell her friend Alice Fletcher, "I can't stand that man, he was no good for Flo."

Nobody had seen Diana, and the speculation was running high—would she have the nerve to show up? How could she look poor, dead Flo in the face? Why didn't she come rushing to Detroit when Flo was down and out?

I rode to church in the funeral procession. There were a bunch of limos leaving that house, there was a police escort, and when we got two or three blocks from the church you couldn't move. About five thousand people were lining the street, all looking in the cars to see the celebrities. When I finally got inside the church there was Mary, her mother, her sister, and oddly enough Diana's mother all standing together. I thought, Diana must be somewhere around here.

I looked around. People had come in evening gowns, sequins, backless dresses, mink coats, sable—it was like a pageant. Just the flowers alone—Flo must have had hundreds of wreaths there and some of them weren't wreaths, some of them were more like advertisements than memorials. You had GLADYS KNIGHT AND THE PIPS spelled out in red roses. You had I LOVE YOU BLONDIE, signed DIANA and spelled out across a huge bleeding heart of white carnations. There was MOTOWN THE SOUND OF

YOUNG AMERICA all done up in flowers, there was one big one that just said THE FOUR TOPS. They'd even managed to spell out TEMPTATIONS in flowers, it was the size of a theater marquee.

And I was thinking, my God, just the money that was spent on floral arrangements could have changed Flo's life a few months ago. Where was everybody then? When suddenly I heard a complete pandemonium of boos, people shouting "the black bitch," and at the same time cheering and clapping. And I said, Lord have mercy, it must be Diana Ross.

A limo had roared up to the church door with the horn blaring. The crowd scampered out the way, the limo door shot open, bodyguards jumped out, there was a big hush, and out stepped Diana. Her entrance seemed rehearsed—the timing was perfect. Berry wasn't with her—in fact he didn't come to Flo's funeral.

Diana looked appropriately tragic. The suit she had on was perfect, how did she do it? She entered the church and looked straight ahead. Applause and boos broke out, people were cursing in that church.

Diana looked straight ahead, her face immobile. She glided past her mother, past Mary, she walked past Tommy, even past Flo's family. She didn't look at any of them. She came in as if she were the chief mourner, with the guards on each side of her, and she glided down the aisle, reached the exact middle of the church and then, only then did she let out a blood-curdling scream. She threw her hands up, went limp, fell out, was picked up by the security guards and taken immediately to the front row pew where she was fanned and revived. She had that, no-makeup I've-been-up-crying-my-eyes-out-all-night look and then she sat there clutching Flo's youngest daughter, Lisa, to her bosom the whole time.

Aretha Franklin's father, the Reverend Franklin, kept trying to continue the eulogy. But the crowd was completely out of control. They were looking at the stars, they were constantly getting up to view Flo's body, people outside were chanting and screaming, "We Want Diana, We Want Diana." It was a circus, and Reverend Franklin was urging everyone to have some respect for the dead, but I think it finally dawned on him just to keep going.

The screaming outside was getting ugly, then I heard glass shatter and everyone turned around. They had shattered the windows on a star's limo. Things were getting ready to flip and the Reverend Franklin brought the service quickly to a close. But before anybody got up, Diana got up and everyone and everything stopped.

Everyone was thinking, what's she gonna do? She gets up and she tells Aretha Franklin's father up in the pulpit, "Give me the mike please," then she announces, "I have a few things I want to say. Mary will you come up here please."

It looked like they had planned something, but then again Mary appeared kind of taken aback, she just stood there while Diana made a little speech about how Flo will live within us all for ever, Flo's gone but she's not forgotten. Then, without as much as a turn of her head she held the mike out toward Mary and without ever letting go of that mike she said, "Here Mary."

Of course Mary didn't have any speech ready because Diana hadn't planned a thing with her. I thought Mary should have slapped her in the face, but all Mary said was that she loved Flo very much. Then they went over to the casket and Diana stood elegantly dabbing her eyes while Mary, who had been weeping openly, stood there like she was in a coma. Finally she just reached out and touched Flo's cheek.

But it wasn't over, because when they went to close down Flo's casket all the screaming started again. It was so emotionally draining I just fainted, and when I was revived I heard the choir start up on a gospel version of "Someday We'll Be Together," which of course was a song neither Flo nor Mary ever recorded. People started singing along with the music while the Four Tops as pallbearers, and Stevie Wonder as honorary pallbearer, tried to get the heavy steel casket out of the church, through the swarming crowds and into the hearse.

And all of a sudden, just as they came out onto the church steps with the ornate silver-gray and powder-blue casket, a streak of sun came out of the sky. It came out just for that one moment and it hit the casket like a shooting star, the casket flashed blue. The whole crowd gasped.

They were rushing the casket like crazy people. Flo's casket had to be backed up into the church again and they had to throw floral arrangements into the crowd to distract the people until they finally got that casket into the hearse. It was mass hysteria, it was more adulation and sympathy and solidarity and love than Flo had ever seen in her lifetime. Everybody was with her now.

By the time we reached the cemetery it had turned windy and gray. A few stray, beat-up wreaths were thrown around the grave and the casket was put in a concrete box for burial. The minister offered a quick ceremony. You could hardly hear him for all the moaning and crying. Flo's three children, being so young, didn't seem to know what was going on.

I looked around to see where Diana was positioned. I was wondering what she was going to do next, I was thinking, she'll probably hurl herself down in the grave and scream and faint. But Diana wasn't there. I later found out that she'd slipped out through a door of the church and disappeared.

Mary was standing by herself with her ring of bee-hive diamonds and a skullcap studded with little mirrors that she'd worn on the back of her last album cover, a boa affair around her neck and a veil that was just a piece of netting pinned to the hat. She didn't look all perfectly put together like Diana, and yet she was striking. She looked like she didn't know where she was going as she just stood there next to the grave by herself. She whispered something, threw her flowers in, and walked away.

I was one of the last mourners to leave. I was going to stay there until they had closed Flo's grave and the whole time I was standing there I heard Diana's song from *Mahogany* going around my head, I couldn't shake it and it was saying, "Do you know, where you're going to . . . ?" I remembered a time when everything was perfect.

Before the cemetery crew started moving dirt back onto Flo's grave, I went and looked down into it, and I said, "Flo, this don't make no sense at all."

The next day things started to calm down. The news reports said it was the end of an era, and Detroit went back to work. I went over to the house and Tommy said, "Yeah, you know I'm writing an epilogue to Flo's book, you know she was very bitter when she wrote it so I'm gonna soften it up a bit."

"But you know," he continued, "Gordy paid for this whole funeral and Gordy's gonna take care of everything and do the right thing by me, and I'm gonna put that book in a safe deposit box, and I'm gonna use that book as my ace in the hole against Motown. If they don't do the right thing by me I'm gonna put that book out and they're gonna be sorry."

Next thing I knew Tommy had left Detroit, Flo's mother had moved into the house and was taking care of the kids. Diana set up a trust fund for Flo's daughters. Tommy claimed that the principal would revert back to her when the youngest child, Lisa, turned twenty-one.

There was a lot of speculation surrounding Flo's death. Had there been foul play? Was it suicide? The theories seemed to cover all possibilities. All I knew for certain was what the autopsy said, that the cause of death was cardiac arrest. I decided to look into the manuscript that Flo and Tommy had told me about, but less than six months after Flo's death nobody had heard of it. The family knew nothing, nobody at Motown knew anything. I called Doubleday, who I'd heard had changed their mind about publishing the book be-

cause it was too hot to handle, and they knew nothing.
I called Bantam, who were supposed to have picked it
up after Doubleday dropped it, and they knew nothing. I couldn't find anyone that knew anything about
Flo's book.

About a year and a half later I found out from
Tommy that he had sold Flo's book to Motown for ten
thousand dollars. He was down and out, he was scared,
he sold the book for fast money and went down South.
I figured, it probably ended up in Motown file number
thirteen, the shredder file, and I forgot about it. Flo
was dead and like she said before she died, "Leave it,
let it go, forget all of that bitterness."

Then in 1984, when I was helping Mary Wilson remember and research her life as a Supreme for her
book, *Dreamgirl*, we located Tommy. I spoke to him
by phone. He told me he wanted to speak with Mary,
he was so sorry for the way he had acted, he hadn't
done right by his wife, and he said, "Tony, Motown
scared me off and they came in and took control of
my wife's funeral, they just used it as publicity for the
company and Diana, and that little piece of money
Diana gave to my daughters was just publicity too."

He said, "When you and Mary get down here I'm
gonna tell you the whole story because I remember
what my wife wrote and I want Mary to tell it. I want
her to tell how Motown killed my wife, they abused
her, they robbed her, they drove her crazy, they set her
up, they blacklisted her, she could have been a big star
and Berry Gordy used everything to keep her down,
and now he wants everything hushed up."

So I made arrangements for Mary and me to meet
him in a month and I thought, boy, are we gonna get
a story from Tommy! Mary said, "I can't wait to get
down there," but we had to wait, we had to wait because Mary was scheduled to appear near there in a
month.

We were on the road when, about two weeks after I
had contacted Tommy and two weeks before he was
supposed to meet us, I got a call from my friend, J.R.

He said, "Tony, someone called you at the house to-day."

"Who was it?" I asked.

He said, "All the man said was, Tommy Chapman is dead."

"WHAT!" I screamed.

"Tony, somebody shot him in his head in a pool hall. They don't know who did it or what but he got shot, the whole thing is over, Tommy's dead and bur-ied."

Looking at Mary, I hung up the phone.

Epilogue

I grew up watching three giggly girls from Detroit become women, on three different rides. All they shared was the miracle of the Supremes. They shared that name, their friendship, and the experience of coming from nothing to a whole lot of everything. They could all be grand, they could all be bitchy, they were all spoiled, they all wanted to be stars—they had little else in common.

Diana was the one who did the little bit extra. She wanted it all: the applause, the glory of stardom, the whole package. And she was willing to work for it.

Flo was the one with the voice. In her mind, that one voice was everything, and could get her everything.

Mary was the sexy one. All she ever wanted was to maintain the Supremes' lifestyle, the party. That was the dream for which she had stood way in the background all those years, for which she had rocked no boats, made no waves, until she woke up to find the party over.

But the Supremes story was not yet over for Mary, nor for me.

In 1981 I was living on Long Island and working in real estate when Mary Wilson called me. After the official disbanding of the Supremes in 1977 she had tried to make it as a solo, but by now her roller coaster had nearly hit rock bottom. She had little left; no contract with Motown, few bookings, no manager, no husband. Pedro Ferrer, her ex-manager/husband, had drained her of almost everything she had and was now leaving her—a physically abused woman with three children and a taste for cocaine.

Mary was terrified of sliding downhill like Flo. Being a Supreme was the only thing she knew, it had been her whole life since she was a teenager. Blessed with looks and talent, she had gotten lucky, she had become a superstar, and having clung to that dream for so long she wasn't about to let go of it.

She picked herself up. She got off the coke, arranged a loan from Diana, and with that bought a small house and put her show on the road again. And after years in court she won her own case against Motown—the judge decided that if someone was a Supreme for twenty years, nobody could stop her from using that name.

Mary asked me to come and work with her as her road manager and personal assistant, and of course I agreed. I knew Mary couldn't pay top dollar, but like several people who worked for her, I had another job and could take time out to tour with her when there was work. I would have done it for next to nothing. After all, this was my dream too.

Mary Wilson *was* the Supremes now, she was the last Supreme. She was no longer in the background, she was now "Mary Wilson of the Supremes," center stage with her own band and two back-up singers way behind her. We were like a family. During the five years I worked for Mary, we struggled, we prayed, we toured. We roamed all over the world, living any place and yet no place. Mary seemed very much a woman alone. She was singing lead on the old Supremes songs and wearing the old Supremes gowns. The dream continued.

We talked Supremes constantly, the funny things and

the sad things—we left nothing out. Sometimes Mary asked me to tell the stories because she couldn't remember them all herself. Sometimes it seemed as if she was under the illusion that it was still 1967, and everything was still arriving on a silver tray.

We had our ups, we had our downs, there were times we didn't get paid, times I had to curse the promoters out, times I had to curse Mary out, times she had to curse me out. One year, we didn't speak to each other from March until August. But it passed, as our disagreements always did. I loved Mary, even if I didn't like some of the things I saw in her. After all that had happened, she was still the same person that I had met all those years ago, still with the same blind, supreme faith that everything will always work out.

Mary could overlook the fact that sometimes her show was held together with spit and a safety pin, whereas I always wanted everything to be exactly right, even as a kid. I had watched Diana Ross and Berry Gordy, and had learned from them to pay attention to detail, to leave nothing to chance. But Mary wasn't big on rehearsals, and as time went by I began to grow tired of the hit and miss, touch and go. Working under these uncertain conditions made me nervous. Yet in some ways maybe I was a bit like Mary. I never wanted to get off that ride.

In 1986, Mary's *Dreamgirl: My Life as a Supreme* was published and Mary was very optimistic that with the book's success she was going to get a huge recording contract. It didn't happen. Mary seemed reluctant to update her show, and the bookings dwindled.

We continued to tour, and Mary continued to resist change. At times she could be shockingly demanding, expecting things to be done as they once had been. Being an original Supreme had made her a legend, but nobody made a big fuss over a Supreme any more, the bottles of French champagne weren't arriving any more, and slowly I began to wake up to the realization that we were caught in a fading reflection of how life used to be.

In 1987 the paperback edition of Mary's book came out and still nobody was rushing to sign her. After she opened for Bill Cosby in Atlantic City, we went to Brazil where Mary started to get belligerent. She cursed out the background singers, the band, and me, wearing only a crinoline slip and a bra. I advised her against cursing out people in such attire, and she started getting extremely difficult with me. I couldn't understand why things were changing between us—maybe Mary was feeling the pressure, maybe I was feeling bitchy, perhaps I was ready to wake up from the dream.

She was telling me things like, "Who do you think you are, Mr. Popularity? Get your own show!" I knew she was drunk at the time, but I also knew that it was more than the champagne talking. Some of the staff said she was jealous of me because I was so comical that I was getting more attention than she was.

I was reminded of Diana and Gregory, the hair-dresser.

It progressed, and it worsened. From Brazil we went to Lake Tahoe, where Mary opened for Joan Rivers. From there we went to Europe. It was exhausting. We were always together, on and off planes and tour buses, in and out of hotels, and every day was uglier than the last until suddenly, for some reason, it hardly seemed worth fighting any more.

We were on the tour bus, everybody talking, Mary lounged across two seats looking as if she were asleep, and the moment I opened my mouth she screamed at me, accusing me of trying to be the center of attraction. Normally I would have stood my ground and cursed her out but this time I stayed calm, I rose above the pettiness.

The tension built. I was siting with Karen Ragland, one of Mary's pseudo Supremes, in a large, empty restaurant somewhere on the Scottish moors when Mary strolled in, walked over to the table next to us, picked up my new mink coat from the chair where I had put it, hurled it to the floor, and sat down. I looked at the coat and carried on eating. Mary didn't say a word, and neither did I.

Nobody could understand why Mary was acting this way, nor why I was so calm in the face of it. They couldn't see that I no longer cared. We went to yet another new location, I told everybody to be downstairs for the bus by eight o'clock. Someone must have changed the plan without informing me, because when I came down at ten to eight I found Mary and company gone.

I turned around and went back upstairs to my room. All I could think was, I gotta get off before I get stabbed in the back like Flo. This was no longer no dream, girl!

The phone rang. It was the bus driver, he had driven forty-five minutes, all the way back to get me. He said, "I told her you were not on the bus, all the others told her, and she said to drive off."

The ride was ending, closing down. I no longer understood this dreamgirl's reasoning, but I knew and feared the nightmare.

He insisted that I let him drive me to the club. "I've been watching," he said, "I don't know how you could stand working for that woman. Did you just get the job?"

I answered, "I have known her since 1964, and it's now 1987. Okay?"

We drove to the club, I did my job, got back on the tour bus. Scarcely a word was spoken, but through that silence I was busy wondering what kind of a ride I had been on most of my life, and where it was headed.

It was the week before Christmas. We stopped in a brand-new hotel in Edinburgh, where we were to stay and perform. The show was sold out, fans were gathering outside, it was time for rehearsal and the promoter's assistant came up to inform me that there was no backstage dressing room, how did Mary want to handle it. I went to find Mary.

"Mary, there's no backstage dressing room. Where would you like to dress?"

"Whaaat!" Everybody stopped to look.

I told her again.

"Whadya mean!" She screamed.

I was asking a simple question, but Mary wouldn't listen. I kept on asking, and she just kept on screaming that she didn't like the way I told her. I kept my voice down, almost to a whisper, "How many ways can you say, there is no dressing room?"

"Well, I don't wanna hear it!" She shouted, and stormed off.

That was the last straw. In that instant I knew, Supreme, this dream is over. I wanted to get off in a hurry. It was as if I had been carrying something around with me for as long as I could remember, and had suddenly discovered that I could simply put it down.

I asked Mary's office manager, Hazel, to come with me. I needed a witness. We followed briskly behind Mary, "Mary, I want to talk to you."

She didn't want to talk. We'd reached the other side of the lobby, she wasn't listening, she just kept shouting that she didn't want to hear it, she didn't want to hear it, until she heard me say, I quit.

She stopped cold in her tracks. "What do you mean?"

I said, "Good luck, God bless you, and goodbye." And I left.

I went up to my room and packed. I had just left twenty-three years behind, it was an old, tired dream now, and it was long over. I was completely at peace.

I went to the airport, got on a flight for London, waited for a connection to New York, got on the plane, and during that long, long journey back home I thought about the journey I had been a part of all those years. I had seen the good, the bad, and the ugly, and I didn't regret a minute of it.

I could have missed it all and still be in the projects, I could be a dope addict, I could have gone to Vietnam, I could be dead, I could have been a lot of things.

I might have sat there happily and never have learned all the things I did if Flo hadn't told me, "Honey, don't just sit here, learn something from somebody. Find out what everybody is doing."

I've been to Japan a few times, I've been all over Europe, South America, the Far East, the Middle East, and I didn't go wearing an army badge, I went with a Supreme ticket. It was great fun, it was tragic, it was hectic, it was horrible, it was the best life in the world and I am still thrilled that the good Lord sent me to Thirty-fourth Street at the exact right time and I got out of Macy's at the exact moment I did, I walked at the exact right pace, I peeked in this window, I crossed the street exactly right, I hit the steps of B. Altman's, opened the door, and there was this goddess.

And something made me stop right then and there, at the exact right time and in the exact right place, and we could have stood there for an eternity had she not said, "Help me get a cab." Not so much as a hello, or a what are you looking at, you never seen a lady look as good as me before? It was a pleasant command and she was my guiding spirit, and from that moment my life was set.

I thought about all of this, I thought about the original Supremes who were like sisters, how new and bright it all had been. I thought about the changes, the roller-coaster rides that went in three different directions, probably never again to meet, I thought about the heartaches, the dissolution, I thought about those gowns that had been packed and unpacked and packed and unpacked in so many different places and for so many different reasons, and the closer the jet got to New York the more relieved I felt. I had something more important than hearing some Supremes song for the millionth time. I had myself.

I was happy, I was tired, I was renewed, relieved. The vision, the dream was done, and all that remained of the Supremes was a shattered illusion.

Finally I saw the whole thing clearly—all that glittered wasn't gold. Finally I understood what Flo had been talking about through all the pills and the booze and the misery. Finally I took a good look at what Mary had struggled so long to maintain.

I thought of Diana. I thought, she knew where she was going and she knew how to get there. I heard her song again, the same song that came to me at Flo's funeral, "Where are you going to, do you know . . . ?"

And I remembered what my grandmother used to say, "Anthony, the smartest thing that anyone can learn, is knowing when to leave."

Once, it was all right.

Index

About the Author

TONY TURNER, a native New Yorker, has worked with a number of musical acts, including the Temptations, Mary Wilson and The Three Degrees. He divides his time between homes in New York and the Gulf of Mexico. BARBARA ARIA is a freelance writer with several books to her credit, including *Misha: The Mikhail Baryshnikov Story.*